HOW CHILDREN SUCCEED

CONFIDENCE, CURIOSITY AND THE HIDDEN POWER OF CHARACTER

PAUL TOUGH

arrow books

Published by Arrow Books 2014

2 4 6 8 10 9 7 5 3 1

First published in the United States in 2012 by Houghton Mifflin Harcourt
First published in Great Britain in 2013 by Random House Books
Random House, 20 Vauxhall Bridge Road,
London SW1V 2SA

www.randomhouse.co.uk

Addresses for companies within The Random House Group Limited can be found at:
www.randomhouse.co.uk/offices.htm

The Random House Group Limited Reg. No. 954009

A CIP catalogue record for this book
is available from the British Library

ISBN 9780099588757

The Random House Group Limited supports the Forest Stewardship Council® (FSC®),
the leading international forest-certification organisation. Our books carrying
the FSC label are printed on FSC®-certified paper. FSC is the only forest-
certification scheme supported by the leading environmental organisations,
including Greenpeace. Our paper procurement policy can be found at:
www.randomhouse.co.uk/environment

Printed and bound by CPI Group (UK) Ltd, Croydon, CR0 4YY

For Ellington,

who prefers books about dump trucks

Contents

HOW CHILDREN SUCCEED

Introduction

In the summer of 2009, a couple of weeks after my son, Ellington, was born, I spent the day in a prekindergarten classroom in a small town in New Jersey. The two events were unrelated — I was visiting room 140 at the Red Bank Primary School not to scope out the class as a new parent but to try to understand it as a journalist. At first glance, the classroom seemed entirely ordinary. The cinder-block walls were painted a cheery yellow; an American flag stood next to the white-board. Around the room, four-year-olds were happily engaged in the customary diversions of pre-K students: building towers of Legos and driving trucks through sand tables and piecing together jigsaw puzzles. But as the day progressed, I realized that what was going on in room 140 was in fact quite unusual, in ways both self-evident and subtle. To begin with, the students were remarkably calm and orderly. There were no tears that day, no meltdowns, no tantrums, no fights. Oddly, though, the teacher, a young, dark-haired woman named Ms. Leonardo, didn't seem to be going out of her way to maintain order, or even to guide the children's conduct in any overt fashion. There were no admonitions, no gold stars, no time-outs, no "I like the way Kellianne is paying attention!" — indeed, no rewards for good behavior or punishments for bad at all.

The students in room 140 were enrolled in a program called Tools of the Mind, a relatively new kindergarten and prekindergarten curriculum that was created by two educators in Denver and based on an unorthodox theory of child development. Most early-childhood classrooms in the United States today are designed to develop in children a set of specific pre-academic skills, mostly related to deciphering text and manipulating numbers. Tools of the Mind, by contrast, doesn't focus much on reading and math abilities. Instead, all of its interventions are intended to help children learn a different kind of skill: controlling their impulses, staying focused on the task at hand, avoiding distractions and mental traps, managing their emotions, organizing their thoughts. The founders of Tools of the Mind believe that these skills, which they group together under the rubric *self-regulation,* will do more to lead to positive outcomes for their students, in first grade and beyond, than the traditional menu of pre-academic skills.

Tools of the Mind students are taught a variety of strategies, tricks, and habits that they can deploy to keep their minds on track. They learn to use "private speech": talking to themselves as they do a difficult task (like, say, forming the letter *W*), to help them remember what step comes next (*down, up, down, up*). They use "mediators": physical objects that remind them how to complete a particular activity (for instance, the two cards, one with a pair of lips and one with an ear, that signify whose turn it is to read aloud in buddy reading and whose turn it is to listen). Every morning, they fill out "play plans," forms on which they write or draw descriptions of that day's play: *I am going to drive the train; I am going to take the dollies to the beach.* And they spend long hours engaged in "mature dramatic play": extended, complex make-believe scenarios that the designers of Tools of the Mind believe naturally teach children how to follow rules and regulate impulses.

As I watched the kids in room 140, I found myself thinking, inevitably, about Ellington, the tiny life form cooing and burping and wailing away thirty miles to the north, in our studio apartment in

Manhattan. I knew I wanted him to have a happy, successful life, but I didn't really know what, exactly, I meant by that, or just what my wife and I were supposed to be doing to help guide him there. I wasn't alone in my confusion. Ellington was born into a particularly anxious moment in the history of American parenting. And that anxiety had grown especially keen in cities like New York, where the competition over slots in favored preschools verged on the gladiatorial. A pair of economists from the University of California recently dubbed this nationwide contest for early academic achievement the Rug Rat Race, and each year, the race seems to be starting earlier and growing more intense. Two years before Ellington's birth, the Kumon chain of tutoring centers opened New York City's first Junior Kumon franchise, where children as young as two spent their mornings filling out worksheets and completing drills on letter and number recognition. "Age 3 is the sweet spot," Kumon's chief financial officer told a reporter for the *New York Times.* "But if they're out of a diaper and can sit still with a Kumon instructor for 15 minutes, we will take them."

Ellington would be growing up in a culture saturated with an idea you might call the cognitive hypothesis: the belief, rarely expressed aloud but commonly held nonetheless, that success today depends primarily on cognitive skills — the kind of intelligence that gets measured on IQ tests, including the abilities to recognize letters and words, to calculate, to detect patterns — and that the best way to develop these skills is to practice them as much as possible, beginning as early as possible. The cognitive hypothesis has become so universally accepted that it is easy to forget that it is actually a relatively new invention. You can trace its contemporary rise, in fact, to 1994, when the Carnegie Corporation published *Starting Points: Meeting the Needs of Our Youngest Children,* a report that sounded an alarm about the cognitive development of our nation's children. The problem, according to the report, was that children were no longer receiving enough cognitive stimulation in the first three years of life, in part because of the increasing number of single-parent families and working mothers — and so they were arriving in kindergarten unready to learn. The report launched an entire industry of brain-building "zero-to-three" products for worried parents. Billions of dollars' worth of books and activity gyms and Baby Einstein videos and DVDs were sold.

The Carnegie findings and the studies that followed in their wake had a powerful effect on public policy, too, as legislators and philanthropists concluded that disadvantaged children were falling behind early on because of insufficient cognitive training. Psychologists and sociologists produced evidence linking the academic underperformance of poor children to a lack of verbal and mathematical stimulation at home and at school. One of the most famous of these studies (which I wrote about in my first book, *Whatever It Takes*) was conducted by Betty Hart and Todd R. Risley, two child psychologists who, beginning in the 1980s, intensively studied a group of forty-two children from professional, working-class, and welfare families in Kansas City. Hart and Risley found that the crucial difference in the children's upbringings, and the reason for the divergence in their later outcomes, boiled down to one thing: the number of words that the children heard from their parents early in life. By age three, Hart and Risley determined, the children raised by professional parents had heard thirty million words spoken to them; the children with parents on welfare had heard just ten million. That shortfall, they concluded, was at the root of the poorer kids' later failures in school and in life.

There is something undeniably compelling about the cognitive hypothesis. The world it describes is so neat, so reassuringly linear, such a clear case of inputs *here* leading to outputs *there*. Fewer books in the home means less reading ability; fewer words spoken by parents means a smaller vocabulary for their kids; more math worksheets at Junior Kumon means better math scores. The correlations at times seemed almost comically exact: Hart and Risley calculated that a child who grew up on welfare would need precisely forty-one hours of language-intensive intervention each week in order to close the vocabulary gap with a working-class child.

But in the past decade, and especially in the past few years, a disparate congregation of economists, educators, psychologists, and neuroscientists have begun to produce evidence that calls into question many of the assumptions behind the cognitive hypothesis. What matters most in a child's development, they say, is not how much information we can stuff into her brain in the first few years. What matters, instead, is whether we are able to help her develop a very different set of qualities, a list that includes persistence, self-control, curiosity, conscientiousness, grit, and self-confidence. Economists refer to these as noncognitive skills, psychologists call them personality traits, and the rest of us sometimes think of them as character.

For certain skills, the stark calculus behind the cognitive hypothesis — that what matters in developing a skill is starting *earlier* and practicing *more* — is entirely valid. If you want to perfect your foul shot, shooting two hundred free throws every afternoon is indeed going to be more helpful than shooting twenty free throws every afternoon. If you're in fourth grade, reading forty books over the summer is going to improve your reading ability more than reading four books. Some skills really are pretty mechanical. But when it comes to developing the more subtle elements of the human personality, things aren't so simple. We can't get better at overcoming disappointment just by working harder at it for more hours. And children don't lag behind in curiosity simply because they didn't start doing curiosity drills at an early enough age. The pathways through which we acquire and lose these skills are certainly not random — psychologists and neuroscientists have learned a lot in the past few decades about where these skills come from and how they are developed — but they are complex, unfamiliar, and often quite mysterious.

This book is about an idea, one that is growing clearer and gathering momentum in classrooms and clinics and labs and lecture halls across the country and around the world. According to this new way of thinking, the conventional wisdom about child development over the past few decades has been misguided. We have been focusing on the wrong skills and abilities in our children, and we have been using the wrong strategies to help nurture and teach those skills. To call this a new school of thought is probably premature. In many cases the researchers adding to this growing store of knowledge are working in isolation. But increasingly, these scientists and educators are finding one another and making connections across the boundaries of academic disciplines. The argument they are piecing together has the potential to change how we raise our children, how we run our schools, and how we construct our social safety net.

If there is one person at the hub of this new interdisciplinary network, it is James Heckman, an economist at the University of Chicago. Heckman might seem an unlikely figure to be leading a challenge to the supremacy of cognitive skill. He is a classic academic intellectual, his glasses thick, his IQ stratospheric, his shirt pocket bristling with mechanical pencils. He grew up in Chicago in the 1940s and 1950s, the son of a middle manager at a meatpacking company. Neither of his parents was college educated, but they both recognized early on that their son possessed a precocious mind. At the age of eight, Heckman devoured his father's copy of the popular self-help book *30 Days to a More Powerful Vocabulary,* and at nine, he saved up his pennies and ordered *Mathematics for the Practical Man* from the back of a comic book. Heckman turned out to be a natural at math, more at home with equations than with anything or anyone else. As a teenager, for fun, he made a habit of taking long numbers and dividing them in his head into the prime numbers that made up their smallest factors — what mathematicians call resolving into primes. At age sixteen, he told me, when his Social Security number arrived in the mail, the first thing he did was resolve it into primes.

Heckman became a professor of economics, first at Columbia University and then at the University of Chicago, and in 2000 he won the Nobel Prize in Economics for a complex statistical method he had invented in the 1970s. Among economists, Heckman is known for his skill in econometrics, a particularly arcane type of statistical analysis that is generally incomprehensible to anyone except other econometricians. I sat in on several of Heckman's graduate classes, and though I did my best to keep up, most of the lectures were, for a layman like me, all but impossible to follow, thick with bewildering equations and phrases like *generalized Leontief functions* and *Hicks-Slutsky substitution elasticity* that made me want to put my head down on my desk and just close my eyes.

Although Heckman's techniques may seem impenetrable, the subjects he has chosen to focus on are anything but obscure. In the years since winning the Nobel, Heckman has used the clout and cachet the honor brought him not to cement his reputation within his field but to expand his pursuits, and his influence, into new areas of study that he previously knew little or nothing about, including personality psychology, medicine, and genetics. (He actually has a copy of *Genetics for Dummies* on his overstuffed office bookshelves, wedged in between two thick texts of economic history.) Since 2008, Heckman has been convening regular invitation-only conferences populated by equal numbers of economists and psychologists, all engaged in one way or another with the same questions: Which skills and traits lead to success? How do they develop in childhood? And what kind of interventions might help children do better?

Heckman oversees a group of two dozen mostly foreign-born graduate students and researchers scattered across a couple of buildings on the Chicago campus; they refer to their tribe, only half jokingly, as Heckmanland. Together, they're always working on several projects at once, and when Heckman talks about his work, he jumps from one topic to another, equally excited by the monkey study in Maryland, the twin study in China, and his collaboration with a philosopher down the hall on the true nature of virtue. (In one conversation with Heckman, I asked him to explain how the various strands of his research fit together. Afterward, as his assistant was walking me out, she turned to me and said, "If you find out, let us know.")

The transformation of Heckman's career has its roots in a study he undertook in the late 1990s on the General Educational Development program, better known as the GED program, which was at the time becoming an increasingly popular way for high-school dropouts to earn the equivalent of high-school diplomas. In many quarters, it was seen as a tool to level the academic playing field, to give low-income and minority students, who were more likely to drop out of high school, an alternative route to college.

The GED's growth was founded on a version of the cognitive hypothesis: the belief that what schools develop, and what a high-school degree certifies, is cognitive skill. If a teenager already has the knowledge and the smarts to graduate from high school, he doesn't need to waste his time actually *finishing* high school. He can just take a test that measures that knowledge and those skills, and the state will certify that he is, legally, a high-school graduate, as well prepared as any other high-school graduate to go on to college or other post-secondary pursuits. It is an attractive notion, especially to young people who can't stand high school, and the program has expanded rapidly since its introduction, in the 1950s. At the high-water mark, in 2001, more than a million young people took the test, and nearly one in every five new high-school "graduates" was actually a GED holder. (The figure is now about one in seven.)

Heckman wanted to examine more closely the idea that young people with GEDs were just as well prepared for further academic pursuits as high-school graduates. He analyzed a few large national databases, and he found that in many important ways, the premise was entirely valid. According to their scores on achievement tests, which correlate closely with IQ, GED recipients were every bit as smart as high-school graduates. But when Heckman looked at their path through higher education, he discovered that GED recipients weren't *anything* like high-school graduates. At age twenty-two, Heckman found, just 3 percent of GED recipients were enrolled in a four-year university or had completed some kind of post-secondary degree, compared to 46 percent of high-school graduates. In fact, Heckman discovered that when you consider all kinds of important future outcomes—annual income, unemployment rate, divorce rate, use of illegal drugs—GED recipients look exactly like high-school dropouts, despite the fact that they have earned this supposedly valuable extra credential, and despite the fact that they are, on average, considerably more intelligent than high-school dropouts.

From a policy point of view, this was a useful finding, if a depressing one: In the long run, it seemed, as a way to improve your life, the GED was essentially worthless. If anything, it might be having a *negative* overall effect by inducing young people to drop out of high school. But for Heckman, the results also posed a confounding intellectual puzzle. Like most economists, Heckman had believed that cognitive ability was the single most reliable determinant of how a person's life would turn out. Now he had discovered a group — GED holders — whose good test scores didn't seem to have any positive effect on their lives.

What was missing from the equation, Heckman concluded, were the psychological traits that had allowed the high-school graduates to make it through school. Those traits — an inclination to persist at a boring and often unrewarding task; the ability to delay gratification; the tendency to follow through on a plan — also turned out to be valuable in college, in the workplace, and in life generally. As Heckman explained in one paper: "Inadvertently, the GED has become a test that separates bright but nonpersistent and undisciplined dropouts from other dropouts." GED holders, he wrote, "are 'wise guys' who lack the ability to think ahead, persist in tasks, or to adapt to their environments."

What the GED study didn't give Heckman was any indication of whether it was possible to help children develop those so-called soft skills. His search for an answer to that question led him, almost a decade ago, to Ypsilanti, Michigan, an old industrial town west of Detroit. In the mid-1960s, in the early days of the War on Poverty, a group of child psychologists and education researchers undertook an experiment there, recruiting low-income, low-IQ parents from the town's black neighborhoods to sign up their three- and four-year-old kids for the Perry Preschool. The recruited children were divided randomly into a treatment group and a control group. Children in the treatment group were admitted to Perry, a high-quality, two-year preschool program, and kids in the control group were left to fend for themselves. And then the children were tracked — not just for a year or two, but for decades, in an ongoing study that is intended to follow them for the rest of their lives. The subjects are now in their forties, which means that researchers have been able to trace the effects of the Perry intervention well into adulthood.

The Perry Preschool Project is famous in social science circles, and Heckman had encountered it, glancingly, several times before in his career. As a case for early-childhood intervention, the experiment had always been considered something of a failure. The treatment children did do significantly better on cognitive tests while attending the preschool and for a year or two afterward, but the gains did not last, and by the time the treatment children were in the third grade, their IQ scores were no better than the control group's. But when Heckman and other researchers looked at the long-term results of Perry, the data appeared more promising. It was true that the Perry kids hadn't experienced lasting IQ benefits. But *something* important had happened to them in preschool, and whatever it was, the positive effects resonated for decades. Compared to the control group, the Perry students were more likely to graduate from high school, more likely to be employed at age twenty-seven, more likely to be earning more than twenty-five thousand dollars a year at age forty, less likely ever to have been arrested, and less likely to have spent time on welfare.

Heckman began to rummage more deeply into the Perry study, and he learned that in the 1960s and 1970s, researchers had collected some data on the students that had never been analyzed: reports from teachers in elementary school rating both the treatment and the control children on "personal behavior" and "social development." The first term tracked how often each student swore, lied, stole, or was absent or late; the second one rated each student's level of curiosity as well as his or her relationships with classmates and teachers. Heckman labeled these *noncognitive skills,* because they were entirely distinct from IQ. And after three years of careful analysis, Heckman and his researchers were able to ascertain that those noncognitive factors, such as curiosity, self-control, and social fluidity, were responsible for as much as two-thirds of the total benefit that Perry gave its students.

The Perry Preschool Project, in ot...
ferently than everyone had believed. Th...
set it up in the sixties thought that they...
raise the intelligence of low-income childr...
believed that was the way to help poor ki...
Surprise number one was that they created...
do much in the long term for IQ but did imp...
cial skills. Surprise number two was that it he... ...he
kids in Ypsilanti, those skills and the underlying ...ey reflected
turned out to be very valuable indeed.

In the course of reporting this book, I spent a lot of time discussing success and skills with a variety of economists, psychologists, and neuroscientists, many of whom were linked to James Heckman by one or two degrees of separation. But what grounded their research for me, what brought it to life and gave it meaning, was a different kind of reporting that I was doing at the same time, in public schools and pediatric clinics and fast-food restaurants, where I was talking with young people whose lives embodied and illustrated, in one way or another, the complex question of which children succeed and how.

Take Kewauna Lerma. When I met her, in the winter of 2010, she was living on the South Side of Chicago — not too far, as it turned out, from the University of Chicago campus where Heckman spent his days. Kewauna had been born on the South Side, into poverty, seventeen years earlier, the second daughter of a mother who had her first child, Kewauna's older sister, when she was still a teenager. Kewauna had a rootless, unsettled childhood. When she was a baby, her mother moved the family to Mississippi, then to Minnesota, then back to Chicago as she drifted in and out of relationships and in and out of trouble. When things were bad, the family spent periods in shelters or bouncing from one friend's couch to another's. Sometimes Kewauna's great-grandmother would take the kids for a while and let Kewauna's mother try to sort out her life on her own.

"I didn't really have a *family* family," Kewauna told me the first

e were sitting in a coffee shop in the Kenwood
d. It was the middle of a harsh Chicago winter, and the
s were fogged over. Kewauna has dark skin, big, sympathetic
s, and straight, dark hair, and she sat forward, warming her hands on a foam-topped mug of hot chocolate. "I was scattered all over the place, no father, with my grandma sometimes. It was all messed up. Jacked up."

Growing up, Kewauna said, she hated school. She never learned to read well, and in elementary school she fell farther and farther behind each year, getting in trouble, skipping class, and talking back to teachers. When she was in sixth grade, living outside of Minneapolis, she collected seventy-two referrals for poor behavior by the middle of the year, and so she was assigned to the slow class. She hated that too. A few weeks before the end of the year, she was kicked out of school for fighting.

When I met Kewauna, I had been reporting for several years on children growing up in poverty, and I had heard plenty of stories like hers. Every unhappy family may be unhappy in its own way, but in families that stay trapped in poverty for generations, the patterns can become depressingly familiar, a seemingly endless cycle of absent or neglectful parents, malfunctioning schools, and bad decisions. I knew how stories like Kewauna's generally turned out. Girls with her history, whatever their good intentions, usually drop out of high school. They get pregnant while they are still teenagers. Then they struggle to raise families on their own, and before long, their own children are sliding down the same slope to failure.

But somewhere along the way, Kewauna's life took a different turn. Just before her sophomore year of high school, a few weeks after Kewauna was arrested for the first time, for scuffling with a police officer, Kewauna's mother told her that she wanted to have a talk. Kewauna knew it was serious, because her great-grandmother was there, too, the one member of her family Kewauna had always respected. The two women sat Kewauna down, and her mother uttered one of the hardest sentences for any parent to say: "I don't want you to end up like me." The three of them talked for hours, discussing the past and the future, digging up some long-buried secrets. Kewauna's mother said she recognized the path that Kewauna was on: She also had been kicked out of school as a teenager; she, too, had been arrested for fighting with the police. But the next chapter of Kewauna's story, her mom said, could be a different one. She could avoid unplanned pregnancies, unlike her mother. She could go to college, unlike her mother. She could have a career, unlike her mother.

Kewauna's mom cried through practically the whole conversation, but Kewauna herself never shed a tear. She just listened. She wasn't sure what to think. She didn't know if she could change, and she didn't know if she wanted to. When she got back to school, though, she started to pay more attention in class. In freshman year, she had run around with a rough crowd, girls into gangs and boys into drugs and everyone into skipping school. Now she pulled herself away from those friends, spending more time alone, doing homework and thinking about her future. At the end of her freshman year, her GPA was a miserable 1.8. By the middle of her sophomore year, it had climbed to 3.4.

That February, her English teacher encouraged her to apply for an intensive three-year college-prep program that had recently been introduced at the school. Kewauna applied, and she was accepted, and the support the program gave her made her work even harder. When I met her, she was in the middle of her junior year. Her GPA was 4.2, and she was preoccupied with the question of which colleges to apply to.

So what happened? If you had met Kewauna on the first day of her sophomore year, you could have been forgiven for thinking that she had virtually no chance to succeed. Her destiny seemed sealed. But something in her changed. Was it really just one stern talk with her mom? Was that all it took? Was it her great-grandmother's positive influence? The intervention of her English teacher? Or was there something deep within her own character that inclined her toward the idea of hard work and success, despite all the obstacles she had faced and the mistakes she had made?

· · ·

How do our experiences in childhood make us the adults we become? It is one of the great human questions, the theme of countless novels, biographies, and memoirs; the subject of several centuries' worth of philosophical and psychological treatises. This process — the experience of growing up — can appear at times to be predictable, even mechanical, and at other times to be arbitrary and capricious; we've all encountered grown men and women who seem trapped in a destiny preordained by their childhoods, and we've all met people who seem to have almost miraculously transcended harsh beginnings.

Until recently, though, there has never been a serious attempt to use the tools of science to peel back the mysteries of childhood, to trace, through experiment and analysis, how the experiences of our early years connect to outcomes in adulthood. That is changing, with the efforts of this new generation of researchers. The premise behind the work is simple, if radical: We haven't managed to solve these problems because we've been looking for solutions in the wrong places. If we want to improve the odds for children in general, and for poor children in particular, we need to approach childhood anew, to start over with some fundamental questions about how parents affect their children; how human skills develop; how character is formed.

At its core, this book is about an ambitious and far-reaching campaign to solve some of the most pervasive mysteries of life: Who succeeds and who fails? Why do some children thrive while others lose their way? And what can any of us do to steer an individual child — or a whole generation of children — away from failure and toward success?

1

HOW TO FAIL
(AND HOW NOT TO)

1. Fenger High School

Nadine Burke Harris grew up surrounded by privilege in Palo Alto, California, the daughter of educated, professional Jamaican immigrants who had moved the family from Kingston to Silicon Valley when Burke Harris was four. As a girl, she often felt like an outsider, one of the only black students at her Palo Alto high school, where the kids were mostly white and well-off, and where the girls cried in the cafeteria if they didn't get the right kind of car for their sixteenth birthdays.

Elizabeth Dozier grew up just outside Chicago in far more modest circumstances, the product of an unlikely and illicit romance between her father, an inmate at the state prison in Joliet, Illinois, and her mother, a nun who was assigned to visit prisoners as part of her religious duty and who wound up falling in love. After Dozier was born, her mother raised her alone, teaching at the local Catholic school and working summers as a motel maid to supplement her meager income.

Burke Harris and Dozier emerged from these very different childhoods with the same goal: to help young people succeed, especially young people in trouble. Burke Harris went to medical school, became a pediatrician, and opened a clinic in the poorest part of San Francisco. Dozier became a teacher, and then a principal, in schools in some of the poorest neighborhoods in Chicago. When I met them both, separately, a couple of years ago, what drew me to them was not just their similar sense of mission but a deeper frustration they seemed to share. Both women had recently come to the conclusion that the best tools available to them in their chosen professions were simply not up to the challenges they faced. And so they were both at turning points in their careers and their lives. They were looking for new strategies: in fact, they were looking for a whole new playbook.

In August of 2009, when Dozier was named the principal of Christian Fenger High School, the school was in a moment of crisis — though if you looked back at its history over the previous twenty years, it was hard to find a moment when Fenger was *not* in crisis. The school had stood for more than eighty years in the heart of Roseland, on Chicago's South Side, a once-prosperous area that is now one of the worst-off neighborhoods in the city by just about every measure you can find — poverty rate, unemployment rate, crime rate, or even just the barren, empty feel of the streets. Where thriving businesses and homes once stood there are now vacant lots, overrun with weeds. Roseland is geographically isolated (close to Chicago's southern border, way down past the last stop on the El) and racially segregated: in a city where the total population is roughly evenly divided among whites, African Americans, and Latinos, Roseland is 98 percent black. And like most big public high schools in high-poverty neighborhoods, Fenger High School has always had a dismal record: consistently low test scores, poor attendance, chronic discipline problems, and a high dropout rate.

When you hear stories about schools like Fenger, they are often told in the language of neglect: a school on the margins, students who have been forgotten and ignored by the bureaucrats downtown and in Washington. But the strange thing about Fenger High School is that it *hasn't* been ignored. Not at all. Instead, over the course of the past two decades, it has been the focus of repeated ambitious and well-financed reforms by some of the most respected education officials and philanthropists in the country. Just about every strategy anyone has come up with for improving failing public high schools has been tried, in some form or another, at Fenger.

Fenger's contemporary history begins in 1995, when Chicago's mayor, Richard M. Daley, was granted control of the city's schools by the Illinois state legislature. To reflect the businesslike approach he favored, Daley decided that the top official in the school system would no longer be called the superintendent; instead, he would be the CEO. For his first CEO, Daley selected his hard-charging budget director, Paul Vallas, who turned his attention immediately to improving Fenger and other underperforming city high schools. Vallas created a citywide evaluation system that ranked schools by how much help they needed, and he placed Fenger in the most dire category: probation. Vallas had been a student at Fenger for two years as a teenager, and perhaps that was why he focused his efforts so intently on the school. He introduced a restructuring plan for Fenger that included hiring an outside contractor to coach the school's teachers in reading and writing instruction. He created a freshman academy at the school, a separate, dedicated floor where incoming students would get special attention for their entire freshman year. In 1999, he created a math-and-science academy at the school, complete with a $525,000 NASA-sponsored science lab. Two years later, he made Fenger a magnet school, specializing in technology.

Each of Vallas's reform initiatives came and went, but things never seemed to improve much for the students at Fenger. And the same was true under Vallas's successor, Arne Duncan. In 2006, Duncan chose Fenger as one of the pilot schools for a large-scale collaboration between the Chicago school system and the Bill and Melinda Gates Foundation, an undertaking called High School Transformation, which the foundation initially financed with a twenty-one-million-dollar grant. (After three years, the total bill for the citywide project had grown to eighty million.) When the initiative was announced, Duncan said it was "a truly historic day, not just for the Chicago Public Schools and the city, but for the country." But a little more than two years later, with evidence mounting that High School

Transformation wasn't producing results, Fenger was switched over to Duncan's latest reform initiative: High School Turnaround. Under Turnaround, a school's principal and at least half its teachers were removed, and a whole new team was brought in. And when Turnaround arrived at Fenger, in 2009, the brand-new principal was Elizabeth Dozier.

Vallas and Duncan, it's important to note, are not garden-variety school-system bureaucrats; they are two of the most celebrated educational leaders in the country. After Vallas left Chicago, he ran the schools in Philadelphia, and then he gained national fame as the man responsible for rebuilding and transforming the New Orleans school system after it was washed away by Hurricane Katrina. Duncan's post-Chicago career is even more illustrious: President Obama chose him as his education secretary in 2009. But throughout all of the two men's well-intentioned and often quite expensive reforms in Chicago, the grim statistics from Fenger High School stayed more or less where they had been in 1995: Between half and two-thirds of each incoming freshman class dropped out before the end of senior year. The minority of students who did make it to graduation were only rarely academically successful: in 2008, Duncan's final year in Chicago, fewer than 4 percent of Fenger students met or exceeded standards on the statewide college-readiness tests given to juniors and seniors. During Duncan's tenure, the school never once made "adequate yearly progress" under the federal No Child Left Behind law. And Vallas's probation designation, originally intended to indicate a temporary state of emergency, became a fact of life at Fenger; in 2011, the school was placed on probation for the sixteenth year in a row.

When Dozier first arrived at Fenger, an ambitious and determined thirty-one-year-old, she believed that the basic tool kit of the modern education reformer contained everything she needed to turn things around for the school's students. She had spent a year in a highly competitive principal-training program called New Leaders for New Schools, which emphasized to trainees that a dynamic leader could raise students' achievement to high levels, no matter what their socioeconomic circumstances, as long as she had a committed staff. Dozier cleaned house at Fenger, replacing several administrators and most of the teachers; when I first sat down with her in her office at Fenger, a little more than a year after she took the job, her seventy-member staff included only three teachers from the school's pre-Turnaround days. Most of the new teachers were young, ambitious, and non-tenured, which meant they would be relatively easy for Dozier to replace if they didn't measure up to her standards.

When we spoke, though, Dozier said that her thinking about schools had been changed by her time at Fenger. "I used to always think that if a school wasn't performing, that it was strictly because there was a bad principal, or there were bad teachers," she explained. "But the reality is that at Fenger, we're a neighborhood school, so we're just a reflection of the community. And you can't expect to solve the problems of a school without taking into account what's happening in the community."

As Dozier got to know the students at Fenger, she found herself repeatedly taken aback by the severity of the problems they faced at home. "The majority of our students are living in poverty, from check to check," she told me. "A lot of them live in neighborhoods with gang problems. I can't think of a single kid at the school who doesn't face some kind of serious adversity." A quarter of the female students were either pregnant or already teenage mothers, she said. And when I asked her to estimate how many of her students lived with both biological parents, a quizzical look came over her face. "I can't think of one," she replied. "But I know we have them."

The threat of violence seemed always to be looming over Fenger's students as well. Chicago's murder rate is twice as high as the rate in Los Angeles and more than double the rate in New York City. Gangs have a bigger and more lethal presence in Chicago than in any other major American city, and when Dozier came to Fenger, there had been a recent spike in gun violence among young people: in 2008, eighty-three school-age teenagers were murdered in the city, and more than six hundred were shot but survived.

Though Dozier had been expecting the turnaround of Fenger to be a challenge, nothing prepared her for what happened on her six-teenth day on the job. A major fight broke out a few blocks from the school, involving maybe fifty teenagers, mostly Fenger students. There were no guns or knives, but some kids picked up railroad ties and started using them as clubs. A sixteen-year-old Fenger student named Derrion Albert who had waded into the fight was hit on the head with a railroad tie and then punched in the face and knocked unconscious. While he was on the ground, a few other young men kicked him in the head, and the combined blunt-force trauma killed him.

In its most basic elements, Derrion Albert's death in September of 2009 was not all that different from any of the dozens of other violent deaths of Chicago high-school students that year. But the fight and Albert's killing were captured on video by a bystander, and that fall the video became first a YouTube sensation and then a cable-news fixture. Local and national media descended on Fenger. For weeks, the streets around the school were lined with TV satellite trucks, and prayer vigils and protests were held in front of the school. The U.S. at-torney general, Eric Holder, came to meet with students. Then in Oc-tober, Fenger made news again when three vicious gang fights broke out simultaneously on three separate floors of the school. Dozens of police cars arrived, five students were arrested, and the whole build-ing was put on lockdown for three hours.

After the schoolwide brawl, Dozier instituted what she called a zero-tolerance policy for violent behavior and behavior that might lead to violence: If students threw up gang signs or exchanged gang handshakes in the hallway, Dozier gave them automatic ten-day sus-pensions. If they fought, she called the police and had them arrested, and then she did her best to expel them from Fenger permanently. When I started spending time at Fenger, more than a year after Al-bert's death, the halls were generally quite orderly, though they cer-tainly didn't seem normal. There were always thick-armed security guards patrolling the hall; students couldn't go anywhere without their IDs on Fenger lanyards around their necks, and when a student needed to go to the bathroom in the middle of class, she had to carry a giant hall pass, two feet long and bright yellow. Between classes, the synthesizer-laden theme from *Beverly Hills Cop* played on speakers in the hallways; students knew they had to make it to the next class before the last note sounded. Despite the firm rules, there were still disruptions; the first time I came to Fenger to interview Dozier, we were interrupted twice by shouts in the hallway, arguments that she had to rush off to help adjudicate.

Midway through her second year as principal, Dozier told me that she was beginning to feel that the most important tools at her disposal were ones that didn't have much to do with classroom instruction. In the wake of Derrion Albert's murder, Holder and Arne Duncan pledged $500,000 in federal money to set up afterschool programs in anger management and trauma counseling at Fenger, and the school began to refer to counseling not just students but their families as well. Dozier enrolled twenty-five of her most troubled students in an intensive mentoring program. She was looking for any kind of intervention that might address what now seemed to her to be the most pressing crisis at Fenger — not her students' academic deficits, though those remained acute and distressing, but a deeper set of problems, born out of her students' troubled and often traumatic home lives, that made it difficult for them to get through each day. "When I came into this job, I discounted questions like 'What families do kids come from?' and 'What effect does poverty have on children?'" Dozier said to me one morning. "But since I started working at Fenger, my thinking has evolved."

2. Nadine Burke Harris

What effect does poverty have on children? Halfway across the country, this was the question Nadine Burke Harris was asking as well. But she was a doctor, not an educator, and so she approached the question from the perspective of her patients' physical health. Since 2007, Burke Harris had been the lead pediatrician of the Bayview Child Health Center in the Bayview–Hunters Point neighborhood of San Francisco, a bleak industrial area tucked away in the city's southeast corner that is home to some of the city's biggest and most violent housing projects. When Burke Harris founded the clinic, she was a recent graduate of the Harvard School of Public Health, a fresh young idealist hired by the California Pacific Medical Center, a well-funded private hospital chain, to take on a vaguely defined but noble-sounding mission: to identify and address health disparities in the city of San Francisco. Those disparities were not hard to find, especially in Bayview–Hunters Point: the rate of hospitalization for congestive heart failure there was five times as high as it was in the Marina District, a few miles away. And before Burke Harris's clinic opened, there was only one pediatrician in private practice in a community with more than ten thousand children.

Burke Harris had studied health disparities at Harvard, and she knew what the public-health playbook said you should do to remediate them: improve access to health care, especially primary care, for low-income families. When the clinic opened its doors, Burke Harris targeted the low-hanging fruit of pediatrics, the health issues where the disparities between rich and poor children were most obvious and best understood: asthma management, nutrition, vaccinations for diphtheria and whooping cough and tetanus. And in just a few months, she made significant headway. "It turned out to be surprisingly easy to get our immunization rates way up and to get our asthma hospitalization rates way down," she told me when I first visited her clinic. And yet, she explained, "I felt like we weren't actually addressing the roots of the disparity here. I mean, as far as I know, no child in this community has died of tetanus in a very, very long time."

Burke Harris found herself in a situation much like Dozier's. Here she was, in her dream job. She had ample resources, she was well trained, she was working hard — and yet she didn't seem to be making much of a difference in the lives of the young people she was trying to help. They were still surrounded by violence and chaos, at home and in the streets, that was clearly taking a grave toll on them, both physically and emotionally. Many of the children she saw in the clinic seemed depressed or anxious, and some of them were downright traumatized, and the stress of their daily lives expressed itself in a variety of symptoms, from panic attacks to eating disorders to suicidal behavior. She sometimes felt less like a primary-care pediatrician and more like a battlefield surgeon, patching up her patients and sending them back to war.

Burke Harris went looking for answers, and her quest took her into a new and unfamiliar conversation about poverty and adversity, one that was taking place not in public-policy magazines and at political science symposiums but in medical journals and at neuroscience conferences. Gradually, Burke Harris became convinced of what had at first seemed a radical idea: that in neighborhoods like Bayview–Hunters Point and Roseland, many of the problems we generally think of as social issues — the province of economists and sociologists — are actually best analyzed and addressed on the molecular level, down deep in the realm of human biology.

3. The ACE Study

Burke Harris's journey began with a medical-journal article that Whitney Clarke, a psychologist on the clinic's staff, dropped on her desk one day in 2008: "The Relationship of Adverse Childhood Experiences to Adult Health: Turning Gold into Lead." The author was Vincent Felitti, the head of the department of preventive medicine at Kaiser Permanente, the giant health maintenance organization based in California, and the article described the Adverse Childhood Experiences study, commonly called the ACE study, that Felitti had conducted in the 1990s with Robert Anda, an epidemiologist at the Centers for Disease Control in Atlanta. When Burke Harris read the paper, she told me, something clicked: "The clouds parted," she said with a smile. "Angels sang. It was like that scene at the end of *The Matrix* where Neo can see the whole universe bending and changing."

Beginning in 1995, patients enrolled in the Kaiser HMO who came in for comprehensive medical exams were mailed questionnaires asking them to relate their personal histories in ten different categories of adverse childhood experiences, including physical and sexual abuse, physical and emotional neglect, and various measures of household dysfunction, such as having divorced or separated parents or family members who were incarcerated or mentally ill or addicted. Over the course of a few years, more than seventeen thousand patients completed and returned the questionnaires — a response rate of almost 70 percent. As a group, the respondents represented a very mainstream, middle- to upper-middle-class demographic: 75 percent were white; 75 percent had attended college; the average age was fifty-seven.

When Anda and Felitti tabulated the responses, they were surprised, first, by the sheer prevalence of childhood trauma among this generally well-off population. More than a quarter of the patients said they had grown up in a household with an alcoholic or a drug user; about the same fraction had been beaten as children. When the doctors used the data to assign each patient an ACE score, giving them one point for each category of trauma they had experienced, they found that two-thirds of the patients had experienced at least one ACE, and one in eight had an ACE score of 4 or more.

The second and more significant surprise came when Anda and Felitti compared the ACE scores with the voluminous medical histories that Kaiser had collected on all the patients. The correlations between adverse childhood experiences and negative adult outcomes were so powerful that they "stunned us," Anda later wrote. What's more, those correlations seemed to follow a surprisingly linear dose-response model: the higher the ACE score, the worse the outcome on almost every measure from addictive behavior to chronic disease. Anda and Felitti produced one bar chart after another from the data, and each one traced more or less the same shape. Along the bottom of each chart, the x-axis, the doctors plotted the number of ACEs that patients had experienced. Along the y-axis, they indicated the prevalence of a specific undesirable outcome: obesity, depression, early sexual activity, history of smoking, and so on. On each chart, the bars rose steadily and consistently from left (0 ACEs) to right (more than 7 ACEs). Compared to people with no history of ACEs, people with ACE scores of 4 or higher were twice as likely to smoke, seven times more likely to be alcoholics, and seven times more likely to have had sex before age fifteen. They were twice as likely to have been diagnosed with cancer, twice as likely to have heart disease, twice as likely to have liver disease, four times as likely to suffer from emphysema or chronic bronchitis. On some charts, the slopes were especially steep: adults with an ACE score above 6 were thirty times more likely to have attempted suicide than those with an ACE score of 0. And men with an ACE score above 5 were forty-six times more likely to have injected drugs than men with no history of ACEs.

The behavior outcomes, though surprising in their intensity, at least made some intuitive sense. Psychologists had long believed that traumatic events in childhood could produce feelings of low self-esteem or worthlessness, and it was reasonable to assume that those feelings could lead to addiction, depression, and even suicide. And some of the health effects that turned up in the ACE study, like liver disease and diabetes and lung cancer, were most likely the result, at least in part, of self-destructive behaviors like heavy drinking, over-eating, and smoking. But Felitti and Anda found that ACEs had a profound negative effect on adult health even when those behaviors *weren't* present. When they looked at patients with high ACE scores (7 or more) who didn't smoke, didn't drink to excess, and weren't overweight, they found that their risk of ischemic heart disease (the single most common cause of death in the United States) was still 360 percent higher than those with an ACE score of 0. The adversity these patients had experienced in childhood was making them sick through a pathway that had nothing to do with behavior.

4. The Firehouse Effect

That initial ACE study led Burke Harris to other research papers, and before long she was immersed, staying up late every night reading articles from medical journals and tracking down footnotes and references on PubMed, the online medical database. The research she compiled during those furious months of study now sits in four fat binders on the shelf of her office at the clinic. The papers within span many scientific disciplines, but most of them are rooted in two fairly obscure medical fields: neuroendocrinology (the study of how hormones interact with the brain) and stress physiology (the study of how stress affects the body). Although Anda and Felitti initially didn't understand the biological mechanisms at work in their ACE data, scientists have reached a consensus in the past decade that the key channel through which early adversity causes damage to developing bodies and brains is *stress.*

Our bodies regulate stress using a system called the HPA axis. HPA stands for "hypothalamic-pituitary-adrenal," and that tongue-twisting phrase describes the way that chemical signals cascade through the brain and the body in reaction to intense situations. When a potential danger appears, the first line of defense is the hypothalamus, the region of the brain that controls unconscious biological processes like body temperature, hunger, and thirst. The hypothalamus emits a chemical that triggers receptors in the pituitary gland; the pituitary releases signaling hormones that stimulate the adrenal glands; and the adrenal glands then send out stress hormones called glucocorticoids that switch on a host of specific defensive responses. Some of these responses we can recognize in ourselves as they happen: emotions like fear and anxiety, and physical reactions like increased heart rate, clammy skin, and a dry mouth. But many effects of the HPA axis are less immediately apparent to us, even when we're the ones experiencing them: neurotransmitters activate, glucose levels rise, the cardiovascular system sends blood to the muscles, and inflammatory proteins surge through the bloodstream.

In his insightful and entertaining book *Why Zebras Don't Get Ulcers,* the neuroscientist Robert Sapolsky explains that our stress-response system, like that of all mammals, evolved to react to brief and acute stresses. That worked well when humans were out on the savanna running from predators. But modern humans rarely have to contend with lion attacks. Instead, most of our stress today comes from mental processes: from worrying about things. And the HPA axis isn't designed to handle that kind of stress. We "activate a physiological system that has evolved for responding to acute physical emergencies," Sapolsky writes, "but we turn it on for months on end, worrying about mortgages, relationships, and promotions." And over the past fifty years, scientists have discovered that this phenomenon is not merely inefficient but also highly destructive. Overloading the HPA axis, especially in infancy and childhood, produces all kinds of serious and long-lasting negative effects — physical, psychological, and neurological.

The tricky thing about this process, though, is that it's not actually the stress itself that messes us up. It is the body's *reaction* to the stress. In the early 1990s, Bruce McEwen, a neuroendocrinologist at Rockefeller University, proposed a theory of how this works, one that is now broadly accepted in the field. According to McEwen, the process of managing stress, which he labeled *allostasis*, is what creates wear and tear on the body. If the body's stress-management systems are overworked, they eventually break down under the strain. McEwen called this gradual process allostatic load, and he says that you can observe its destructive effects throughout the body. For example, acute stress raises blood pressure to provide adequate blood flow to the muscles and organs that need to respond to a dangerous situation. That's good. But repeatedly elevated blood pressure leads to atherosclerotic plaque, which causes heart attacks. That's not so good.

Although the human stress-response system is highly complex in design, in practice it has all the subtlety of a croquet mallet. Depending on what kind of stress you experience, the ideal response might come from one of any number of defense mechanisms. If you're about to receive a flesh wound, for instance, then it would be a good idea for your immune system to start producing copious antibodies. If you need to run away from an attacker, you want your heart rate and blood pressure to elevate. But the HPA axis can't distinguish between different types of threat, so it activates every defense, all at once, in response to any threat. Unfortunately, this means you often experience stress responses that are not at all helpful — like when you need to speak before an audience, and suddenly your mouth goes dry. Your HPA axis, sensing danger, is conserving fluids, preparing to ward off an attack. And you're standing there looking for a glass of water and swallowing hard.

Think of the HPA axis as a superdeluxe firehouse with a fleet of fancy, high-tech trucks, each with its own set of highly specialized tools and its own team of expertly trained firefighters. When the alarm bell rings, the firefighters don't take the time to analyze exactly what the problem is and figure out which truck might be most appropriate. Instead, all the trucks rush off to the fire together at top speed, sirens blaring. Like the HPA axis, they simply respond quickly with every tool they might need. This may be the right strategy for saving lives in fires, but it can also result in a dozen trucks pulling up to put out a single smoldering trash can — or worse, responding to a false alarm.

5. Scared to Death

Nadine Burke Harris saw the results of this firehouse effect in her patients all the time. One day at the Bayview clinic, she introduced me to one of them, a teenager named Monisha Sullivan who had first come to the clinic when she was sixteen and a new mother. Monisha's childhood was about as stressful as they come: She was abandoned just a few days after she was born by her mother, who was a heavy user of crack cocaine and other drugs. As a child, Monisha lived with her father and her older brother in a section of Hunters Point with a lot of gang violence until her father, too, got lost in a drug habit; when Monisha was ten, she and her brother were removed from their home by the city's child protection bureau, separated from each other, and placed in foster care. Ever since, she had been ricocheting through the system, staying for a week or a month or a year in each foster or group home until, inevitably, tensions escalated over food or homework or TV, and she ran away or her caregivers gave up. Then it was on to another placement. In the previous six years, she had cycled through nine different homes.

When I met Monisha, in the fall of 2010, she had just turned eighteen, and three days earlier, she had been emancipated from the foster-care system in which she had spent almost half her life. Her most painful experience, she told me, was the day she was placed in foster care. Without any warning, she was pulled out of class by a social worker she had never met and driven to a strange new home. It was months before she was able to have any contact with her father. "I remember the first day like it was yesterday," she told me. "Every detail. I still have dreams about it. I feel like I'm going to be damaged forever."

As we sat in the therapy room at the clinic, I asked Monisha to describe for me what that damage felt like. She is unusually articulate about her emotional state — when she feels sad or depressed, she writes poems — and she enumerated her symptoms with precision. She had insomnia and nightmares, she said, and at times her body inexplicably ached. Her hands sometimes trembled uncontrollably. Her hair had recently started falling out, and she was wearing a pale green headscarf to cover up a thin patch. More than anything, she felt anxious: anxious about school, anxious about her young daughter, anxious about earthquakes. "I think about the weirdest things," she said. "I think about the world ending. If a plane flies over me, I think they're going to drop a bomb. I think about my dad dying. If I lose him, I don't know what I'm going to do." She was even anxious about her anxiety. "When I get scared, I start shaking," she said. "My heart starts beating. I start sweating. You know how people say 'I was scared to death'? I get scared that that's really going to happen to me one day."

The firehouse metaphor might help us understand what was happening with Monisha Sullivan. When she was a child, her fire alarm went off constantly, at top volume: *My mom and stepmom are punching each other; I'm never going to see my dad again; no one's home to make me dinner; my foster family isn't going to take care of me.* Every time the alarm went off, her stress-response system sent out all the trucks, sirens blaring. The firefighters smashed in some windows and soaked some carpets, and by the time Monisha turned eighteen, her biggest problem wasn't the threats that she faced from the world around her. It was the damage the firefighters had done.

When McEwen first proposed the notion of allostatic load, in the 1990s, he didn't conceive of it as an actual numerical index. But recently, he and other researchers, led by Teresa Seeman, a gerontologist at UCLA, have been trying to "operationalize" allostatic load, to produce a single number for each individual that would express the damage that a lifetime of stress management had imposed. Doctors use comparable biological-risk indicators all the time today, most notably blood pressure measurements. Those numbers are obviously useful as predictors of certain medical conditions (which is why your doctor takes your blood pressure every time you visit his or her office, no matter what ailment you might be there for). The problem is, blood pressure readings alone are not precise measures of future health risks. A more accurate allostatic-load index would include not just blood pressure and heart rate but other stress-sensitive measures: levels of cholesterol and high-sensitivity C-reactive protein (a leading marker for cardiovascular disease); readings of cortisol and other stress hormones in the urine and of glucose and insulin and lipids in the bloodstream. Seeman and McEwen have shown that a complex index including all those values would be a much more reliable indicator of future medical risk than blood pressure or any other single-factor measure in use today.

It's an attractive and fascinating notion, and a slightly frightening one: a single number that a doctor could give you in, say, your early twenties that would reflect both the stress you had experienced in life to that point and the medical risks that you now faced as a result of that stress. In some ways it would be a more refined version of your ACE score. But unlike your ACE score, which relies on your own report of your childhood, your allostatic-load number would reflect nothing but cold, hard medical data: the actual physical effects of childhood adversity, written on your body, deep under your skin.

6. Executive Functions

As a medical doctor, Burke Harris was initially interested in the physiological effects that early trauma and unmanaged stress had on her patients: Monisha's trembling hands and hair loss and unexplained pains. But Burke Harris quickly realized that these forces had an equally serious impact in other aspects of her patients' lives. When she used a modified version of the Felitti-Anda ACE questionnaire with more than seven hundred patients at her clinic, she found a disturbingly powerful correlation between ACE scores and problems in school. Among her patients with an ACE score of 0, just 3 percent had been identified as having learning or behavioral problems. Among patients with an ACE score of 4 or higher, the figure was 51 percent.

Stress physiologists have found a biological explanation for this phenomenon as well. The part of the brain most affected by early stress is the prefrontal cortex, which is critical in self-regulatory activities of all kinds, both emotional and cognitive. As a result, children who grow up in stressful environments generally find it harder to concentrate, harder to sit still, harder to rebound from disappointments, and harder to follow directions. And that has a direct effect on their performance in school. When you're overwhelmed by uncontrollable impulses and distracted by negative feelings, it's hard to learn the alphabet. And in fact, when kindergarten teachers are surveyed about their students, they say that the biggest problem they face is not children who don't know their letters and numbers; it is kids who don't know how to manage their tempers or calm themselves down after a provocation. In one national survey, 46 percent of kindergarten teachers said that at least half the kids in their class had problems following directions. In another study, Head Start teachers reported that more than a quarter of their students exhibited serious self-control-related negative behaviors, such as kicking or threatening other students, at least once a week.

Some of the effects of stress on the prefrontal cortex can best be categorized as emotional, or psychological: anxiety and depression of all kinds. I kept in touch with Monisha in the months after our first meeting, and I saw a lot of those emotional symptoms in her. She was plagued by self-doubt — about her weight, her parenting ability, her prospects in general. She was assaulted one night by an ex-boyfriend, a sketchy character she had invited over, against her better judgment, to stave off her loneliness. And she struggled constantly to cope with a flood of emotions that always seemed on the verge of capsizing her.

"Sometimes the stress is just too much for me to bear," she told me one day. "I don't see how people deal with it."

For Monisha, the main effect of stress overload on her prefrontal cortex was that she had a hard time regulating her emotions. For many other young people, though, the main effect of stress is that it compromises their ability to regulate their thoughts. This has to do with a particular set of cognitive skills located in the prefrontal cortex known as executive functions. In wealthy school districts, *executive function* has become the new educational catch phrase, the most recent thing to evaluate and diagnose. But among scientists who study children in poverty, executive functions are a newly attractive field for another reason: improving executive function seems like a potentially promising vehicle for narrowing the achievement gap between poor kids and middle-class kids.

Executive functions, as we now understand them, are a collection of higher-order mental abilities; Jack Shonkoff, the head of the Center on the Developing Child at Harvard University, has compared them to a team of air traffic controllers overseeing the functions of the brain. Most broadly, they refer to the ability to deal with confusing and unpredictable situations and information. One famous test of executive-function ability is called the Stroop test. You see the word *red* written in green letters, and someone asks you what color that word is. It takes some effort to stop yourself from saying *red,* and the skills you're drawing on when you resist that impulse are executive functions. And those skills are especially valuable in school. We're constantly asking kids to deal with contradictory information. The letter *C* is pronounced like a *K* — unless it is pronounced like an *S. Tale* and *tail* sound the same but have different meanings. A zero means one thing on its own and an entirely different thing with a one in front of it. Keeping track of those various tricks and exceptions requires a certain amount of cognitive impulse control, and that is a skill that is neurologically related to emotional impulse control — your ability to refrain from punching the kid who just grabbed your favorite toy car. In both the Stroop test and the toy-car incident, you're using the prefrontal cortex to overcome your immediate and instinctive reaction. And whether you're utilizing your self-control in the emotional realm or the cognitive realm, that ability is crucially important to getting through the school day, whether you're in kindergarten or your senior year of high school.

7. Simon

For a while now, we've known that executive-function ability correlates strongly with family income, but until recently, we didn't know why. Then in 2009, two researchers at Cornell University, Gary Evans and Michelle Schamberg, designed an experiment that for the first time gave us a clear look at exactly how childhood poverty affects executive function. The particular executive-function skill they examined was working memory, which refers to the ability to keep a bunch of facts in your head at the same time. It's quite distinct from long-term memory — working memory is not about remembering the name of your first-grade teacher; it's about remembering everything you're supposed to pick up at the supermarket. The tool that Evans and Schamberg selected to measure working memory was a kitschy one: the electronic children's game Simon. If you grew up in the 1970s, as I did, you might remember this Hasbro game: it's a UFO-looking disk about the size of an LP record but fatter, with four panels that light up and make distinct sounds. The panels illuminate in various sequential patterns, and you have to remember the order of the beeps and the flashes.

Evans and Schamberg used Simon to test the working memory of 195 seventeen-year-olds in rural upstate New York, all part of a group that Evans had been studying since they were born. About half the children had grown up below the poverty line and the other half in working- and middle-class families. Evans and Schamberg's first discovery was that the amount of time that children spent in poverty when they were growing up predicted how well they would do on the Simon test, on average — kids who had spent ten years in poverty, in other words, did worse than kids who had spent just five years in poverty. This, on its own, was not too surprising; researchers had previously found correlations between poverty and working memory.

But then Evans and Schamberg did something new: They introduced some biological measures of stress. When the children in the study were nine years old, and again when they were thirteen, Evans's researchers took a number of physiological readings from each child, including blood pressure, body mass index, and levels of certain stress hormones, including cortisol. Evans and Schamberg combined those biological data to create their own measure of allostatic load: the physical effects of having an overtaxed stress-response system. When they sat down with all the data and compared each child's Simon score, poverty history, and allostatic-load reading, they found that the three measures correlated — more time in poverty meant higher allostatic-load numbers and lower scores on Simon. But then came the surprise: When they used statistical techniques to factor out the effect of allostatic load, the poverty effect disappeared completely. It wasn't poverty itself that was compromising the executive-function abilities of the poor kids. It was the stress that went along with it.

This was, potentially at least, a big deal in terms of our understanding of poverty. Picture two boys sitting together playing Simon for the first time. One is from an upper-middle-class home, and one is from a low-income home. The kid from the upper-middle-class home is doing a lot better at memorizing the patterns. We might be inclined to assume that the reason for this effect is genetic — maybe there's a Simon gene that rich kids are more likely to possess. Or maybe it has to do with material advantages in the upper-middle-class kid's home — more books, more games, more electronic toys. Or maybe his school is a better place to learn short-term memory skills. Or perhaps it's some combination of the three. But what Evans and Schamberg found is that the more significant disadvantage the low-income boy faces is in fact his elevated allostatic load. And if another low-income boy came along with low levels of allostatic load — if, for whatever reason, he had had a less stressful childhood, despite his family's poverty — he would in all probability do just as well at the

Simon competition as the rich kid. And why does a low Simon score matter? Because in high school, college, and the workplace, life is filled with tasks where working memory is crucial to success.

The reason that researchers who care about the gap between rich and poor are so excited about executive functions is that these skills are not only highly predictive of success; they are also quite malleable, much more so than other cognitive skills. The prefrontal cortex is more responsive to intervention than other parts of the brain, and it stays flexible well into adolescence and early adulthood. So if we can improve a child's environment in the specific ways that lead to better executive functioning, we can increase his prospects for success in a particularly efficient way.

8. Mush

It is in early childhood that our brains and bodies are most sensitive to the effects of stress and trauma. But it is in adolescence that the damage that stress inflicts on us can lead to the most serious and long-lasting problems. Partly, that's just a practical fact of growing up. When you have trouble controlling your impulses in elementary school, the consequences are relatively limited: you might get sent to the principal's office; you might alienate a friend. But the kind of impulsive decisions you are tempted to make in adolescence — driving drunk, having unprotected sex, dropping out of high school, stealing a wallet — can often have lifelong consequences.

What's more, researchers have found that there is something uniquely out of balance about the adolescent brain that makes it especially susceptible to bad and impulsive decisions. Laurence Steinberg, a psychologist at Temple University, has analyzed two separate neurological systems that develop in childhood and early adulthood that together have a profound effect on the lives of adolescents. The problem is, these two systems are not well aligned. The first, called the incentive processing system, makes you more sensation seeking, more emotionally reactive, more attentive to social information. (If you've ever been a teenager, this may sound familiar.) The second, called the cognitive control system, allows you to regulate all those urges. The reason the teenage years have always been such a perilous time, Steinberg says, is that the incentive processing system reaches its full power in early adolescence while the cognitive control system doesn't finish maturing until you're in your twenties. So for a few wild years, we are all madly processing incentives without a corresponding control system to keep our behavior in check. And if you combine that standard-issue whacked-out adolescent neurochemistry with an overloaded HPA axis, you've got a particularly toxic brew.

This combination of forces in many of her students was exactly what Elizabeth Dozier felt unable to manage at Fenger High School. After the near riot at the school in October of 2009, she decided there were certain students she simply needed to remove from the school for good. At the top of her list was a sixteen-year-old boy named Thomas Gaston, known to all as Mush. As Dozier saw it, Mush was a ringleader, a high-ranking gang member who was able to spark giant brawls at Fenger with a single glance at one of his lieutenants. "He was hell on wheels," Dozier told me. "He would step into this building, and it would just go up. He set the school up for a whole lot of nonsense."

I got to know Mush because he was enrolled, along with two dozen or so other Fenger students, in an intensive mentoring program paid for by the Chicago public schools and run by a nonprofit organization called Youth Advocate Programs, or YAP. In the fall of 2010 and the winter and spring of 2011, I spent a lot of time in Roseland with various YAP advocates and the students they were mentoring, including Mush. My main guide was Steve Gates, the deputy director of YAP in Chicago, a laid-back, burly guy in his late thirties with short, tight dreadlocks; a loose beard; and watery, pale blue eyes. Like Mush, Gates lived in Roseland, just a few blocks from Fenger; he had grown up there, in fact, in similar circumstances and had made a lot of the same mistakes that Mush was making now, twenty years later: running with a gang, carrying a gun, risking his life and his future every day. Gates's delinquent past gave him a unique understanding of the pressures Mush faced as well as a heightened feeling of urgency as he tried to steer Mush and other Roseland teenagers enrolled in YAP toward a better future.

YAP had come to Chicago at the invitation of Ron Huberman, who replaced Arne Duncan as the CEO of the Chicago school system in 2009. When Mayor Daley named Huberman to the post, Daley was concerned about the rising rate of gun violence among young people in the city, and he gave Huberman an unusual mission for a schools chief: Keep our students from killing one another. Huberman was a firm believer in data; his first job out of college had been with Chicago's police department, where he was trained in the gospel of CompStat, the high-tech data-analysis system that has been credited with leading to the steep drop in crime in New York City in the 1990s. His first step as schools CEO was to hire a team of consultants to do a CompStat-like analysis on homicide and shootings among students in Chicago. The consultants created a statistical model that, they said, enabled them to identify the students in the city who were most likely to become victims of gun violence over the course of the next two years. They found twelve hundred students in Chicago high schools who, according to their model, had at least a one-in-thirteen chance of being shot before the summer of 2011; within that group of twelve hundred, two hundred "ultra-high-risk" students were identified, each of whom had at least a one-in-five chance of being a victim of gun violence over the next two years. Those were the students who were handed over to YAP and assigned an advocate for as many as twenty hours a week of mentoring and support.

Mush was on that list, which meant that in the fall of 2009, Steve Gates went looking for him to get him enrolled in YAP and assigned to an advocate. At the same time, though, Elizabeth Dozier was trying to kick Mush out of Fenger. Soon after he signed up with YAP, she managed to remove him from her school, at least temporarily, exiling him for a semester to Vivian E. Summers Alternative High School, a small, grim, prisonlike facility eight blocks away from Fenger. Though Mush didn't like Vivian Summers much, that winter and spring he seemed to thrive under the watchful eyes of the mentors at YAP. Mush's first advocate got him a job in a local auto-body shop, where he was able to develop his artistic side working on paint jobs, and for a while it seemed like Mush had turned his back on his troublemaking past and was starting to move toward a more productive life.

Then, one night in June of 2010, Mush's advocate dropped him off at home late and assumed he was in for the night. But Mush decided to slip back out to the streets. A few hours later he was in the Cook County jail along with his friend Bookie, both of them charged with aggravated vehicular hijacking, meaning carjacking with a gun. He and Bookie were each looking at a potential sentence of twenty-one years, but YAP's attorney somehow persuaded the judge to give them eight months in boot camp instead. Boot camp was a tough ride for Mush — a military-style regimen, pushups and ten-mile runs at dawn — but he drew on some inner discipline that he had seemed to lack at Fenger, and he made it through his sentence.

When I first started spending time with YAP advocates and their students, Mush was still locked up, and well before I encountered him in the flesh, I heard a lot about him — from Gates, from Dozier, from his friends in YAP, even from his mom, whom Gates and I dropped in to see one night while Mush was in boot camp. Dozier spoke about Mush with awe, as if he were some kind of delinquent Svengali. Gates told me that grown men were scared to death of him. His mom, of course, was less impressed with his gangland reputation; she took great pleasure in telling me that she used to buy him boxers with Arthur, the cartoon aardvark, printed on them, to embarrass her boy into keeping his pants pulled up. Still, when the time came for me to meet him, I was a little nervous; it felt like meeting a celebrity. In person, though, Mush looked like an average South Side teenager, but smaller — not much more than five feet tall, and skinny even after eight months of pushups — and he walked with a stiff-jointed, splay-footed, almost Chaplinesque shuffle. He wore a string of rosary beads around his neck, a Yankees cap pulled low on his forehead, and an oversize jacket that could have easily held two or three Mushes.

We went to a diner on Western Avenue to eat eggs and drink coffee and talk. Like all of his friends, Mush grew up with a single mother, the one who bought him the Arthur boxers, a woman Gates described to me as "a beautiful person, but not necessarily equipped with the best parenting skills." His extended family had a history of violence and legal trouble, and Mush rattled off a long list of siblings and cousins and other relations who were dead or in jail. When he was nine, Mush told me, his uncle was shot and killed in Mush's home. "It was crazy," he said. "It happened right in front of me." As we talked, I found myself silently adding up Mush's ACE score, each childhood trauma clicking the counter higher.

Mush's personal history differed from Monisha Sullivan's in its particulars — he witnessed much more violence growing up than she did, but the family disruptions she experienced were more profound: abandoned by her mother, separated from her father, her entire adolescence spent in foster care. Both of their childhoods, though, were unrelentingly stressful, and each of them was damaged by that stress in a deep and lasting way. Though neither had the opportunity (or the inclination) to submit to the kind of allostatic-load measurements that McEwen and Evans and Schamberg and other researchers performed on their subjects, we can assume that if they did, their readings would be off the charts. And yet, while the damage done to their bodies and brains by childhood trauma may have been comparable, there was a big difference in the way that damage expressed itself in their lives. Monisha took her stress and turned it inward, where it manifested as fear, anxiety, sadness, self-doubt, and self-destructive tendencies. Mush, by contrast, turned his outward: fighting, acting up in class, and, eventually, breaking the law in a variety of ways.

Mush started getting in trouble early: he was kicked out of elementary school for fighting with the principal. But his behavior got significantly worse when he was fourteen and his brother, who had enlisted in the army to escape the violence of the South Side, was shot and killed in a robbery near his base in Colorado Springs. "That's what messed me up," Mush told me. "I stopped caring about a lot of stuff after that." As Mush described it, the only way he could escape the pain of his brother's death was by gangbanging. "I was holding in so much," he said. "I was like a ticking time bomb. And to clear my mind, I would just be out there on the block, acting bad, playing with guns and all that."

Researchers from Northwestern University recently gave psychiatric evaluations to more than a thousand young detainees at the Cook County Juvenile Temporary Detention Center in Chicago — a facility where the majority of YAP students had spent at least a little time — and found that 84 percent of the detainees had experienced two or more serious childhood traumas and that the majority had experienced six or more. Three-quarters of them had witnessed someone being killed or seriously injured. More than 40 percent of the girls had been sexually abused as children. More than half of the boys said that at least once, they had been in situations so perilous that they thought they or people close to them were about to die or be badly wounded. And these repeated traumas, not surprisingly, had had a devastating effect on the detainees' mental health: two-thirds of the males had one or more diagnosable psychiatric disorders. Academically, they were severely behind the curve: the detained youth had average scores on standardized vocabulary tests at the fifth percentile, meaning they were below 95 percent of their peers nationwide.

When I talked with Mush and other young residents of Roseland, I often found myself thinking about the research in neuroscience and stress physiology that had so changed Nadine Burke Harris's perspective. She and I drove one afternoon through the housing projects in Bayview–Hunters Point, exchanging looks with the young men on the corners, and Burke Harris talked as if she could see the cortisol and oxytocin and norepinephrine ebbing and flowing through their bodies and brains. "When we look at these kids and their behavior, it can all seem so mysterious," she said. "But at some point, what you're seeing is just a complex series of chemical reactions. It's the folding of a protein or the activation of a neuron. And what's exciting about that is that those things are treatable. When you get down to the molecules, you realize, that's where the healing lies. That's where you're discovering a solution."

Burke Harris told me the story of one particular patient, a teenage boy who, like so many of her patients, lived in a stress-filled home that had inflicted on him a particularly high ACE score. She had run her clinic long enough that she had essentially been able to watch him grow up. When he first came to the clinic, he was ten, an unhappy child in an unhappy family but still a boy, someone who had withstood some blows but who still seemed to have a chance to escape his bleak destiny. But now this boy was fourteen, an angry black teenager on his way to being six feet tall, and he was hanging out on the street, getting into trouble — a hoodlum in training, if not a criminal already. The reality is that most of us are inclined to feel nothing but sympathy and understanding toward the ten-year-old — he is a boy, after all, and clearly a victim. But toward the fourteen-year-old — not to mention the eighteen-year-old he will soon become — we usually feel something darker: anger and fear, or at least despair. What Burke Harris could see, of course, with the advantage of time and with her clinician's perspective, was that the ten-year-old and the fourteen-year-old were the same child, reacting to the same environmental influences, buffeted by the same powerful neurochemical processes.

Spending time with the kids in YAP, I often found myself wrestling with questions of guilt and blame: When does the innocent boy become the culpable man? I had no objection to the proposition that aggravated vehicular hijacking is a genuinely bad thing, and that people who do it, even sensitive, thoughtful guys like Mush, should suffer the consequences. But I could also see Steve Gates's point of view: that these were young men caught in a terrible system that constrained their decisions in a way that was almost impossible for them to withstand. Gates defined that system mostly in social and economic terms; Burke Harris saw it neurochemically. But the more time I spent in Roseland, the more those two perspectives seemed to converge.

9. LG

Much of the new information about childhood and poverty uncovered by psychologists and neuroscientists can be daunting to anyone trying to improve outcomes for disadvantaged children. We now know that early stress and adversity can literally get under a child's skin, where it can cause damage that lasts a lifetime. But there is also some positive news in this research. It turns out that there is a particularly effective antidote to the ill effects of early stress, and it comes not from pharmaceutical companies or early-childhood educators but from parents. Parents and other caregivers who are able to form close, nurturing relationships with their children can foster resilience in them that protects them from many of the worst effects of a harsh early environment. This message can sound a bit warm and fuzzy, but it is rooted in cold, hard science. The effect of good parenting is not just emotional or psychological, the neuroscientists say; it is biochemical.

The researcher who has done the most to expand our understanding of the relationship between parenting and stress is a neuroscientist at McGill University named Michael Meaney. Like many in the field, Meaney does much of his research with rats, as rats and humans have similar brain architecture. At any given time, the Meaney lab houses hundreds of rats. They live in Plexiglas cages, and usually each cage holds a mother rat, called a dam, and her small brood of baby rats, called pups.

Scientists in rat labs are always picking up baby rats to examine them or weigh them, and one day about ten years ago, researchers in Meaney's lab noticed a curious thing: When they put the pups back in the cages after handling them, some dams would scurry over and spend a few minutes licking and grooming their pups. Others would just ignore them. When the researchers examined the rat pups, they discovered that this seemingly insignificant practice had a distinct physiological effect. When a lab assistant handled a rat pup, researchers found, it produced anxiety, a flood of stress hormones, in the pup. The dam's licking and grooming counteracted that anxiety and calmed down that surge of hormones.

Meaney and his researchers were intrigued, and they wanted to learn more about how licking and grooming worked and what kind of effect it had on the pups. So they kept watching the rats, spending long days and nights with their faces pressed up against the Plexiglas, and after many weeks of careful observation, they made an additional discovery: different mother rats had different patterns of licking and grooming, even in the absence of their pups' being handled. So Meaney's team undertook a new experiment, with a new set of dams, to try to quantify these patterns. This time, they didn't handle any of the pups. They just closely observed each cage, an hour at a time, eight sessions a day, for the first ten days of the pups' lives. Researchers counted every instance of maternal licking and grooming. And after ten days, they divided the dams into two categories: the ones that licked and groomed a lot, which they labeled high LG, and the ones that licked and groomed a little, which they labeled low LG.

The researchers wanted to know what the long-term effects of these variations in parenting behavior might be. So when the pups were twenty-two days old, they were weaned, separated from their mothers, and housed for the rest of their adolescence with same-sex siblings. When the pups were fully mature, about a hundred days old, Meaney's team gave them a series of tests that compared the offspring of the high-licking-and-grooming dams with the rats that hadn't received a lot of licking and grooming as pups.

The main evaluation they used was something called an openfield test, a common procedure in animal-behavior studies: A rat is placed in a large, round, open box for five minutes and allowed to explore at will. Nervous rats tend to stay close to the wall, circling around and around the perimeter; bolder rats dare to venture away from the wall and explore the whole field. In a second test, designed to measure fearfulness, hungry rats were placed in a new cage for ten minutes and offered food. Anxious rats, like jittery guests at a fancy dinner party, tend to take longer to work up the nerve to try any food, and they eat less than the calmer, more confident rats do.

On both tests, the difference between the two groups was striking. The rats who hadn't been licked and groomed much as pups spent, on average, fewer than five seconds of their five minutes daring to explore the inner part of the open field; the rats who had been licked and groomed a lot as pups spent, on average, thirty-five seconds in the inner field — seven times as long. In the ten-minute food test, high-LG rats began eating, on average, after just four tentative minutes, and they ate for more than two minutes in total. The low-LG rats took, on average, more than nine minutes to start eating, and once they did, they ate for only a few seconds.

The researchers ran test after test, and on each one, the high-LG offspring excelled: They were better at mazes. They were more social. They were more curious. They were less aggressive. They had more self-control. They were healthier. They lived longer. Meaney and his researchers were astounded. What seemed like a tiny variation in early mothering style, so small that decades of researchers hadn't noticed it, created huge behavioral differences in mature rats, months after the licking and grooming had taken place. And the effect wasn't just behavioral; it was biological too. When Meaney's researchers examined the brains of the adult rats, they found significant differences in the stress-response systems of the high-LG and low-LG rats, including big variations in the size and shape and complexity of the parts of the brain that regulated stress.

Meaney wondered if a dam's licking-and-grooming frequency was just a proxy for some genetic trait that was passed on from mother to child. Maybe nervous dams produced temperamentally nervous pups, and those dams also coincidentally happened to be less inclined to lick and groom. To test that hypothesis, Meaney and his researchers did a number of cross-fostering experiments, in which they removed pups at birth from a high-LG dam and put them in the litter of a low-LG dam, and vice versa, in all kinds of combinations. Whatever permutation they chose, though, however they performed the experiment, they found the same thing: what mattered was not the licking-and-grooming habits of the biological mother; it was the licking-and-grooming habits of the *rearing* mother. When a pup received the comforting experience of licking and grooming as an infant, it grew up to be braver and bolder and better adjusted than a pup who hadn't, whether or not its biological mother was the one who had done the licking and grooming.

10. Attachment

Meaney and other neuroscientists have found intriguing evidence that something like the LG effect takes place in humans as well. In collaborations with geneticists over the past decade, Meaney and his researchers have been able to demonstrate that a dam's licking and grooming doesn't affect her pups just on the level of their hormones and brain chemicals. It goes much deeper than that, all the way down to the control of gene expression. Licking and grooming a rat pup in its earliest days of life affects the way certain chemicals are affixed to certain sequences on the pup's DNA, a process known as methylation. Using gene-sequencing technology, Meaney's team was able to establish which part of a pup's genome got "switched on" by licking and grooming, and it turned out to be the precise segment that controlled the way the rat's hippocampus would process stress hormones in adulthood.

That discovery alone caused a sensation in the world of neuroscience. It showed that, in rats at least, subtle parental behaviors had predictable and long-lasting DNA-related effects that could actually be traced and observed. What made the discovery relevant beyond the rodent world was an experiment that Meaney's team then went on to do using the brain tissue of human suicides — some from suicides who had been maltreated and abused in childhood, and some from suicides who had not. The researchers sliced into the brain tissue and examined the sites on the DNA that are related to the stress response in the hippocampus — the human equivalent of the rat DNA sequence that was switched on by early parental behavior, profoundly affecting the rat's future reactions. They discovered that the suicides who had been maltreated and abused in childhood had experienced methylation effects on that exact segment of their DNA, though the abuse had the opposite effect of licking and grooming: it had switched off the healthy stress-response function that licking and grooming had switched on in the rat pups.

The suicide study is definitely intriguing, but on its own, it does not amount to conclusive evidence about the effect of parenting on stress function in humans. But more solid evidence is beginning to emerge, thanks to some innovative studies that build on Meaney's research. Clancy Blair, a researcher in psychology at NYU, has been conducting a large-scale experiment in which he has followed almost from birth a group of more than twelve hundred infants. Every year or so, beginning when the infants were just seven months old, Blair measured the way their cortisol levels spiked in reaction to stressful situations—a simple way to evaluate how well a child is handling stress, kind of a bare-bones index of allostatic load. Blair found that environmental risks, like family turmoil and chaos and crowding, did have a big effect on children's cortisol levels—but only when their mothers were inattentive or unresponsive. When mothers scored high on measures of responsiveness, the impact of those environmental factors on their children seemed almost to disappear. High-quality mothering, in other words, can act as a powerful buffer against the damage that adversity inflicts on a child's stress-response system, much as the dams' licking and grooming seemed to protect their pups.

Gary Evans, the Cornell scientist who tested the Simon-playing ability of the cohort of children in upstate New York he has been studying for almost two decades, conducted a similar experiment as Blair's, though his subjects were in middle school. He collected three different kinds of data for each child: a cumulative-risk score that took into account everything from the ambient noise in a child's home to the results of a questionnaire about family friction; an allostatic-load measure that incorporated blood pressure, the level of stress hormones in urine, and body mass index; and a rating of maternal responsiveness, which combined the child's answers to a series of questions about his or her mother with a researcher's observations of the mother and child playing Jenga together (another Hasbro game!). Evans found mostly what you'd expect: the higher the environmental-risk score, the higher the allostatic-load score—*unless* a child's mother was particularly responsive to her child. If that was the case, the effect of all of those environmental stressors, from overcrowding to poverty to family turmoil, was almost entirely eliminated. If your mom was particularly sensitive to your emotional state during a game of Jenga, in other words, all the bad stuff you faced in life had little to no effect on your allostatic load.

When we consider the impact of parenting on children, we tend to think that the dramatic effects are going to appear at one end or the other of the parenting-quality spectrum. A child who is physically abused is going to fare far worse, we assume, than a child who is simply ignored or discouraged. And the child of a supermom who gets lots of extra tutoring and one-on-one support is going to do way better than an average well-loved child. But what Blair's and Evans's research suggests is that regular good parenting—being helpful and attentive during a game of Jenga—can make a profound difference for a child's future prospects.

Some psychologists believe that the closest parallel to licking and grooming in humans can be found in a phenomenon called attachment. Attachment theory was developed in the 1950s and 1960s by a British psychoanalyst named John Bowlby and a researcher from the University of Toronto named Mary Ainsworth. At the time, the field of child development was dominated by behaviorists, who believed that children developed in a mechanical way, adapting their behavior according to the positive and negative reinforcement they experienced. Children's emotional lives were not very deep, behaviorists believed; an infant's apparent yearning for his mother was nothing more than an indication of his biological needs for nourishment and physical comfort. The dominant advice to parents in the 1950s, based on behavioral theory, was to avoid "spoiling" infants by picking them up or otherwise comforting them when they cried.

In a series of studies in the 1960s and early 1970s, Ainsworth showed that the effect of early nurturance was exactly the opposite of what the behaviorists expected. Babies whose parents responded readily and fully to their cries in the first months of life were, at one year, more independent and intrepid than babies whose parents had ignored their cries. In preschool, the pattern continued—the children whose parents had responded most sensitively to their emotional needs as infants were the most self-reliant. Warm, sensitive parental care, Ainsworth and Bowlby contended, created a "secure base" from which a child could explore the world.

Although psychologists in the 1960s had at their disposal many tests to evaluate the cognitive abilities of infants and children, they had no reliable way to measure a child's emotional capacities. So Ainsworth invented a method to do just that, an unusual procedure called the Strange Situation. At Johns Hopkins University, in Baltimore, where Ainsworth was a professor, a mother would bring her twelve-month-old child into a lab set up as a playroom. After playing with her infant for a while, the mother left the room, sometimes leaving the child with a stranger, sometimes leaving him or her alone. After a brief interval, she would return. Ainsworth and her researchers observed the whole procedure through one-way mirrors, and then categorized the children's reactions.

Most children greeted the returning mother happily, running to her and reconnecting with her, sometimes tearfully, sometimes with joy. These children Ainsworth labeled securely attached, and in subsequent experiments over the past few decades, psychologists have come to believe that they make up about 60 percent of American children. Children who did not have a warm reunion — pretending to ignore the mother when she returned; lashing out at her; falling to the floor in a heap — were labeled anxiously attached. Ainsworth found that a child's reaction in the Strange Situation was directly related to his parents' degree of responsiveness in that first year of life. Parents who were attuned to their child's mood and responsive to his cues produced securely attached children; parenting that was detached or conflicted or hostile produced anxiously attached children. And early attachment, Ainsworth said, created psychological effects that could last a lifetime.

11. Minnesota

But Ainsworth's contention that early attachment had long-term consequences was, at that point, just a theory. No one had figured out a reliable way to test it. And then in 1972, one of Ainsworth's research assistants, Everett Waters, graduated from Johns Hopkins and entered the PhD program in child development at the University of Minnesota. There he met Alan Sroufe, a rising young star at the university's Institute of Child Development. Sroufe was intrigued by what Waters told him about Ainsworth's work, and he quickly embraced her ideas and her methods, setting up a lab with Waters where they could perform the Strange Situation test with mothers and children. Before long, the institute had become a leading center of attachment research.

Sroufe joined forces with Byron Egeland, a psychologist at the university who had received a grant from the federal government to conduct a long-term study on low-income mothers and their children. From the local public-health clinic in Minneapolis, they recruited 267 pregnant women, all about to become first-time mothers, all with incomes below the poverty line. Eighty percent of the mothers were white, two-thirds were unmarried, and half were teenagers. Egeland and Sroufe began tracking this group of children at birth, and they have been studying them ever since. (The subjects are now in their late thirties; both Egeland and Sroufe recently retired.) The evidence the study produced, which Egeland and Sroufe and two coauthors summarized most completely in their 2005 book *The Development of the Person,* stands as the fullest evaluation to date of the long-lasting effects of early parental relationships on a child's development.

Attachment classification, the Minnesota researchers found, was not absolute destiny — sometimes attachment relationships changed in the course of childhood, and some children with anxious attachments went on to thrive. But for most children, attachment status at one year of age, as measured by the Strange Situation and other tests, was highly predictive of a wide range of outcomes later in life. Children with secure attachment early on were more socially competent throughout their lives: better able to engage with preschool peers, better able to form close friendships in middle childhood, better able to negotiate the complex dynamics of adolescent social networks.

In preschool, two-thirds of children in the Minnesota study who had been securely attached in infancy were categorized by their teachers as "effective" in terms of their behavior, meaning they were attentive and engaged and rarely acted out in class. Among children who had been observed to be anxiously attached a few years earlier, only one in eight was placed in the effective category; the large majority of those children were classified by their teachers as having one or more behavior problems. (The teachers didn't know how the kids had done on the Strange Situation.) Children whose parents had been judged disengaged or emotionally unavailable in early assessments of their parenting style did the worst in preschool, and teachers recommended special education or grade retention for two-thirds of them. When teachers ranked students on indicators of dependency, 90 percent of the children with an anxious-attachment history fell in the more dependent half of the class, compared with just 12 percent of children with secure histories. When teachers and other children were surveyed, the anxiously attached children were more often labeled mean, antisocial, and immature.

When the children in the study were ten, researchers invited a randomly selected group of forty-eight students to four-week-long sessions at a summer camp, where they were closely observed and discreetly studied. Counselors (again, unaware of the students' attachment classifications at one year) rated campers who had had secure attachment in infancy as more self-confident, more curious, and better able to deal with setbacks. The ones with anxious-attachment histories spent less time with peers, more time with the counselors, and more time alone.

Finally, the researchers followed the children through high school, where they found that early parental care predicted which students would graduate even more reliably than IQ or achievement-test scores. Using measures of early parenting only and ignoring the students' own characteristics and abilities, the researchers found they could have predicted with 77 percent accuracy, when the children were not yet four years old, which ones would later drop out of high school.

It is easy to see parallels between what Michael Meaney's researchers found in their rat pups in Montreal and what Alan Sroufe and

Byron Egeland found in the children they studied in Minnesota. In both cases, certain mothers performed certain specific idiosyncratic parenting behaviors in the earliest days of their children's lives. And those behaviors — licking and grooming in the rats, responding sensitively to infants' cues in the humans — seem to have had a powerful and long-lasting effect on the children's outcomes in a variety of similar ways: the human and rat babies who received the extra dose of early care were, later on, more curious, more self-reliant, calmer, and better able to deal with obstacles. The early nurturing attention from their mothers had fostered in them a resilience that acted as a protective buffer against stress. When the regular challenges of life emerged, even years later — an open-field test, a disagreement among strong-willed kindergartners — they were able, rats and humans alike, to assert themselves, draw on reserves of self-confidence, and make their way forward.

12. Parenting Interventions

There is a direct link between Mary Ainsworth's research on attachment and Nadine Burke Harris's clinic in Bayview–Hunters Point, and that link is a San Francisco psychologist named Alicia Lieberman. In the mid-1970s, Lieberman studied with Ainsworth at Johns Hopkins University in Baltimore. It was the era when Ainsworth was conducting her first big study of parenting and attachment, and under Ainsworth's direction, Lieberman, then a graduate student, spent long hours watching and coding videotape of new mothers interacting with their babies, looking for the small, specific examples of sensitive and responsive maternal behavior that promoted secure attachment for the infants. Today, Lieberman runs the Child Trauma Research Program at the University of California at San Francisco, where she has become, in recent years, a close collaborator with Nadine Burke Harris.

Lieberman told me that while she admires the study that Sroufe and Egeland did in Minnesota, she feels there are two important ideas missing from their analysis. The first is an explicit recognition of how plainly difficult it is for many parents in neighborhoods like Bayview–Hunters Point to form secure attachments with their children. "Often, the circumstances of a mother's life overwhelm her natural coping capacity," Lieberman told me when I visited one of the clinics where she works in San Francisco. "When you are bombarded by poverty, uncertainty, and fear, it takes a superhuman quality to provide the conditions for a secure attachment." In addition, a mother's own attachment history can make her parenting challenge even greater: research from the Minnesota study and elsewhere shows that if a new mother experienced insecure attachment with her parents as a child (no matter what her class background), then it will be exponentially more difficult for her to provide a secure, nurturing environment for her own children.

The other thing that is underemphasized in the Minnesota study, Lieberman said, is the fact that parents can *overcome* histories of trauma and poor attachment; that they can change their approach to their children from one that produces anxious attachment to one that promotes secure attachment and healthy functioning. Some parents can accomplish this transformation on their own, Lieberman said, but most need help. And that is what she has spent most of her career doing: figuring out how best to provide that help. In the years after she left Johns Hopkins, she developed a treatment, called child-parent psychotherapy, that combines Ainsworth's theories on attachment with more recent research on traumatic stress. In child-parent psychotherapy, therapists work with at-risk parents and their infant children simultaneously to improve attachment relationships and protect both parents and children from the effects of trauma. Two therapists in Lieberman's program now work on site at Burke Harris's clinic, providing the treatment to dozens of patients.

Lieberman's treatment is relatively intensive, administered in weekly sessions that can continue for as long as a year. But the principle behind it — improving children's outcomes by promoting stronger relationships between children and their parents — is increasingly in use across the country in a wide variety of interventions. And the results, when these interventions are evaluated, are often powerful.

In one study, Dante Cicchetti, a psychologist at the University of Minnesota, tracked a group of 137 families with documented histories of previous child maltreatment; these were families, in other words, where children were at very high risk. Each family had a one-year-old child who was the focus of the intervention. At the beginning of the study, all the infants were evaluated in the Strange Situation procedure, and the results were predictably awful: just one of the 137 infants demonstrated secure attachment, and 90 percent of them were classified as having disorganized attachment, the most problematic type of anxious attachment. Then the families were divided randomly into a treatment group and a control group. The treatment group was given a year of Lieberman's child-parent psychotherapy, and the control group received the standard community services provided to families reported for maltreatment. When the children were two years old, 61 percent of the ones in the treatment group had formed a secure attachment with their mothers, while in the control group, only 2 percent of the children were securely attached. Attachment-promoting parenting, Cicchetti had shown, can be nurtured in even the most troubled parents, and the benefit to both them and their children can be profound.

Other studies have shown an effect on not only children's attachment classification but also the health of their stress-response systems, and researchers have demonstrated this effect with interventions that are less intensive than Lieberman's treatment. An intervention called Multidimensional Treatment Foster Care for Preschoolers, run by a psychologist in Eugene, Oregon, named Philip Fisher, gives foster parents six months of training and consultation in techniques to manage confrontation and difficult situations in the home. Children in foster care often have trouble regulating their stress-response systems (just as Monisha Sullivan did), but in one experiment, after six months of treatment, the kids in Fisher's program not only showed increased evidence of secure attachment; they also had cortisol patterns that had shifted from dysfunctional to entirely normal.

Another intervention for foster parents of young children, called

Attachment and Biobehavioral Catch-up, or ABC, was developed by Mary Dozier, a psychologist at the University of Delaware. ABC encourages foster parents to respond to their infants' cues more attentively and warmly and calmly. After just ten home visits, children in ABC show higher rates of secure attachment, and their cortisol levels are indistinguishable from those of typical, well-functioning, non-foster-care children. What is perhaps most remarkable about Dozier's intervention is that only the parents receive the treatment, not the children in their care — and yet it has a profound effect on the HPA-axis functioning of the children.

13. Visiting Makayla

I saw the attachment-promotion approach in action one recent spring afternoon on the South Side of Chicago when I visited a sixteen-year-old girl named Jacqui and her eight-month-old baby, Makayla, at the house where they lived with Jacqui's mother. I wasn't the only visitor — an older African American woman named Anita Stewart-Montgomery was there too, an employee of Catholic Charities who regularly visited at-risk parents (usually single mothers) and their children through a program run by the Ounce of Prevention Fund, a Chicago-based philanthropy. After the visit, I spoke to Nick Wechsler, an infant specialist who has overseen the Ounce's home-visiting programs for more than two decades. He explained that while he and his staff do care about the traditional issues that home visitors discuss with new parents — infant nutrition and smoking cessation and vocabulary growth — they are convinced by the research that improving attachment is the most powerful lever they have for improving child outcomes. And so attachment is what they emphasize.

In fact, Wechsler said, he often has to remind home visitors in the program that it is not their job to try to fix all the many problems they see in the lives of the young parents they visit — just this one. "It's a tremendous challenge for home visitors, because your instinct is that you want to do more," Wechsler told me. "But even if you can't always take away bad housing or bad schooling, you can build in the parent an inner strength and resilience, so they can be the best parent they can be."

It was true that there was plenty to fix in Makayla's world. As I watched her and Jacqui and Stewart-Montgomery playing and talking on the living-room rug, I found myself wishing that the house were quieter and the furniture had fewer sharp corners, that she and her mom and grandmother didn't live next to an abandoned lot on a rough-looking block, and that we couldn't smell the cigarette smoke from next door. But Stewart-Montgomery, to her credit, focused on Jacqui, watching her watch Makayla, making encouraging comments, expressing to Jacqui exactly the kind of warm and nurturing support that she hoped Jacqui would pass on to Makayla.

A previous generation of early-childhood interventions, developed under the influence of Hart and Risley's research on the importance of early language skills, focused primarily on encouraging the parents to take steps to expand their children's vocabulary. The frustrating reality about those interventions, though, is that if you are a parent and you have a limited vocabulary, which many low-income parents do, it is very hard for you to nurture in your children a rich vocabulary. Reading to them more is certainly helpful, but infants absorb language from their parents not just in dedicated vocabulary-building moments but at every moment. This is why vocabulary deficits are often handed down from one generation to the next — a cycle that a great preschool and a great kindergarten can do a lot to interrupt but that is hard to break with a parent-based intervention alone.

But what Fisher and Dozier and Cicchetti and Lieberman have demonstrated is that the potential for growth and improvement is much greater when it comes to attachment. Unlike a subpar vocabulary, anxiety-producing parenting can be undone with a relatively minor intervention. Which means that the cycle of poor attachment can be broken for good. If a low-income mother with attachment issues gets the right kind of intervention, she can become a mother who forms a secure attachment with her child. And that will potentially make a huge difference in that child's life. If Anita Stewart-Montgomery is able to help Jacqui and Makayla form a secure attachment bond, then Makayla will not just be more likely to be a happy child. She will also be more likely to graduate from high school, to stay out of jail, to delay pregnancy, and to have a more positive relationship with her own children.

14. Steve Gates

Soon after Ron Huberman, Chicago's schools CEO, announced his plan to hire YAP's advocates to mentor the city's ultra-high-risk teenagers, Heather Mac Donald, an Olin fellow at the conservative Manhattan Institute, wrote a long article in the institute's quarterly publication, *City Journal,* about youth violence in the city. She was critical of Huberman and YAP — and of Barack Obama, for that matter — for ignoring what she called the primary cause of Roseland's dysfunction: "the disappearance of the black two-parent family." She associated YAP with the work of Saul Alinsky, the left-wing twentieth-century political organizer, and complained about the "assiduously nonjudgmental" interventions she believed YAP advocates were undertaking. In their place, she proposed an intervention in which advocates acted like "Scoutmasters" and "provided their charges with opportunities to learn self-discipline and perseverance, fired their imaginations with manly virtues, and spoke to them about honesty, courtesy, and right and wrong." That kind of tough talk, Mac Donald wrote, "might make some progress in reversing the South Side's social breakdown."

Oddly, though, for all of Mac Donald's heated criticism of what she imagined YAP was doing, the reality that I heard and saw from YAP advocates looked an awful lot like what Mac Donald was proposing. Far from avoiding talk of family breakdown, advocates like Steve Gates seemed preoccupied with it, and they were quite explicit that they wouldn't need to be doing the work they were doing if Roseland's families were functioning the way families should.

"Take a close look at our kids' family structures, and you get a perfectly clear picture of why they are the way they are," Gates told me one morning. "There is a very direct correlation between family issues and what the kids present in school. The lapses in parenting, the dysfunction — it all spills over to the kids, and then they take that to school and the streets and everywhere else."

Gates is not blind to the many other problems that young people face in Roseland; he is keenly aware of the social and economic and political forces that have so devastated the neighborhood during his lifetime. In fact, he often takes them personally. White flight, for example: In the early 1970s, when Gates arrived in Roseland as a newborn with his parents, they were one of the only black families on the block. That didn't last long. "By the time I could walk," Gates told me, "all the Caucasian kids were gone." And it wasn't just his block. In 1960, there were more than 45,000 white people living in Roseland; in 1990, there were 493. Meanwhile, the South Side's vibrant manufacturing sector, which employed Gates's grandfather, father, and uncles, evaporated as well, as one factory after another closed its doors or moved away. What was left behind in Roseland was a tangle of social pathologies that seemed to grow only worse each year, each problem reinforcing itself and feeding a host of others, from welfare dependency to drug addiction to gang violence.

But while Gates is careful not to blame Roseland's parents for the neighborhood's crisis, he has decided that for him, at least, the most effective vehicle for improving children's outcomes is not the school or the church or even the job center; it is the family — or, if necessary, the creation of substitute or supplemental family structures for children who don't have them. This approach certainly doesn't have a 100 percent success rate, and in the months that I spent watching Steve Gates, he experienced countless setbacks and tragedies: teenagers he was mentoring were arrested, jailed, shot, or even killed. But sometimes it did work, and the transformations that YAP's advocates were able to inspire in their clients were often stunning.

15. Keitha Jones

The YAP student whose future seemed the most hopeful was also the one whose life story I found the most painful to hear. Keitha Jones was, when I met her in Elizabeth Dozier's office in the fall of 2010, a

seventeen-year-old Fenger High School senior. She had a hard look
about her — tattoos up and down her arms, a metal stud through
her lower lip, and an angry streak of red dye down the front of her
choppy haircut. She lived in her mother's house on Parnell Avenue at
113th Street, a couple of blocks south of Fenger in a section of Roseland known as the Hundreds. The house, a small, worn bungalow,
was, when Keitha was growing up, invariably loud and crowded and
full of conflict, populated by a rotating crew of lodgers: siblings, half
siblings, uncles, cousins. On rare occasions, the cast would include
Keitha's father, who was, as she described him, a "player," a local me-
chanic with a wife and family living a few blocks away, girlfriends
(including Keitha's mom) scattered all over the neighborhood, and a
total of nineteen kids. Growing up, Keitha would occasionally meet a
girl who looked suspiciously like herself, and she'd think: *Well, there's
another sister.* Keitha's mother had been a Fenger student back in the
eighties until she got kicked out in her senior year for showing up at
school drunk. Now she was addicted to crack, Keitha told me, as were
many others in her extended family. Some of them dealt cocaine as
well, and when Keitha was young, police raided the house on Parnell
frequently, looking for drugs or guns, and they knocked over dressers
and threw pots and pans around and then usually dragged one relative or another away in handcuffs.

When Keitha was in the sixth grade, she told me, she was sexually
molested by a relative, an older man she called Cousin Angelo, also
a crack addict, who lived with her family throughout her childhood.
"I was real young, and I was scared," she recalled. "So I was just, like,
Whatever you're going to do, you need to do it and get it over with."
The abuse, which went on for years, ate away at her. She hoped her
mother would somehow notice and intervene, but Keitha never actually said anything — she was afraid that if she did tell her mother, her
mother wouldn't believe her, and that would be more than Keitha
could bear. So she kept quiet and just got angrier and angrier. She
and her mother argued all the time, but they never came to blows;
Keitha believed it was wrong to strike an adult. "So that's why I used
to come to school, just to fight," she told me. "That was the way for

me to relieve the stress. I didn't talk to people about my problems. I just let them build up inside until I was ready to explode. And so when I got to school, as soon as someone said something to me that I didn't like, I'd take my anger out on them, because I knew I couldn't hit my mama." In her freshman year at Fenger, Keitha piled up multiple disciplinary infractions, one ten-day suspension after another, until she had a reputation as one of the most violent kids at a violent school. "That's how everybody thought of me," she said. "As a fighter. I used to brag on it."

In June of 2010, Dozier requested that Keitha be assigned to a YAP advocate. The first advocate Steve Gates paired Keitha with wasn't the right fit — she was too "old-fashioned," in Keitha's opinion. So Gates tried again, assigning Keitha to a part-time advocate named Lanita Reed, a thirty-one-year-old Roseland resident who was mentoring just one other YAP client. Reed had a full-time job running her own beauty salon, a cozy, welcoming place called Gifted Hanz that cheered up an otherwise desolate block of 103rd Street. Keitha had always had in the back of her mind the idea that she wanted to cut hair, so Reed put her to work in the salon as a shampoo girl, washing hair and sweeping up and occasionally helping out with molding or braiding or doing twisties, the short, tight dreads that many of the neighborhood boys wore.

Reed is a spiritual person, a regular churchgoer, but she also believes in the importance of a young lady's physical appearance, so she undertook with Keitha what amounted to a simultaneous inner and outer makeover. When you meet her, Keitha does not seem like the manicure type, but Reed convinced her to get her nails done and have her hair styled, and she taught her about makeup and false eyelashes and nice clothes. The two of them spent hours at Gifted Hanz or out together in the neighborhood, eating or bowling or just sitting and talking: an extended, ongoing salon-therapy session. Reed, Keitha told me, was like the perfect big sister. She organized Sunday-night dinners at the salon for Keitha and a few other girls enrolled in the YAP program where they could trade stories about neglectful mothers and absent fathers, about boys and drugs and anger. Keitha, who had never talked about anything to anybody, opened up. "My whole outlook on life changed," Keitha told me.

At Reed's suggestion, Keitha started praying. "I asked God just to heal me," she said, "to forgive all the bad things I did." She stopped arguing with her mother and quit fighting at school. When a couple of sophomore girls started mouthing off to her in the hallways, she kept her cool and asked Reed what to do about it. Reed helped to arrange a sit-down with the girls in Dozier's office, and much to Keitha's surprise, they were able to work through their problems. "When we sat down to talk about it," Keitha told me, "it turned out it was all over nothing."

And then another distressing development: That fall, Keitha's youngest sister, who was just six years old, told Keitha that Cousin Angelo had tried to touch her. "When she said that, I just couldn't stop crying," Keitha told me. "I felt so guilty. Because if I had said something when I was younger, then maybe he would have been gone, and it wouldn't ever have happened to my sister." Keitha told Reed, and Reed told Gates, and Gates told Reed that she was obligated to inform the Illinois Department of Child and Family Services, or DCFS; like almost all social workers and teachers, YAP advocates were mandated reporters, meaning they were legally required to report physical or sexual abuse to the proper authorities. Reed was beside herself. In Roseland, DCFS were the bad guys: they were the people who took your kids away. And troubled though Keitha's home was, Reed believed that Keitha and her siblings belonged with their mother, not in foster care.

Reed told Gates she didn't want to make the report. She threatened to quit. She didn't know what to do. "The street in me wanted to go get somebody and just beat Angelo up," Reed told me. "But the God in me said you have to deal with this situation the best you can." Reed finally let Gates place the call. She managed to negotiate with the social workers from DCFS, and in the end Angelo was removed from the home—he ended up in jail, charged with sexual assault on a minor—and Keitha and her siblings stayed with their mother.

As Keitha had feared, her mother wasn't very supportive about Keitha's decision to speak out about Angelo. She complained about losing the three hundred dollars a month that Angelo had been contributing to the rent, and she sometimes seemed to Keitha to be more concerned about how Angelo would survive in prison than about the daughters he molested. But Keitha had resolved to change her life, and the incident with Angelo made her all the more determined. "I'm not going to let my past affect my future," she told me. "I'm going to think about it every now and then, but I'm not going to let it take a toll. The worst has already been done. I'm looking for the positive now. I'm so tired of living the way I'm living that I'm going to do everything in my power to change things."

Though she was behind on credits at school, Keitha set her mind on graduating with her class in the summer of 2011, and the school system made it possible for her. If you are an underperforming big-city high-school student these days, there are plenty of mechanisms available that let you gather credits quickly: makeup work, night school, online credit-recovery courses like Aventa that let students complete a semester-long course in a month or two. Many education advocates are skeptical about these innovations, which often seem to be nothing more than a new way for school systems to get rid of their most-difficult-to-teach students, sending them out into the world with diplomas but not real educations. But for Keitha, who was more than ready to get away from Fenger, the courses were a godsend, and for the first time in her academic career, she actually worked hard at her classes; she attended night school five days a week and often stayed at Fenger from eight in the morning till seven at night. In June of 2011, Keitha graduated from Fenger and enrolled in Truman College, a community college on the North Side of Chicago, where she began studying for a cosmetology degree.

One day in the spring of 2011, with graduation still a few months away, Keitha and I sat in the Fenger cafeteria and she described her plan for the future. After she graduated from Truman and got licensed, she told me, Lanita Reed had promised her a full-time job in her salon. "Five years from now, I picture myself in my own apartment with my own money," Keitha said. "And my little sisters, they can come live with me."

That was what always impressed me the most about Keitha: that her dream was to find a way out not just for herself but for her family too. "I want to show my little sisters that there is a better life than what we see every day," she told me that day in the cafeteria. "It might look to them like this is all you get, because they don't know nothing but Parnell and the Hundreds. But there's more in life than what it is out here, all this fighting and killing and all that. There's more. There's way more."

It is hard to argue with the science behind early intervention. Those first few years matter so much in the healthy development of a child's brain; they represent a unique opportunity to make a difference in a child's future. But one of the most promising facts about programs that target emotional and psychological and neurological pathways is that they can be quite effective later on in childhood too — much more so than cognitive interventions. Pure IQ is stubbornly resistant to improvement after about age eight. But executive functions and the ability to handle stress and manage strong emotions can be improved, sometimes dramatically, well into adolescence and even adulthood.

The teenage years are difficult for almost every child, and for children growing up in adversity, adolescence can often mark a terrible turning point, the moment when early wounds produce bad decisions, and bad decisions produce devastating results. But teenagers also have the ability — or at least the potential — to rethink and remake their lives in a way that younger children do not. And as Keitha's story shows (and as you'll see again in the chapters ahead), adolescence can be a time for a different kind of turning point, the profoundest sort of transformation: the moment when a young person manages to turn herself away from near-certain failure and begins to steer a course toward success.

2

HOW TO BUILD
CHARACTER

1. Best Class Ever

The thirty-eight young teenagers who graduated from KIPP Academy middle school in the South Bronx in the spring of 1999 might just be the most famous eighth-grade class in the history of American public education. All black and Hispanic, almost all from low-income families, they had been recruited from their fourth-grade classrooms four years earlier by David Levin, a manic, lanky, twenty-five-year-old white Yale graduate who won them (and their parents) over with the pledge that if they enrolled in his brand-new middle school, he would transform them from typical underperforming Bronx-public-school students into college-bound scholars. In their four years at KIPP (which stands for Knowledge Is Power Program), they had experienced a new, immersive style of schooling, one that Levin often seemed to be inventing on the fly, combining long days of high-energy, high-intensity classroom instruction with an elaborate program of attitude adjustment and behavior modification.

Levin's formula seemed to have worked, and remarkably quickly: on the eighth-grade citywide achievement test in 1999, the students of KIPP Academy earned the highest scores of any school in the Bronx and the fifth-highest in all of New York City. Those scores — unheard-of at the time for an open-admission school in a poor neighborhood — led to a front-page story on KIPP in the *New York Times* and a report by Mike Wallace on *60 Minutes,* and they helped convince Doris and Donald Fisher, the founders of the Gap, to put millions of philanthropic dollars behind an effort to turn KIPP into a national network. That project has led to the creation of more than a hundred new KIPP charter schools around the country over the past decade, and it has kept KIPP, for better or worse, at the center of the national debates over charter schools, unionized teachers, standardized tests, and the effect of poverty on learning.

From their very first day of school, back in 1995, the students in that initial cohort at KIPP Academy were reminded — some might say browbeaten — about the importance of higher education. They were labeled the Class of 2003, for the year they would enter college. The school's hallways were lined with college pennants, and each teacher decorated her classroom with paraphernalia from her own alma mater. A giant sign in the stairwell reminded the students of their mission: CLIMB THE MOUNTAIN TO COLLEGE. And when they graduated from KIPP, they seemed poised to do just that: Not only did they leave middle school with outstanding academic results, but most of them had won admission to highly selective private or Catholic high schools, often with full scholarships.

But for many students in that first cohort, things didn't go as planned. "We thought, 'Okay, our first class was the fifth-highest performing class in all of New York City,'" Levin told me. "'We got ninety percent into private and parochial schools. It's all going to be solved.' But it wasn't." Almost every member of the Class of 2003 did make it through high school, and most of them enrolled in college. But then the mountain grew steeper: Six years after their high-school graduation, just 21 percent of the cohort — eight students — had completed a four-year college degree.

Tyrell Vance was part of that original KIPP class, and in many ways his experience was typical. When he first arrived at KIPP, he felt overwhelmed, bewildered by the rituals and rules and energy. "It was like a culture shock," he told me. "I had never seen anything like it." Vance considered homework to be optional, but at KIPP, it was mandatory, and that difference of opinion led to a long series of battles between Vance and the KIPP staff. When the class took off on a trip to Vermont in seventh grade, Vance was left behind to catch up on his homework. Still, it was clear that KIPP's teachers were devoted to him and his fellow students, and he became devoted to them as well. "They were my second family, in essence," he told me. "That's the vibe we all ended up getting, that we were like a family."

Like so many students in that class, Vance was a math star in middle school, acing the citywide test, passing the ninth-grade state math course when he was still in eighth grade. But when he got to high school, he told me, away from KIPP's blast furnace of ambition, he lost his intensity. "I didn't have the drive that I had when I was at KIPP," he explained. He started coasting, and his report cards were soon filled with Cs instead of the As and Bs he'd been getting in middle school. The way Vance sees it today, KIPP set him up for high school very well academically, but it didn't prepare him emotionally or psychologically. "We went from having that close-knit family, where everyone knew what you were doing, to high school, where there's no one on you," he said. "There's no one checking if you did your homework. Then we had to deal with all the stuff that everybody goes through in high school, just growing up. And none of us were really prepared for that."

After high school, Vance enrolled in a four-year public college in upstate New York to study computer information systems, but he found the subject boring, so he switched his major to casino and gaming management. He didn't get along with the head of that department, so he dropped out, took a little time off and worked at a shoe store, and then enrolled in another school in the state system, planning to major in history. Before long, though, his tuition money ran out, and this time Vance dropped out altogether. Now in his mid-twenties, he has spent the last few years working in call centers for

AT&T and Time Warner Cable, answering customer-service questions. He enjoys the work, and he is proud of what he's accomplished, but looking back, he has regrets too. "I had a lot of potential," he told me, "and I probably should have done more with it."

2. Learned Optimism

For David Levin, it was painful to watch those first students struggle through their college experience. Every month or so, it seemed, he would get word that another student had decided to drop out. Levin took the college data personally: What could he have done differently? The whole point of KIPP was to give his students everything they needed to succeed in college. What had he failed to include?

As the dropout reports rolled in, not just from the first KIPP class but from the second and third too, Levin noticed something curious: The students who persisted in college were not necessarily the ones who had excelled academically at KIPP. Instead, they seemed to be the ones who possessed certain other gifts, skills like optimism and resilience and social agility. They were the students who were able to recover from bad grades and resolve to do better next time; who could bounce back from unhappy breakups or fights with their parents; who could persuade professors to give them extra help after class; who could resist the urge to go out to the movies and instead stay home and study. Those traits weren't enough by themselves to earn a student a BA, Levin knew. But for young people without the benefit of a lot of family resources, without the kind of safety net that their wealthier peers enjoyed, these characteristics proved to be an indispensable part of making it to college graduation day.

The qualities that Levin was noticing in his college graduates overlapped considerably with the set of abilities that James Heckman and other economists had identified as noncognitive skills. But Levin liked to use a different term: *character strengths.* Since KIPP's beginnings, in a middle-school classroom in Houston in the early 1990s, Levin and KIPP's cofounder, Michael Feinberg, had explicitly set out to provide students with lessons in character as well as academics. They filled the walls with slogans like "Work Hard" and "Be Nice" and "There Are No Shortcuts," and they developed a system of rewards and demerits designed to instruct their students in not only fractions and algebra but also teamwork and empathy and perseverance. At KIPP Academy, kids wore T-shirts with the slogan "One School. One Mission. Two Skills. Academics and Character."

Levin and Feinberg originally came to Houston as part of the third Teach for America cohort; they were brand-new Ivy League graduates and relatively clueless teachers. Early on, they borrowed academic tricks and tactics from innovative educators they met, especially a woman named Harriett Ball, a veteran teacher down the hall from Levin's classroom whose chants, songs, and drills made it easier to teach every academic subject, from multiplication tables to Shakespeare. But when it came to teaching character, Levin told me, he and Feinberg found no equivalent mentor. The absence of any established structure for teaching character, or even talking about it, meant that each year, the discussions at KIPP schools would start from scratch, with teachers and administrators debating anew which values and behaviors they were trying to nurture in their students, and why, and how.

In the winter of 2002, as the first KIPP Academy graduates were making their way through high school, Levin's brother, a money manager, gave him *Learned Optimism*, a book by Martin Seligman, a professor of psychology at the University of Pennsylvania. Seligman is one of the main scholars behind the school of thought known as positive psychology, and the book, originally published in 1991, is the movement's founding text, teaching that optimism is a learnable skill, not an inborn trait. Pessimistic adults and children can train themselves to be more hopeful, Seligman says, and if they do, they will likely become happier, healthier, and more successful. In *Learned Optimism*, Seligman wrote that for most people, depression was not an illness, as most psychologists believed, but simply a "severe low mood" that occurred "when we harbor pessimistic beliefs about the causes of our setbacks." If you want to avoid depression and improve your life, Seligman counseled, you need to refashion your "explanatory style," to create for yourself a better story about why good and bad things happen to you.

Pessimists, Seligman wrote, tend to react to negative events by explaining them as permanent, personal, and pervasive. (Seligman calls these "the three P's.") Failed a test? It's not because you didn't prepare well; it's because you're stupid. If you get turned down for a date, there's no point in asking someone else; you're simply unlovable. Optimists, by contrast, look for specific, limited, short-term explanations for bad events, and as a result, in the face of a setback, they're more likely to pick themselves up and try again.

As he read the book, Levin recognized many of Seligman's three-P explanatory patterns in himself, in his teachers, and in his students. Levin was famous among students and staff in those days for the long, loud lectures he regularly delivered to misbehaving or underperforming students. ("The man yelled a *lot*," Vance recalled with a laugh.) Now Levin found himself wondering what those diatribes might sound like to a student who tended to hear critical remarks personally, pervasively, and permanently. "Why didn't you do your homework?" could easily be interpreted as meaning "What's wrong with you? You can't do anything right!" Levin bought a copy of *Learned Optimism* for everyone on the staff of the KIPP Academy, and he drew up a list of Questions for Reflection and Concern inspired by the book. On a professional-development day in the summer of 2002, he handed out the list to his teachers for discussion. It included some uncomfortable questions for Levin and his staff, like *Why do some of our students feel not-liked/not-valued/not-believed-in?* and *Why do some of our parents feel belittled/disrespected/spoken down to?* and *How do we continue to develop the spirit and character of the KIPPsters without breaking them?* For Levin, it was the beginning of a long process of reevaluation. He had spent almost a decade trying to develop the character of his students. What if the techniques he was using just weren't working?

3. Riverdale

David Levin attended school in the Bronx, like his students, but in a very different part of the Bronx and at a very different kind of school. If you drive west from KIPP Academy, go past Yankee Stadium, then turn north and head a few miles up the Major Deegan Expressway, you soon arrive in Riverdale, a lush, green neighborhood of steep hills and winding streets that for more than a century has been home to some of New York City's wealthiest families. Among the historic mansions stand three of the city's most prestigious private schools: the Horace Mann school, the Ethical Culture Fieldston School, and, at the top of a tall hill, looking down grandly on Van Cortlandt Park and the city below, the Riverdale Country School. Levin, who grew up on Park Avenue, transferred to Riverdale in eighth grade, and he excelled there, becoming not only a standout student in math and science but also the captain of the basketball team.

When you visit the school today, what impresses you first is its campus, the largest of any school in the city, twenty-seven rolling acres adorned with stone buildings and carefully tended lacrosse fields. There are no uniforms, technically, but the middle- and high-school students share a studiously casual wardrobe of Abercrombie and Fitch jackets and North Face backpacks. (One wet late-winter day when I visited a tenth-grade English class, every girl but one was wearing identical $125 knee-high Hunter rain boots.) John F. Kennedy and Robert F. Kennedy went to Riverdale briefly as boys, and today's student body draws heavily from the Upper East Side and the tonier precincts of Westchester County; it is the kind of place members of the establishment send their kids so they can learn to be members of the establishment. Tuition starts at $38,500 a year, and that's for prekindergarten.

When you first meet him, Dominic Randolph, Riverdale's headmaster, seems like an unusual choice to lead an institution so steeped in status and tradition. He comes across as an iconoclast, a disrupter, even a bit of an eccentric. He dresses for work every day in a black suit with a narrow tie, and the outfit, plus his cool demeanor and flowing, graying hair, makes you wonder if he might have played sax in a ska band in the 1980s. (The English accent helps.) Randolph is a big thinker, always chasing new ideas, and a conversation with him can feel like a one-man TED conference; it is dotted with references to the latest work by behavioral psychologists and management gurus and design theorists. When he became headmaster, in 2007, he swapped offices with his secretary: she got the reclusive inner sanctum where previous headmasters had sat, and he remodeled the small outer reception area into his own open-concept workspace, its walls lined with whiteboards on which he sketches ideas and slogans. One day when I visited, one wall was bare except for a lone sheet of white paper. On it was printed a single black question mark.

For the headmaster of an intensely competitive school, Randolph, who is in his early fifties, is surprisingly skeptical about many of the basic elements of a contemporary high-stakes American education. He did away with Advanced Placement classes soon after he arrived at Riverdale; he encourages his teachers to limit the homework they assign; and he says that the standardized tests that Riverdale and other private schools require for admission to kindergarten and middle school are "a patently unfair system" because they evaluate students almost entirely by IQ. "This push on tests," he told me when I visited his office one fall day, "is missing out on some serious parts of what it means to be a successful human."

The most critical missing piece, Randolph explained, is character. "Whether it's the pioneer in the Conestoga wagon or someone coming here in the 1920s from southern Italy, there was always this idea in America that if you worked hard and you showed real grit, that you could be successful," he said. "Strangely, we've now forgotten that. People who have an easy time of things, who get eight hundreds on their SATs, I worry that those people get feedback that everything they're doing is great. And I think as a result, we are actually setting them up for long-term failure. When that person suddenly has to face up to a difficult moment, then I think they're screwed, to be honest. I don't think they've grown the capacities to be able to handle that."

Like Levin, Randolph has pondered throughout his career as an educator the question of whether and how schools should impart good character. It has often felt like a lonely quest. At the British boarding school Randolph attended as a boy, educators took it for granted that they were teaching character as much as they were teaching math or history. When Randolph moved to the United States, though, he found that American educators were more reluctant to talk about character than their British counterparts. For many years, he followed the national discourse on character, or what passed for it, but it always seemed to him out of step with the needs of a school. In the 1980s, William Bennett made the case for teaching virtue, but that effort quickly became too political for Randolph's taste, co-opted, he says, by neoconservatives. He was intrigued by Daniel Goleman's writing on emotional intelligence in the 1990s, but it seemed too mushy, too touchy-feely, to serve as the basis for a practical system of instruction. "I was looking for something that was going to be serious, that wasn't going to be a fad, that would let you actually shift a school's culture," he told me.

In the winter of 2005, Randolph read *Learned Optimism*, and he became intrigued by the field of positive psychology. He began to read up on the work of not only Seligman but also two of Seligman's frequent collaborators: Christopher Peterson of the University of Michigan and Angela Duckworth, one of Seligman's star protégées at Penn. At the time, Randolph was the assistant head of the Lawrenceville School, a private boarding and day school near Princeton, New Jersey, and he arranged a meeting with Seligman in Philadelphia. As it happened, on the morning that Randolph made the forty-mile drive, Seligman had scheduled a separate meeting with David Levin. When the two educators arrived in his office at about the same time, Seligman decided, impulsively, to combine the two meetings, and he invited the psychologist Peterson, who was also visiting Penn that day, to join him and Randolph and Levin in his office for a freewheeling discussion of psychology and schooling. It turned out to be the beginning of a long and fruitful collaboration.

4. Character Strengths

Levin and Randolph each came to Philadelphia expecting to talk about optimism. But Seligman surprised them by pulling out a new and very different book, which he and Peterson had just finished: *Character Strengths and Virtues: A Handbook and Classification.* The bestselling books that Seligman had published previously were relatively thin works of popularly accessible psychology with subtitles designed to catch the eye in an airport bookstore ("How to Change Your Mind and Your Life"!), but *Character Strengths and Virtues* was an eight-hundred-page scholarly tome that weighed in at three and a half pounds and retailed for eighty dollars. It was intended, according to the authors, to be a "manual of the sanities," a mirror image of the *Diagnostic and Statistical Manual of Mental Disorders,* or the *DSM,* the authoritative taxonomy of psychiatric maladies that sat on the bookshelf of every therapist and psychiatrist. *Character Strengths and Virtues* was an attempt to inaugurate a "science of good character." It was, in other words, exactly what Randolph and Levin had each been looking for, even if neither of them had quite known it.

Character is one of those words that complicate any conversation, mostly because it can mean very different things to different people. It is often used to represent adherence to a particular set of values, which means that its definition will necessarily change over time. In Victorian England, a person of good character was one who displayed values like chastity, thrift, cleanliness, piety, and social propriety. On the American frontier, good character had more to do with courage, self-sufficiency, ingenuity, industriousness, and grit. But Seligman and Peterson aspired in their book to transcend those vagaries of history, to identify qualities that were valued not just in contemporary North American culture but in every society and in every era. They consulted works from Aristotle to Confucius, from the Upanishads to the Torah, from the *Boy Scouts Handbook* to profiles of Pokémon creatures, and they eventually settled on a list of twenty-four character strengths they believed to be universally respected. The list includes some qualities we think of as traditional noble traits, like bravery, citizenship, fairness, wisdom, and integrity; others that veer into the emotional realm, like love, humor, zest, and appreciation of beauty; and still others that are more concerned with day-to-day human interactions, like social intelligence (the ability to recognize interpersonal dynamics and adapt quickly to different social situations), kindness, and gratitude.

In most societies, Seligman and Peterson wrote, character strengths were considered to have a moral valence, and in many cases they overlapped with religious laws and strictures. But moral laws were limiting when it came to character because they reduced virtuous conduct to a simple matter of obedience to a higher authority. "Virtues," they wrote, "are much more interesting than laws." According to Seligman and Peterson, the value of these twenty-four character strengths did not come from their relationship to any particular system of ethics but from their practical benefit — what you could actually gain by possessing and expressing them. Cultivating these strengths represented a reliable path to "the good life," a life that was not just happy but meaningful and fulfilling.

For many of us, *character* refers to something innate and unchanging, a core set of attributes that define one's very essence. Seligman and Peterson defined *character* in a different way: a set of abilities or strengths that are very much changeable — entirely malleable, in fact. They are skills you can learn; they are skills you can practice; and they are skills you can teach.

In practice, though, when educators try to teach character, they often collide with those moral laws. In the 1990s, there was a big national push for character education in the United States, inspired partly by encouraging comments from the First Lady, Hillary Clinton, and from President Clinton, who declared in his 1996 State of the Union address, "I challenge all our schools to teach character education, to teach good values and good citizenship." But before long, the Clintons' character campaign devolved into finger-pointing and mutual suspicion between advocates on both ends of the political spectrum; the right suspected that character-education initiatives were a cloak for creeping political correctness, and the left suspected the initiatives were hidden attempts at Christian indoctrination. Hundreds of American public schools now have some kind of character-education program in place, but most of them are vague and superficial, and those that have been studied rigorously have generally been found to be ineffective. A national evaluation of character-education programs published in 2010 by the National Center for Education Research, part of the federal Department of Education, studied seven popular elementary-school programs over three consecutive years. It found no significant impact at all from the programs — not on student behavior, not on academic achievement, not on school culture.

What intrigued Levin and Randolph about the approach Seligman was taking was that it was focused not on finger-wagging morality but on personal growth and achievement. KIPP is often considered moralistic by both its champions and its critics. In his 2008 book *Sweating the Small Stuff,* the journalist David Whitman approvingly applied the label "the new paternalism" to the methods that KIPP Academy and similar charter schools employed. These schools, Whitman wrote, taught students "not just how to think but how to act according to what are commonly termed traditional, middle-class values." But Levin cringed at this notion. He disliked the idea that KIPP's aim was to instill in its students middle-class values, as though well-off kids had some depth of character that low-income students lacked. "The thing that I think is great about the character-strength approach is that it is fundamentally devoid of value judgment," he told me. "The inevitable problem with the values-and-ethics approach is you get into, well, Whose values? Whose ethics?"

5. Self-Control and Willpower

After that first meeting in Seligman's office, Levin and Randolph kept in touch, calling and e-mailing, swapping articles and web links, and they soon discovered that they shared a lot of ideas and interests despite the very different school environments in which they worked. They decided to join forces and try to tackle the mysteries of character together, and they turned for help to Angela Duckworth, who at the time was a postdoctoral student in Seligman's department. (She is now an assistant professor there.) Duckworth had come to Penn in 2002, at the age of thirty-two, later in life than a typical graduate student. The daughter of Chinese immigrants, she had been a classic multitasking overachiever in her teens and twenties. After completing her undergraduate degree at Harvard (and starting a summer school for low-income kids in Cambridge in her spare time), she had bounced from one station of the mid-nineties meritocracy to the next: intern in the White House speechwriting office, Marshall scholar at Oxford (where she studied neuroscience), management consultant for McKinsey and Company, charter-school adviser. She thought for many years that she might start her own charter school, but she eventually came to believe that charters weren't the right vehicle to change the circumstances of poor children—or at least, they weren't the right vehicle for her to use. When she applied to the PhD program at Penn, she wrote in her application essay that her experiences working in schools had given her "a distinctly different view of school reform" than the one she had started out with in her twenties. "The problem, I think, is not only the schools but also the students themselves," she wrote. "Here's why: learning is hard. True, learning is fun, exhilarating and gratifying—but it is also often daunting, exhausting and sometimes discouraging. . . . To help chronically low-performing but intelligent students, educators and parents must first recognize that character is at least as important as intellect."

At Penn, Duckworth initially studied self-discipline. For her first-year thesis, she rounded up 164 eighth-grade students at Masterman Middle School, a magnet school in downtown Philadelphia, and gave them all both traditional IQ tests and standard assessments of self-discipline. Then, over the course of a school year, she evaluated their performances using a number of academic measures; at the end of the year, to the surprise of many, she found that the students' self-discipline scores from the previous fall were better predictors of their final GPAs than their IQ scores.

Duckworth began to collaborate with Walter Mischel, a professor of psychology at Columbia University who is famous in social-science circles for a study known informally as the marshmallow test. In the late 1960s, Mischel, then a professor at Stanford University, developed an ingenious experiment to test the willpower of four-year-olds. At a nursery school on the Stanford campus, a researcher brought each child into a small room, sat him at a desk, and offered him a treat, such as a marshmallow. On the desk was a bell. The experimenter announced that she was going to leave the room, and the child could eat the marshmallow when she returned. Then she gave him a choice: If he wanted to eat the marshmallow, he needed only to ring the bell; the experimenter would return, and he could have it. But if he waited until the experimenter returned on her own, he would get two marshmallows.

Mischel intended the experiment as a study of the different techniques that children used to resist temptation. But it took on a new dimension more than a decade later when Mischel began to check up on the children in the experiment to see if their ability to delay gratification had predicted any academic or other outcomes. Starting in 1981, he tracked down as many students as he could find, and he continued to follow them for years afterward. The correlations between the children's marshmallow wait times and their later academic success turned out to be striking. Children who had been able to wait for fifteen minutes for their treat had SAT scores that were, on average, 210 points higher than those of children who had rung the bell after thirty seconds.

Duckworth was intrigued by Mischel's results, which her Philadelphia self-control study seemed to corroborate. But she was actually more interested in Mischel's original premise: If you want to maximize your self-control, which tricks and strategies are most effective? And can those techniques be taught? Mischel's experiment had suggested some interesting answers. For instance, both psychoanalytic theory and behavioral theory had held that the best way for a child to motivate himself to wait and get two marshmallows was for him to keep the reward at the center of his attention, to reinforce how delicious those two marshmallows would be when he finally got to eat them. But in fact, the opposite turned out to be true: when the marshmallows were hidden from view, children were able to delay much longer than when the marshmallows were right in front of them. The children who did best at the delay test created their own distractions. Some talked or sang to themselves while they waited for the experimenter to return; some looked away from the treat or put their hands over their eyes. One young master of self-control actually managed to take a nap.

Mischel found that children were able to delay more effectively if they were given simple prompts to encourage them to think differently about the marshmallow. The more abstractly they thought about the treat, the longer they were able to delay. When children were invited to think of the marshmallow as a puffy round cloud instead of a marshmallow, they were able to delay about seven minutes longer. Some children were encouraged to look at a picture of a marshmallow instead of the real marshmallow. They were able to wait longer too. Others looked at the real marshmallows but were told to "put a frame around them in your head, just like a real picture." Those children were able to wait almost eighteen minutes.

But when Duckworth tried to adapt Mischel's findings to a school context, she found it more difficult than she had expected. In 2003, she and some colleagues conducted a six-week-long experiment with forty fifth-grade students at a school in Philadelphia. They led the kids through self-control exercises and gave them rewards for completing their homework. And at the end of the experiment, the students dutifully reported that they now had more self-control than when they started the program. But in fact, they did not: the children who had been through the intervention did no better on a variety of measures than a control group at the same school. "We looked at teacher ratings of self-control, we looked at homework completion, we looked at standardized achievement tests, we looked at GPA, we looked at whether they were late to class more," Duckworth told me. "We got zero effect on everything."

6. Motivation

The problem with self-control techniques like the ones that the most disciplined marshmallow resisters employed is that they work only when a child knows what he or she wants. The long-term goals Duckworth hoped kids would aspire to were less tangible and immediate and attractive than two marshmallows after twenty minutes. So how do you help children acquire the focus and persistence they will need for longer-term, more abstract goals: passing a test or graduating from high school or succeeding in college?

Duckworth finds it useful to divide the mechanics of achievement into two separate dimensions: motivation and volition. Each one, she says, is necessary to achieve long-term goals, but neither is sufficient alone. Most of us are familiar with the experience of possessing motivation but lacking volition: You can be extremely motivated to lose weight, for example, but unless you have the volition — the willpower, the self-control — to put down the cherry Danish and pick up the free weights, you're not going to succeed. If a child is highly motivated, the self-control techniques and exercises Duckworth tried to teach those fifth-grade students might be very helpful. But what if students just aren't motivated to achieve the goals their teachers or parents want them to achieve? Then, Duckworth acknowledges, all the self-control tricks in the world aren't going to help.

But that doesn't mean it's impossible to shift a person's motivation. In the short term, in fact, it can be surprisingly easy. Let's stay in the candy aisle for a bit longer and consider a couple of experiments done decades ago involving IQ and M&M's. In the first test, conducted in northern California in the late 1960s, a researcher named Calvin Edlund selected seventy-nine children between the ages of five and seven, all from "low-middle class and lower-class homes." The children were randomly divided into an experimental group and a control group. First, they all took a standard version of the

Stanford-Binet IQ test. Seven weeks later, they took a similar test, but this time the kids in the experimental group were given one M&M for each correct answer. On the first test, the two groups were evenly matched on IQ. On the second test, the IQ of the M&M group went up an average of twelve points — a huge leap.

A few years later, two researchers from the University of South Florida elaborated on Edlund's experiment. This time, after the first, candy-less IQ test, they divided the children into three groups according to their scores on the first test. The high-IQ group had an average IQ score on the first test of about 119. The medium-IQ group averaged about 101, and the low-IQ group averaged about 79. On the second test, the researchers offered half the children in each IQ category an M&M for each right answer, just as Edlund had; the others in each group received no reward. The medium-IQ and high-IQ kids who got candy didn't improve their scores at all on the second test. But the low-IQ children who were given M&M's for each correct answer raised their IQ scores to about 97, almost erasing the gap with the medium-IQ group.

The M&M studies were a major blow to the conventional wisdom about intelligence, which held that IQ tests measured something real and permanent — something that couldn't be changed drastically with a few candy-covered chocolates. They also raised an important and puzzling question about the supposedly low-IQ children: Did they actually have low IQs or not? Which number was the true measure of their intelligence: 79 or 97?

This is the kind of frustrating but tantalizing puzzle that teachers face on a regular basis, especially teachers in high-poverty schools. You're convinced that your students are smarter than they appear, and you know that if they would only apply themselves, they would do much better. But how do you get them to apply themselves? Should you just give them M&M's for every correct answer for the rest of their lives? That doesn't seem like a very practical solution. And the reality is that for low-income middle-school students, there are *already* tremendous rewards for doing well on tests — not immediately and for each individual correct answer, but in the long term. If a student's test scores and GPA through middle and high school reflect an applied IQ of 97 instead of 79, he is much more likely to graduate from high school and then college and then to get a good job — at which point he can buy as many bags of M&M's as he wants.

But as every middle-school teacher knows, convincing students of that logic is a lot harder than it seems. Motivation, it turns out, is quite complex, and rewards sometimes backfire. In their book *Freakonomics,* Steven Levitt and Stephen Dubner recount the story of a study researchers undertook in the 1970s to see if giving blood donors a small financial stipend might increase blood donations. The result was actually that *fewer* people gave blood, not more.

And while the M&M test suggests that giving kids material incentives to succeed should make a big difference, in practice, it often doesn't work that way. In recent years, the Harvard economist Roland Fryer has essentially tried to extend the M&M experiment to the scale of a metropolitan school system. He tested several different incentive programs in public schools — offering bonuses to teachers if they improved their classes' test results; offering incentives like cellphone minutes to students if they improved their own test results; offering families financial incentives if their children did better. The experiments were painstaking and carefully run — and the results have been almost uniformly disappointing. There are a couple of bright spots in the data — in Dallas, a program that paid young kids for each book they read seems to have contributed to better reading scores for English-speaking students. But for the most part, the programs were a bust. The biggest experiment, which offered incentives to teachers in New York City, cost seventy-five million dollars and took three years to conduct. And in the spring of 2011, Fryer reported that it had produced no positive results at all.

7. The Coding-Speed Test

This is the problem with trying to motivate people: No one really knows how to do it well. It is precisely why we have such a booming industry in inspirational posters and self-help books and motivational speakers: what motivates us is often hard to explain and hard to measure.

Part of the complexity is that different personality types respond to different motivations. We know this because of a series of experiments undertaken in 2006 by Carmit Segal, then a postdoctoral student in the Harvard economics department and now a professor at a university in Zurich. Segal wanted to test how personality and incentives interacted, and she chose as her vehicle one of the easiest tests imaginable, an evaluation of basic clerical skills called the coding-speed test. It is a very straightforward test. First, participants are given an answer key in which a variety of simple words are each assigned a four-digit identifying number. The list looks something like this:

game	2715
chin	3231
house	4232
hat	4568
room	2864

And then a little lower on the page is a multiple-choice test that offers five four-digit numbers as the potential correct answer for each word.

Questions	Answers				
	A	B	C	D	E
1. hat	2715	4232	4568	3231	2864
2. house	4232	2715	4568	3231	2864
3. chin	4232	2715	3231	4568	2864

All you have to do is find the right number from the key above and then check that box (1C, 2A, 3C, etc.). It's a snap, if a somewhat mind-numbing one.

Segal located two large pools of data that included scores from thousands of young people on both the coding-speed test and a standard cognitive-skills test. One pool was the National Longitudinal Survey of Youth, or NLSY, a huge survey that began tracking a cohort of more than twelve thousand young people in 1979. The other was a group of military recruits who took the coding exam as part of a range of tests they had to pass in order to be accepted into the U.S. Armed Forces. The high-school and college students who were part of the NLSY had no real incentive to exert themselves on the tests — the scores were for research purposes only and didn't have any bearing on their academic records. For the recruits, though, the tests mattered very much; bad scores could keep them out of the military.

When Segal compared the scores of the two groups on each test, she found that on average, the high-school and college kids did better than the recruits on the cognitive tests. But on the coding-speed test, it was the recruits who did better. Now, that might have been because the kind of young person who chose to enlist in the armed forces was naturally gifted at matching numbers with words, but that didn't seem too likely. What the coding-speed test really measured, Segal realized, was something more fundamental than clerical skill: the test takers' inclination and ability to force themselves to care about the world's most boring test. The recruits, who had more at stake, put more effort into the coding test than the NLSY kids did, and on such a simple test, that extra level of exertion was enough for them to beat out their more-educated peers.

Now, remember that the NLSY wasn't just a one-shot test; it tracked young people's progress afterward for many years. So next Segal went back to the NLSY data, looked at each student's cognitive-skills score and coding-speed score in 1979, and then compared those two scores with the student's earnings two decades later, when the student was about forty. Predictably, the kids who did better on the cognitive-skills tests were making more money. But so were the kids who did better on the super-simple coding test. In fact, when Segal looked only at NLSY participants who didn't graduate from college, their coding-test scores were every bit as reliable a predictor of their adult wages as their cognitive-test scores. The high scorers on the coding test were earning thousands of dollars a year more than the low scorers.

And why? Does the modern American labor market really put such a high value on being able to compare mindless lists of words and numbers? Of course not. And in fact, Segal didn't believe that the students who did better on the coding test actually had better coding skills than the other students. They did better for a simple reason: they tried harder. And what the labor market *does* value is the kind of internal motivation required to try hard on a test even when there is no external reward for doing well. Without anyone realizing it, the coding test was measuring a critical noncognitive skill that mattered a lot in the grown-up world.

Segal's findings give us a new way of thinking about the so-called low-IQ kids who took part in the M&M experiment in south Florida. Remember, they scored poorly on the first IQ test and then did much better on the second test, the one with the M&M incentive. So the question was: What was the real IQ of an average "low-IQ" student? Was it 79 or 97? Well, you could certainly make the case that his or her true IQ must be 97. You're supposed to try hard on IQ tests, and when the low-IQ kids had the M&M's to motivate them, they tried hard. It's not as if the M&M's magically gave them the intelligence to figure out the answers; they must have already possessed it. So in fact, they weren't low-IQ at all. Their IQs were about average.

But what Segal's experiment suggests is that it was actually their first score, the 79, that was more relevant to their future prospects. That was their equivalent of the coding-test score, the low-stakes, low-reward test that predicts how well someone is going to do in life. They may not have been low in IQ, but they were low in whatever quality it is that makes a person try hard on an IQ test without any obvious incentive. And what Segal's research shows is that that is a very valuable quality to possess.

8. Conscientiousness

So what do you call the quality exhibited by Segal's go-getters, the kids who exerted themselves whether or not there was a potential reward? Well, here's the technical term that personality psychologists use: *conscientiousness.* Over the past couple of decades, a consensus has emerged among personality psychologists that the most effective way to analyze the human personality is to consider it along five dimensions, known as the Big Five: agreeableness, extraversion, neuroticism, openness to experience, and conscientiousness. And when Segal gave the male students in one of her surveys a standard personality test, the ones who didn't respond to material incentives — who did well whether or not there were M&M's involved — scored particularly high on conscientiousness.

Within the world of personality psychology, the reigning expert on conscientiousness is Brent Roberts, a professor at the University of Illinois at Urbana-Champaign who has collaborated with both James Heckman, the economist, and Angela Duckworth, the psychologist. Roberts told me that in the late 1990s, when he was getting out of grad school and deciding what research field to specialize in, no one wanted to study conscientiousness. Most psychologists considered it to be the black sheep of the personality field. Many still do. It's a cultural thing, Roberts explained. Like the word *character,* the word *conscientiousness* has some strong and not always positive associations outside academia. "Researchers prefer to study the things they value," he told me. "And the people in society who value conscientiousness are not intellectuals, and they're not academics, and they're not liberals. They tend to be religious-right conservatives who think people should be more controlled." (According to Roberts, psychologists prefer to study openness to experience. "Openness is just *cool,*" he explained, a little ruefully. "It's about creativity. Plus, it has the strongest correlation with liberal ideology. Most of us in personality psychology — including me, I should say — are liberal. And we like studying ourselves.")

Though academic personality psychologists, with the lonely exception of Roberts, mostly stayed away until recently, Big Five conscientiousness was embraced in the 1990s by a less illustrious psychological specialty: industrial/organizational psychology, or I/O psychology. Researchers in that field rarely hold positions with prestigious universities; most of them work as consultants for human-resource managers in large corporations that have a very specific need, far removed from esoteric academic debates: they want to hire the most productive, reliable, and diligent workers they can find. When I/O psychology began using various personality assessments to help corporations identify those workers, they found consistently that Big Five conscientiousness was the trait that best predicted workplace success.

What intrigues Roberts most about conscientiousness is that it predicts so many outcomes that go far beyond the workplace. People high in conscientiousness get better grades in high school and college; they commit fewer crimes; and they stay married longer. They live longer — and not just because they smoke and drink less. They have fewer strokes, lower blood pressure, and a lower incidence of Alzheimer's disease. "It would actually be nice if there were some negative things that went along with conscientiousness," Roberts told me. "But at this point it's emerging as one of the primary dimensions of successful functioning across the lifespan. It really goes cradle to grave in terms of how well people do."

9. The Downside of Self-Control

Of course, that doesn't mean that everyone agrees that conscientiousness is an entirely positive thing. In fact, some of the first empirical evidence for the connections between conscientiousness and success in school and the workplace came from people who didn't think much of either school or the workplace. In their 1976 book *Schooling in Capitalist America*, the Marxist economists Samuel Bowles and Herbert Gintis argued that American public schools had been set up to perpetuate social-class divisions. In order for capitalists to keep proletarians in their class of origin, they wrote, "the educational system must try to teach people to be properly subordinate." Bowles and Gintis drew on contemporary research by Gene Smith, a psychologist who had found that the test that most reliably predicted a high-school student's future didn't measure IQ; it measured how a student's peers rated him on a trait Smith called "strength of character," which included being "conscientious, responsible, insistently orderly, not prone to daydreaming, determined, persevering." This measure was three times more successful in predicting college performance than any combination of cognitive ratings, including SAT scores and class rank. Intrigued by Smith's results, Bowles and Gintis and a colleague undertook a new research project, subjecting all 237 students in the senior class of a big high school in New York state to a variety of IQ and personality tests. They found, as expected, that cognitive scores were quite predictive of GPA, but an index they derived from a combination of sixteen personality measures, including conscientiousness, had an equivalent predictive power.

To psychologists like Seligman and Peterson and Duckworth and Roberts, these results are a resounding demonstration of the importance of character to school success. To Bowles and Gintis, they were evidence that the school system was rigged to create a docile proletariat. Teachers rewarded repressed drones, according to Bowles and Gintis; they found that the students with the highest GPAs were the ones who scored the lowest on measures of creativity and independence, and the highest on measures of punctuality, delay of gratification, predictability, and dependability. Bowles and Gintis then consulted similar scales for office workers, and they found that supervisors judged their workforce the way teachers judged their students. They gave low ratings to employees with high levels of creativity and independence and high ratings to those workers with high levels of tact, punctuality, dependability, and delay of gratification. To Bowles and Gintis, these findings confirmed their thesis: Corporate America's rulers wanted to staff their offices with bland and reliable sheep, so they created a school system that selected for those traits.

According to Roberts's research, people who score high on conscientiousness tend to share certain characteristics: they are orderly, hard-working, reliable, and respectful of social norms. But perhaps the most important ingredient of conscientiousness is self-control. And when it comes to self-control, Marxist economists are not the only people who are skeptical of its value.

In *Character Strengths and Virtues,* Peterson and Seligman contended that "there is no true disadvantage of having too much self-control"; it is a capacity, like strength or beauty or intelligence, with no inherent downside — the more you have, the better. But an opposing school of thought, led by the late Jack Block, a psychological researcher at the University of California at Berkeley, argued that too much self-control could be just as big a problem as too little. Overcontrolled people are "excessively constrained," Block and two colleagues wrote in one paper. They "have difficulty making decisions [and] may unnecessarily delay gratification or deny themselves pleasure." According to these researchers, conscientious people are classic squares: they're compulsive, anxious, and repressed.

Block's findings are certainly valid; it's easy to see how conscientiousness can descend into compulsiveness. But at the same time, it is hard to argue with the data showing correlations between self-control and positive outcomes. In 2011, that pool of evidence grew further when a team of researchers published the results of a three-decade-long study of more than a thousand young people in New Zealand that showed, in new detail, clear connections between childhood self-control and adult outcomes. When their subjects were between the ages of three and eleven, the researchers, led by the psychologists Avshalom Caspi and Terrie Moffitt and including Brent Roberts, used a variety of tests and questionnaires to measure the children's self-control and then combined those results into a single self-control rating for each child. When they surveyed the subjects at age thirty-two, they found that the childhood self-control measure had predicted a wide array of outcomes. The lower a subject's self-control in childhood, the more likely he or she was at thirty-two to smoke, to have health problems, to have a bad credit rating, and to have been in trouble with the law. In some cases, the effect sizes were huge: Adults with the lowest self-control scores in childhood were three times more likely to have been convicted of a crime than those who scored highest as kids. They were three times more likely to have multiple addictions, and they were more than twice as likely to be raising their children in a single-parent household.

10. Grit

But even Angela Duckworth agrees that self-control has its limitations. It may be very useful for predicting who will graduate from high school, but, she says, it's not as relevant when it comes to identifying who might invent a new technology or direct an award-winning movie. And after publishing her groundbreaking self-control-versus-IQ study in *Psychological Science* in 2005, Duckworth began to sense that self-control wasn't precisely the driver of success that she was looking for. She considered her own career. She was, by objective measures, very intelligent, and she recognized that she had high levels of self-discipline: she got up early; she worked hard; she met deadlines; she made it to the gym on a regular basis. And though she was certainly successful — very few doctoral students have their first-year theses published in a prestigious journal like *Psychological Science* — her peripatetic early career was much less directed than that of, say, David Levin, who had found his life's calling at twenty-two and had persisted at the same goal ever since, overcoming many obstacles and creating, with Michael Feinberg, a successful network of charter schools educating thousands of students. Duckworth felt that Levin, who was about her age, possessed some trait that she did not: a passionate commitment to a single mission and an unswerving dedication to achieve that mission. She decided she needed to name this quality, and she chose the word *grit*.

Working with Chris Peterson, Seligman's coauthor on *Character Strengths and Virtues,* Duckworth developed a test to measure grit, which she called the Grit Scale. It is a deceptively simple test, just twelve brief statements on which respondents must evaluate themselves, including "New ideas and projects sometimes distract me from previous ones"; "Setbacks don't discourage me"; "I am a hard worker"; and "I finish whatever I begin."

For each statement, respondents score themselves on a five-point scale, ranging from 5, "very much like me," to 1, "not like me at all." The test takes about three minutes to complete, and it relies entirely on self-report — and yet when Duckworth and Peterson took it out into the field, they found it was remarkably predictive of success. Grit, Duckworth discovered, is only faintly related to IQ — there are smart gritty people and dumb gritty people — but at Penn, high grit scores allowed students who had entered college with relatively low college-board scores to nonetheless achieve high GPAs. At the National Spelling Bee, Duckworth found that children with high grit scores were more likely to survive to the later rounds. Most remarkable, Duckworth and Peterson gave their grit test to more than twelve hundred freshman cadets as they entered the military academy at West Point and embarked on the grueling summer training course known as Beast Barracks. The military has developed its own complex evaluation, called the whole candidate score, to judge incoming cadets and predict which of them will survive the demands of West Point; it includes academic grades, a gauge of physical fitness, and a leadership potential score. But the more accurate predictor of which cadets persisted in Beast Barracks and which ones dropped out turned out to be Duckworth's simple little twelve-item grit questionnaire.

11. Quantifying Character

As they began consulting with Angela Duckworth and her colleagues on character, David Levin and Dominic Randolph were easily persuaded that self-control and grit were essential character strengths for their students. Yet those didn't seem like the only strengths that mattered. Seligman and Peterson's full list of twenty-four, however, felt too unwieldy, too difficult to turn into a practical system of instruction for their schools. So Levin and Randolph asked Peterson if he could narrow the list down to a more manageable handful, and Peterson identified a set of strengths that were, according to his research, especially likely to predict life satisfaction and high achievement. After a few small adjustments, they settled on a final list of seven:

grit
self-control
zest
social intelligence
gratitude
optimism
curiosity

Over the next year and a half, Duckworth worked with Levin and Randolph to turn the list of seven strengths into a two-page evaluation tool, a questionnaire that could be completed by teachers or by parents or by the students themselves. For each strength, teachers suggested a variety of possible indicators, statements much like the twelve indicators Duckworth chose for her grit questionnaire, and she road-tested several dozen of them at Riverdale and KIPP, asking teachers to rate students and students to rate themselves on a five-point scale for each indicator. She eventually settled on the twenty-four most statistically reliable indicators, from "This student is eager to explore new things" (an indicator of curiosity) to "This student believes that effort will improve his or her future" (optimism).

For Levin, the next step was clear. Back in 2007, at a small, invitation-only conference on positive psychology that Randolph organized at Lawrenceville, he had hit on the idea of grading KIPP students on character in the same way they were graded on math and science and history. Wouldn't it be cool, Levin had mused at the time, if each student graduated from school with not only a GPA but also a CPA (for character point average)? If you were a college-admissions director or a corporate human-resources manager selecting entry-level employees, wouldn't you like to know which ones had scored highest in grit or optimism or zest? And if you were a parent of a KIPP student, wouldn't you want to know how your son or daughter stacked up against the rest of the class in character as well as in reading ability? For Levin, the answer to all these questions was a clear yes, and as soon as he got the final list of indicators from Duckworth and Peterson, he started working to turn it into a specific, concise assessment that he could hand out to students and parents at KIPP's New York City schools twice a year: the first-ever character report card.

Back at Riverdale, though, the idea of a character report card made Randolph nervous. "I have a philosophical issue with quantifying character," he explained to me one afternoon. "With my school's specific population, at least, as soon as you set up something like a report card, you're going to have a bunch of people doing test prep for it. I don't want to come up with a metric around character that could then be gamed. I would hate it if that's where we ended up."

Still, he did agree with Levin that the inventory Duckworth and Peterson had compiled could be a useful tool in communicating with students about character. And so he took what one Riverdale teacher described to me as a "viral approach" to spreading the idea of this new method of assessing character throughout the Riverdale community. He talked about character at parent nights, asked pointed questions in staff meetings, connected like-minded members of his faculty and encouraged them to come up with new programs. In the winter of 2011, Riverdale students in the fifth and sixth grade took the twenty-four-indicator survey, and their teachers rated them as well. The staff discussed the results, but they weren't shared with students or parents, and they certainly weren't labeled report cards.

Randolph's deliberate pace is in part a consequence of his personal style — he enjoys what he calls the dialogic process, meandering conversations that gradually change people's minds. It also has a lot to do with the culture of Riverdale, a school where teachers are hired not for any particular interest in pedagogy but for their mastery of the content of their field. "Teachers come here because they want to have a level of independence," Randolph explained. "In theory, I could probably say, 'We're just going to do this, and that's the way it is.' But everybody would say, 'Get lost.'"

As I spent time at Riverdale, though, it became apparent to me that the debate over character at the school wasn't just about how best to evaluate and improve students' character and how quickly to adopt new ways of doing so. It went deeper than that, to the question of what *character* really meant. When Randolph arrived at Riverdale, the school already had in place a character-education program of a sort. Called CARE, for Children Aware of Riverdale Ethics, the program was adopted in 1988 in the lower school, which at Riverdale means kindergarten through fifth grade. It is a blueprint for a certain kind of well-mannered niceness, mandating that students "treat everyone with respect" and "be aware of other people's feelings and find ways to help those whose feelings have been hurt." Posters in the hallway remind students of the virtues related to CARE (PRACTICE GOOD MANNERS; AVOID GOSSIPING; HELP OTHERS). In the lower school, many teachers describe it proudly as an essential part of what makes Riverdale the school that it is.

When I asked Randolph about CARE, he grimaced, a revolutionary forced to tip his cap to tradition. "I see the character strengths as CARE 2.0," he explained delicately. "I'd basically like to take all of this new character language and say that we're in the next generation of CARE."

In fact, the character-strength approach of Seligman and Peterson isn't an expansion of programs like CARE; if anything, it is a repudiation of them. In 2008, a national organization called the Character Education Partnership published a paper that divided character education into two categories: programs that develop "moral character," which embodies ethical values like fairness, generosity, and integrity; and those that address "performance character," which includes values like effort, diligence, and perseverance. The CARE program falls firmly on the "moral character" side of the divide, but the seven strengths that Randolph and Levin chose for their schools leaned much more heavily toward performance character: while they do have a moral component, strengths like zest, optimism, social intelligence, and curiosity aren't particularly heroic; they make you think of Steve Jobs or Bill Clinton more than Martin Luther King Jr. or Gandhi.

The two teachers Randolph chose to oversee the school's character initiative were K. C. Cohen, the guidance counselor for the middle and upper schools, and Karen Fierst, a learning specialist in the lower school. Cohen was friendly and thoughtful, in her mid-thirties, a graduate of Fieldston, the private school just down the road from Riverdale. She was intensely interested in character development, and, like Randolph, she was worried about the character of Riverdale students. But she was not convinced by the seven character strengths that Riverdale had chosen. "When I think of good character, I think, 'Are you fair? Are you honest in dealings with other people? Are you a cheater?'" she told me. "I don't think so much about 'Are you tenacious? Are you a hard worker?' I think, 'Are you a good person?'"

Cohen's vision of character was much closer to moral character than performance character, and during the months I visited Riverdale, that vision remained the dominant one. When I spent a day at the school in the late winter of 2011, sitting in on a variety of classes and meetings, messages about behavior and values were everywhere, but those messages stayed almost entirely in the moral dimension. It was a hectic day at the middle school — it was pajama day, plus there was a morning assembly, and then on top of that, the kids who were going on the two-week class trip to Bordeaux for spring break had to leave early in order to make their overnight flight to Paris. The topic for the assembly was heroes, and half a dozen students stood up in front of their classmates — about three hundred and fifty kids in all — and each made a brief presentation about a particular hero he or she had chosen: Ruby Nell Bridges, the African American girl who was part of the first group to integrate the schools in New Orleans in 1960; Mohamed Bouazizi, the Tunisian fruit vendor whose self-immolation had helped spark the recent revolt in that country; the actor and activist Paul Robeson; the boxer Manny Pacquiao.

In the assembly, in classes, and in conversations with different students, I heard a lot of talk about values and ethics, and the values that were emphasized tended to be social values: inclusion, tolerance, diversity. (I heard a lot more about black history at Riverdale than I did at the KIPP schools I visited.) A photo exhibit at one end of the school's gorgeous sunlight-drenched cafeteria featured portraits of pointedly diverse families — gay couples, blind parents, mixed-race families, adopted kids. One eighth-grade girl I asked about character said that for her and her friends, the biggest issue was inclusion — who was invited to whose bat mitzvah; who was being shunned on Facebook. Character, as far as I could tell, was defined at Riverdale mostly in terms of helping other people — or at least not hurting their feelings. I heard much less talk about how possessing character strengths might help a person lead a more successful life.

Yet Randolph told me that he had concerns about a character program that didn't go beyond those kinds of nice-guy values. "The danger with character is if you just revert to these general terms — respect, honesty, tolerance — it seems really vague," he said. "If I stand in front of the kids and just say, 'It's really important for you to respect each other,' I think they glaze over. But if you say, 'Well, actually you need to exhibit self-control,' or you explain the value of social intelligence — this will help you collaborate more effectively — then it seems a bit more tangible."

When I spoke to Karen Fierst, the teacher who was overseeing the character project for the Riverdale lower school, she said she was worried that it would be a challenge to convince the students and their parents that there was anything in the twenty-four character strengths that might actually benefit them. For KIPP kids, she said, the notion that character could help them get through college was a powerful lure, one that would motivate them to take the strengths seriously. For kids at Riverdale, though, there was no question that they were going to graduate from college. "It will just happen," Fierst explained. "It happened to every generation in their family before them. And so it's harder to get them to invest in this idea. For KIPP students, learning these strengths is partly about trying to demystify what makes other people successful — kind of like, 'We're letting you in on the secret of what successful people are like.' But kids here already live in a successful community. They're not depending on their teachers to give them the information on how to be successful."

12. Affluence

Dwight Vidale teaches English to middle- and high-school students at Riverdale. He is a Riverdale alumnus, class of 2001, and as an African American, he is something of a rarity in the Riverdale faculty lounge; when I met him, he was the only black teacher at the high school. Vidale grew up in the Bronx and was raised by his mother, a secretary, and his stepfather, an electrician. He came to Riverdale in high school, a scholarship kid, and though he loved the school's vast resources and the academic challenge of the classes, he told me, the wealth of his white classmates was hard to get used to. In ninth grade, he was paired with a girl in his class on a school project, and she invited him to her family's home on the Upper East Side to work on it. "I will never forget walking into her apartment," he told me. "I was just blown away by the opulence." That experience, he said, made him keep some distance between himself and many of his classmates. In all his years at Riverdale, he told me, he never invited his white friends to his house. He felt his life was just too different from theirs.

Now, teaching kids growing up amid similar wealth, Vidale finds he has a more nuanced view of affluent childhoods. Though he came from what he calls "very humble beginnings," he drew strength from the fact that his mother was always in his corner, always there when he needed to talk. Many of his students seem to have more distant relationships with their parents. He sees a lot of what the Riverdale staff call helicopter parents—"always hovering around, ready to swoop in for the rescue"—but, he said, "that doesn't mean they're making emotional connections with their kids, or even spending time with their kids."

On one professional-development day when I was at Riverdale, Dominic Randolph arranged a screening for his entire faculty of *Race to Nowhere*, a movie about the stresses facing mostly privileged American high-school students that had become an underground hit in many wealthy suburbs, where one-time showings at schools, churches, and community centers were bringing out hundreds or even thousands of concerned parents. The movie paints a grim portrait of contemporary adolescence, rising to an emotional crescendo with the story of an overachieving teenage girl who committed suicide, apparently because of the ever-increasing pressure to succeed that she felt both at school and at home. At Riverdale, the film seemed to have a powerful effect on many of the staff; one teacher came up to Randolph afterward with tears in her eyes.

Race to Nowhere has helped to coalesce a growing movement of psychologists and educators who believe that the systems and methods in place to raise and educate well-off kids in the United States are in fact devastating them. One of the central figures in the movie is Madeline Levine, a psychologist in Marin County who is the author of a bestselling book, *The Price of Privilege: How Parental Pressure and Material Advantage Are Creating a Generation of Disconnected and Unhappy Kids*. In her book, Levine cites a variety of studies and surveys to back up her contention that children of affluent parents now exhibit "unexpectedly high rates of emotional problems beginning in junior high school." This is no accident of demographics, Levine says; it is a direct result of the child-rearing practices that prevail in well-off American homes. Wealthy parents today, she argues, are more likely than others to be emotionally distant from their children while at the same time insisting on high levels of achievement, a potentially toxic blend of influences that can create "intense feelings of shame and hopelessness" in affluent children.

Levine's book draws on research done by Suniya Luthar, a psychology professor at Columbia University's Teachers College, who for the past decade or so has made a specialty of researching the specific psychological challenges of children growing up in affluence. (She attended the Lawrenceville conference in 2007 at Randolph's invitation.) When Luthar began her research, she was interested primarily in the problems of low-income adolescents. But in the late 1990s, she decided she needed to find a comparison group to help her better understand how the patterns she was seeing in disadvantaged urban neighborhoods compared to those of less troubled demographic groups. And so she undertook a study comparing more than two hundred mostly white, mostly wealthy suburban tenth-graders with a similar number of mostly African American, low-income urban tenth-grade students. To Luthar's surprise, she found the affluent teenagers used alcohol, cigarettes, marijuana, and harder illegal drugs *more* than the low-income teens. Thirty-five percent of the suburban girls had tried all four substances, compared with just 15 percent of the inner-city girls. The wealthy girls in Luthar's survey also suffered from elevated rates of depression; 22 percent of them reported clinically significant symptoms.

Luthar was soon asked to consult at another middle school in an even more affluent town, where she followed a cohort of middle-school students for several years. About a fifth of these high-income students, she found, had multiple persistent problems, including substance use, high levels of depression and anxiety, and chronic academic difficulties. This time, in addition to collecting information about psychological distress and delinquent behavior, Luthar polled students on their relationships with their parents. She found that parenting mattered at both socioeconomic extremes. For both rich and poor teenagers, certain family characteristics predicted children's maladjustment, including low levels of maternal attachment, high levels of parental criticism, and minimal afterschool adult supervision. Among the affluent children, Luthar found, the main cause of distress was "excessive achievement pressures and isolation from parents — both physical and emotional."

Dan Kindlon, an assistant professor of child psychology at Harvard, found further evidence of the specific pressures on well-off children in a nationwide survey of affluent families he conducted for a book he published in 2000. Like Luthar, Kindlon discovered disproportionately high levels of anxiety and depression among wealthy students, especially in adolescence, and he found that the emotional disconnection that existed between many affluent parents and their children often meant that the parents were unusually indulgent of their children's bad behavior. In Kindlon's survey, parents making more than one million dollars a year were, by a wide margin, the group most likely to say that they were less strict than their own parents.

K. C. Cohen told me that she and other teachers at Riverdale have talked a lot about affluence and its potentially detrimental effect on students' character development; in fact, she brought Kindlon to Riverdale to speak to students and teachers on the subject. Both Cohen and Fierst told me that many parents at Riverdale, while pushing their children to excel, inadvertently shield them from exactly the kind of experience that can lead to character growth. As Fierst put it, "Our kids don't put up with a lot of suffering. They don't have a threshold for it. They're protected against it quite a bit. And when they do get uncomfortable, we hear from their parents. We try to talk to parents about having to sort of make it okay for there to be challenge, because that's where learning happens."

Cohen explained that in the middle school, "If a kid is a C student, and their parents think that they're all A's, we do get a lot of pushback: 'What are you talking about? This is a great paper!' We have parents calling in and saying, for their kids, 'Can't you just give them two more days on this paper?' Overindulging kids, with the intention of giving them everything and being loving, but at the expense of their character — that's huge in our population. I think that's one of the biggest problems we have at Riverdale."

This is an issue for all parents, of course, not just affluent ones. It is a central paradox of contemporary parenting, in fact: we have an acute, almost biological impulse to provide for our children, to give them everything they want and need, to protect them from dangers and discomforts both large and small. And yet we know — on some level, at least — that what kids need more than anything is a little hardship: some challenge, some deprivation that they can overcome, even if just to prove to themselves that they can. As a parent, you struggle with these thorny questions every day, and if you make the right call even half the time, you're lucky. But it's one thing to acknowledge this dilemma in the privacy of your own home; it's quite another to have it addressed in public, at a school where you send your kids at great expense.

This is the problem that Randolph is up against at Riverdale as he tries to propel this new kind of conversation about character forward. When you work at a public school, whether it's a charter or a traditional public school, you're paid by the state, responsible, on some level, to your fellow citizens for the job you do preparing your students to join the adult world. When you work at a private school like Riverdale, though, you are always conscious that you're working for the parents who pay the tuition. Which makes a campaign like the one that Randolph is trying to launch all the more complicated. If your premise is that your students are lacking in deep traits like grit and gratitude and self-control, you're implicitly criticizing the parenting they've received—which means you're implicitly criticizing your employers.

Although they would almost certainly not express it this way, wealthy parents choose a school like Riverdale for their children, at least in part, as a risk-management strategy. If you look at the list of successful Riverdale alumni, you'll see some impressive names on it—Carly Simon, Chevy Chase, Robert Krulwich, the governor of Pennsylvania, and the junior U.S. senator from Connecticut—but for a school that has been producing highly privileged graduates for 104 years, it boasts very few real world-changers. (Sorry, Chevy.) Traditionally, the purpose of a school like Riverdale is not to raise the ceiling on a child's potential achievement in life but to raise the floor, to give him the kinds of connections and credentials that will make it very hard for him ever to fall out of the upper class. What Riverdale offers parents, above all else, is a high probability of nonfailure.

The problem, as Randolph has realized, is that the best way for a young person to build character is for him to attempt something where there is a real and serious possibility of failure. In a high-risk endeavor, whether it's in business or athletics or the arts, you are more likely to experience colossal defeat than in a low-risk one—but you're also more likely to achieve real and original success. "The idea of building grit and building self-control is that you get that through failure," Randolph explained. "And in most highly academic environments in the United States, no one fails anything."

David Levin says that this is one area where he believes KIPP students have an advantage over their peers at Riverdale. "The day-to-day challenges that our kids go through to obtain an education are very, very different than the day-to-day challenges of the kids who go to Riverdale," he told me. "As a result, the grit of our students is significantly higher in many respects than the grit of the students who go to Riverdale."

As Karen Fierst observed, most Riverdale students can see before them a clear path to a certain type of success. They'll go to college, they'll graduate, they'll get well-paying jobs — and if they fall along the way, their families will almost certainly catch them, often well into their twenties or even thirties if necessary. But despite these students' many advantages, Randolph isn't convinced that the education they are currently receiving at Riverdale or the support they are receiving at home will provide them with the skills to negotiate the path to the deeper success that Seligman and Peterson hold up as the ultimate product of good character: a happy, meaningful, productive life. Randolph wants his students to succeed, of course — it's just that he believes that in order for them to do so, they first need to learn how to fail.

13. Discipline

"At KIPP, we've always said that character is just as important as academics," Tom Brunzell was saying. It was six o'clock on a warm Wednesday night in October, and Brunzell was standing at the front of a large auditorium pitching the character report card to an audience of KIPP parents. "We think that even if your children have the academic skills they need — and we're doing our best to make sure they do — if our young adults grow up and they don't also have strong character skills, then they don't have very much. Because we know that character is what keeps people happy and successful and ful-filled."

Brunzell, who was in his mid-thirties, was the dean of students at KIPP Infinity middle school; it was the third KIPP school in New York City when it opened, in 2005, on one floor of the Roberto Clemente Middle School on West 133rd Street, across from a giant city bus depot. As Infinity's resident disciplinarian, Brunzell had a very effective stern side, but on this night, he was all smiles, dressed in a pressed button-down shirt and a tie and crisp jeans, looking a little nervous as he clicked his way through the PowerPoint slides on his laptop that were projected on a screen behind him. Brunzell had become the person in the KIPP organization most directly responsible for the character report card; he chaired the monthly meetings of what had come to be called the KIPP/Riverdale character working group. In many ways, though, he was an unusual choice for the job—he had come to KIPP as something of a conscientious objector, an outspoken critic of its system of discipline.

From KIPP's earliest days, Levin and Feinberg, the founders, were famous—and infamous—for regulating student behavior in direct and often intense ways, prescribing precisely how students should sit and talk and pay attention and walk through the halls. In *Sweating the Small Stuff,* David Whitman wrote that "paternalistic" schools like KIPP's "tell students exactly how they are expected to behave, and their behavior is closely monitored, with real rewards for compliance and penalties for noncompliance." In Jay Mathews's account of the founding of KIPP, *Work Hard. Be Nice,* he describes some of Levin's harsher moments of discipline, like the time Levin caught a student throwing a wadded-up piece of paper. Levin sat the offender on a chair at the front of the class, put a garbage can on the floor in front of him, and told the other students they were free to throw in the garbage any stray pieces of paper they could find—some of which narrowly missed the student. (Mathews says that Levin later regretted that incident.)

When Brunzell arrived at KIPP Infinity, in 2005, he was completing a graduate degree at Bank Street College, a school of education known for its progressive bent. His thesis, which he researched and wrote in his first year and a half working at Infinity, was a thorough critique of the school's discipline regime. Infinity's "compliance-based" system "models an atmosphere of punitive dependence," Brunzell wrote, "which ultimately negates student decision-making." As a result, he noted, KIPP Infinity students often demonstrated the shallowest kind of good conduct — not contemplating in a deep way the consequences of their actions but ostentatiously behaving well when teachers were watching and then trying to get away with as much as possible as soon as the teachers' backs were turned.

Though Brunzell was calling into question some of the fundamental elements of the KIPP tradition, he received a surprisingly encouraging response from both Levin and Joseph Negron, the young principal of Infinity, which in its first year achieved remarkable results, even by KIPP standards. The school opened with just a fifth-grade class, recruited from the housing projects and bodegas of West Harlem and Washington Heights and chosen by random lottery. Only 24 percent of the incoming students had passed the state's fourth-grade English test at their previous public schools; just 35 percent had mastered the fourth-grade math standards. But after a year at KIPP, 81 percent passed the fifth-grade English test and 99 percent passed the fifth-grade math test. And yet, Negron told me, he agreed with Brunzell that things at Infinity weren't quite right that first year. "We had kids who were doing the right thing for the wrong reasons," he said. "We didn't have that many student issues, and we had good results, which was great. But we just didn't feel like we were the type of school where we were creating happy and fulfilled lives."

When I met Brunzell, in the fall of 2010, he had been at KIPP Infinity for more than five years, and over that time Infinity had changed, partly in response to his criticisms. Punishments were less severe and of shorter duration, and discipline conversations between students and administrators, though still often intense, were conducted less publicly and with more emphasis on making sure students felt heard and respected. The character report card was, for Brunzell, a critical part of those reforms, providing a different structure for conversations about behavior, one that allowed for deeper reflection and, potentially, more growth.

At the same time, Brunzell had tempered some of his original critique. He told me he had come to appreciate some of the elements of the KIPP behavior-modification system that had once struck him as overly authoritarian. One example was SLANT, a set of classroom habits that KIPP students were drilled on at the beginning of fifth grade, their first year at KIPP. For Brunzell, SLANT, which stands for Sit up, Listen, Ask questions, Nod, and Track the speaker with your eyes, was a useful way to teach code-switching, the ability, highly prized at KIPP and at many other low-income urban schools, to recognize and accurately perform the behaviors appropriate to each different cultural setting. It's okay to be street on the street, according to the theory of code-switching, but if you're in a museum or a college interview or a nice restaurant, you need to know exactly how to act or you're going to miss out on important opportunities. "At KIPP, we are teaching the professional code of behavior, the college code of behavior, the cultural-dominant code of behavior," Brunzell said, "and we have to teach that every moment of the day."

This is an area where KIPP's teachers and Riverdale's diverged especially sharply. K. C. Cohen, the Riverdale guidance counselor, told me that over the course of the school year, she had perceived a growing disagreement between the two schools over certain indicators on the character report card. It wasn't that she and other Riverdale teachers valued strengths like self-control less than the folks at KIPP did, she said. It was just that they were beginning to realize that they might define those strengths differently. "If you're showing self-control at KIPP, for example, you sit up straight and you track the teachers," she explained. "Here, you can sit in a ball in your chair, and no one cares. We don't care if you lie on the floor."

As we spoke in her office, Cohen read through the list of twenty-four indicators on KIPP's character report card and mentioned a few others that she thought would resonate differently at each school. "Take 'Student is polite to adults and peers,'" she said (an indicator for self-control). "That's great, but at Riverdale, kids come up to me and pat me on the back and say, 'Hey, K.C.!' And that's okay. At KIPP, though, teachers are always Mr. This and Mrs. That. There's a sort of formality." It's the confusing thing about code-switching: the kids who are actually part of the dominant culture don't necessarily act like it at school — or perhaps it is more accurate to say that at a school like Riverdale, slouching and wearing your shirt untucked and goofing around with teachers *is* dominant-culture behavior.

"We have kids who have to chew gum because they're so hyperactive," Cohen went on. "They chew gum, and it calms them down. You would never allow that at KIPP. It's almost like, we assume our kids already have manners here, so if they need to sit funny in their chair, that's okay. Whereas at KIPP, it's like, No, no, no, everyone has to conform, because the conformity is supposed to help them succeed."

It's true that gum-chewing is a transgression at KIPP — but it's also true that as a result of KIPP's ongoing conversation about character development, some teachers have found a way to make discussions about an infraction like gum-chewing into something more meaningful than a simple matter of conformity. A couple of days before my talk with Cohen, I spoke to Sayuri Stabrowski, a thirty-year-old seventh- and eighth-grade reading teacher at KIPP Infinity, and she mentioned that she had caught a girl chewing gum in her class earlier that day. "She denied it," Stabrowski told me. "She said, 'No, I'm not, I'm chewing my tongue.'" Stabrowski rolled her eyes as she told me the story. "I said, 'Okay, fine.' Then later in the class, I saw her chewing again, and I said, 'You're chewing gum! I see you.' She said, 'No, I'm not, see?' and she moved the gum over in her mouth in this really obvious way, and we all saw what she was doing. Now, a couple of years ago, I probably would have blown my top and screamed. But this time, I was able to say, 'Gosh, not only were you chewing gum, which is kind of minor, but you lied to me twice. That's a real disappointment. What does that say about your character?' And she was just devastated."

Stabrowski was worried that the girl, who often struggled with her behavior, might have a mini-meltdown — a baby attack, in KIPP jargon — in the middle of the class, but in fact, the girl spit out her gum and sat through the rest of the class and then afterward came up to her teacher with tears in her eyes. "We had a long conversation," Stabrowski told me. "She said, 'I'm trying so hard to just grow up. But nothing ever changes!' And I said, 'Do you know what *does* change? You didn't have a baby attack in front of the other kids, and two weeks ago, you would have.'"

To Tom Brunzell, what is going on in a moment like that isn't academic instruction at all, or even discipline; it's therapy. Specifically, it's a kind of cognitive-behavioral therapy, the practical psychological technique that provides the theoretical underpinning for the whole positive psychology field. Cognitive-behavioral therapy, or CBT, involves using the conscious mind to recognize negative or self-destructive thoughts or interpretations and to (sometimes literally) talk yourself into a better perspective.

"The kids who succeed at KIPP are the ones who can CBT themselves in the moment," Brunzell told me. As he saw it, part of the job for him and the other KIPP teachers was giving their students the tools to do that. "All kids this age are having mini-implosions every day," he said. "I mean, it's middle school, the worst years of their lives. But the kids who make it are the ones who can tell themselves, 'I can rise above this little situation. I'm okay. Tomorrow is a new day.'"

14. Good Habits

Cognitive-behavioral therapy is just one example of what psychologists call metacognition, an umbrella term that means, broadly, thinking about thinking. And one way to look at the character report card is as a giant metacognitive strategy. One of the things that first appealed to David Levin about *Learned Optimism,* in fact, was Martin Seligman's assertion that the most fruitful time to transform pessimistic children into optimistic ones was "before puberty, but late enough in childhood so that they are metacognitive (capable of thinking about thinking)" — in other words, right around when students arrive at a KIPP middle school. Talking about character, thinking about character, evaluating character: these are all metacognitive processes.

But Angela Duckworth believes that thinking and talking about character isn't enough, especially for adolescents. It's one thing to know abstractly that you need to improve your grit or your zest or your self-control. It's another thing to actually have the tools to do so. This is the flip side of the distinction Duckworth draws between motivation and volition, or willpower. Just as a strong will doesn't help much if a student isn't motivated to succeed, so motivation alone is insufficient without the volitional fortitude to follow through on goals. Duckworth is now trying to help young people develop those volitional tools—a project that is in many ways an extension of her work with Walter Mischel studying the strategies kids used to resist the lure of the marshmallow—and one fall day, I sat in on a professional-development workshop that she led for teachers at KIPP Infinity to brief them on a specific nuts-and-bolts metacognitive strategy that she had tested, over the course of a school year, with the fifth-grade students there.

The intervention, which goes by the rather clunky name of Mental Contrasting with Implementation Intentions, or MCII, was developed by NYU psychologist Gabriele Oettingen and her colleagues. Oettingen discovered in her research that people tend to use three strategies when they are setting goals and that two of those strategies don't work very well. Optimists favor indulging, which means imagining the future they'd like to achieve (for a middle-school student, that might mean getting an A in math next year) and vividly envisioning all the good things that will go along with it—the praise, the self-satisfaction, the future success. Oettingen found that indulging feels really good when you're doing it—it can trigger a nice dopamine surge—but it doesn't correlate at all with actual achievement.

Pessimists tend to use a strategy Oettingen calls dwelling, which involves thinking about all the things that will get in the way of their accomplishing their goals. If our prototypical middle-school student hoping for an A in math was a dweller, he might think about how he never finishes his homework, and there's never anywhere quiet for him to study anyway, and besides, he always gets distracted in class. Unsurprisingly, dwelling doesn't correlate well with achievement either.

The third method is called mental contrasting, and it combines elements of the other two methods. It means concentrating on a positive outcome and simultaneously concentrating on the obstacles in the way. Doing both at the same time, Duckworth and Oettingen wrote in a recent paper, "creates a strong association between future and reality that signals the need to overcome the obstacles in order to attain the desired future." The next step to a successful outcome, according to Oettingen, is creating a series of "implementation intentions" — specific plans in the form of if/then statements that link the obstacles with ways to overcome them, such as "*If* I get distracted by TV after school, *then* I will wait to watch TV until after I finish my homework." Oettingen has demonstrated the effectiveness of MCII in a variety of experiments: the strategy has helped dieters eat more fruits and vegetables, high-school juniors prepare more diligently for the practice SAT, and chronic-back-pain patients gain more mobility.

"Just fantasizing about doing your math homework every day next semester — that feels really good right then," Duckworth explained to the KIPP teachers in her workshop. "But you don't go out and do anything. When I go into a lot of schools, I see posters that say 'Dream it and you can achieve it!' But we need to get away from positive fantasizing about how we're all going to grow up to be rich and famous, and start thinking about the obstacles that now stand in the way of getting to where we want to be."

What MCII amounts to is a way to set *rules* for yourself. And as David Kessler, the former commissioner of the FDA, notes in his recent book *The End of Overeating*, there is a neurobiological reason why rules work, whether you're using them to avoid fried foods (as Kessler was) or the lure of *American Idol* (as our imaginary KIPP math student might have been). When you're making rules for yourself, Kessler writes, you're enlisting the prefrontal cortex as your partner against the more reflexive, appetite-driven parts of your brain. Rules, Kessler points out, are not the same as willpower. They are a metacognitive *substitute* for willpower. By making yourself a rule ("I never eat fried dumplings"), you can sidestep the painful internal conflict between your desire for fried foods and your willful determination to resist them. Rules, Kessler explains, "provide structure, preparing us for encounters with tempting stimuli and redirecting our attention elsewhere." Before long, the rules have become as automatic as the appetites they are deflecting.

When Duckworth talks about character, as she did that day at the KIPP workshop, she often cites William James, the American philosopher and psychologist, who wrote that the traits we call *virtues* are no more and no less than simple habits. "Habit and character are essentially the same thing," Duckworth explained to the KIPP teachers. "It's not like some kids are good and some kids are bad. Some kids have good habits and some kids have bad habits. Kids understand it when you put it that way, because they know that habits might be *hard* to change, but they're not *impossible* to change. William James says our nervous systems are like a sheet of paper. You fold it over and over and over again, and pretty soon it has a crease. And I think that's what you at KIPP are doing. When your students leave KIPP, you want to make sure they have the kind of creases that will lead them to success later on."

According to Duckworth, conscientious people don't go around consciously deciding to act virtuously all the time. They've just made it their default response to do the "good" thing, meaning the more socially acceptable or long-term-benefit-enhancing option. In any given situation, the most conscientious path is not always the smartest option. On Carmit Segal's coding-speed test, for example, the students who scored highest worked really hard at a really boring task and got nothing in return. One word for that behavior is *conscientious*. Another is *foolish*. But in the long run, it serves most people well to have conscientiousness be their default option. Because when it *does* matter — when you have to study for a final exam or show up on time for a job interview or decide whether to yield to temptation and cheat on your wife — then you will probably make the right choice, and you won't have to exert yourself and exhaust yourself in order to do so. Strategies like MCII, or the act of imagining a picture frame around a marshmallow—in the end, these are just tricks to make the virtuous path easier to follow.

15. Identity

When I visited KIPP Infinity in the winter of 2011, halfway through the inaugural year of the character report card, character language was everywhere. Kids wore sweatshirts with the slogan "Infinite Character" and all the character strengths listed on the back. One pro-self-control T-shirt even included a nod to Walter Mischel: "Don't Eat the Marshmallow!" The walls were covered with signs that read GOT SELF-CONTROL? and I ACTIVELY PARTICIPATE! (one of the indicators for zest). There was a bulletin board in the hallway topped with the words *Character Counts;* tacked on the board were Spotted! cards, notecards that students filled out whenever they noticed fellow students performing actions that demonstrated character. (Jasmine R. cited William N. for zest: *William was in math class and he raised his hand for every problem.*)

I asked David Levin about the message saturation. Didn't he think it was a little much? Not at all, he replied. "In order to succeed," he explained, "this has to permeate everything in the school, from the language people use to lesson plans to how people are rewarded and recognized to signs on the wall. If it's not woven into the DNA of an institution, it will have minimal impact."

Wall-to-wall messaging is nothing new at KIPP, of course; right from the start, Levin and Feinberg used posters and slogans and signs and T-shirts to create a powerful school culture at KIPP, to instill in students a sense that they were different, and that they belonged. Duckworth told me she thinks that KIPP's approach to group identity is a central part of what makes the schools effective. "What KIPP does is create a social role shift, so that a child will suddenly switch into a totally different mindset," she said. "They play on the in-group/out-group thing: 'We know what SLANTing is and you don't know what SLANTing is, because you don't go to KIPP.'"

Psychologists have demonstrated that group identity can have a powerful effect on achievement — both a positive and a negative one. In the early 1990s, Claude Steele, a psychologist who is now the dean of the school of education at Stanford University, identified a phenomenon that he called stereotype threat. If you give a person a subtle psychological cue having to do with his group identity before a test of intellectual or physical ability, Steele showed, you can have a major effect on how well he performs. Researchers have since demonstrated this effect in countless different settings. When white students at Princeton were told before trying a ten-hole mini golf course that it was a test of natural ability in sports (which they feared they didn't possess), they scored four strokes worse than a similar group of white students who were told it was a test of their ability to think strategically (which they were confident they did possess). For black students, the effect was the opposite: when they were told the mini golf course was a test of their strategic intelligence, their scores were four strokes worse. Steele's theory is that when you are worried about confirming a stereotype about your group — that white people aren't athletic; that black people aren't smart — you get anxious, and as a result, you do worse.

Other researchers have found stereotype threat in pursuits much more serious than miniature golf. When people in their sixties and seventies and eighties were instructed to read an article about how memory fades with age before they took a memory test, they remembered 44 percent of the words in the test; members of a similar group who weren't told to read the article before the test remembered 58 percent of the words. Before a challenging math test, female college students need only be reminded that they are female for them to do worse on the test than female students who don't receive that identity cue.

The good news about stereotype threat is that, just as it can be triggered by subtle cues, it can be defused by subtle interventions. One of the most effective techniques, which has now been tested in a variety of settings, is exposing students at risk of stereotype threat to a very specific message: that intelligence is malleable. If students internalize that idea, these studies show, they gain confidence, and their test scores and GPAs often rise too.

The most intriguing fact about these interventions is that the question of the malleability of intelligence is actually hotly debated by psychologists and neuroscientists. Although scores on achievement tests like the SAT can certainly be affected by training of different kinds, the purest kind of intelligence is not very malleable at all. But a psychologist at Stanford named Carol Dweck has discovered a remarkable thing: Regardless of the facts on the malleability of intelligence, students do much better academically if they *believe* intelligence is malleable. Dweck divides people into two types: those who have a fixed mindset, who believe that intelligence and other skills are essentially static and inborn, and those who have a growth mindset, who believe that intelligence can be improved. She has shown that students' mindsets predict their academic trajectories: those who believe that people can improve their intelligence actually do improve their grades.

And whether or not intelligence is malleable, mindset certainly is. Dweck and others have shown that with the right kind of intervention, students can be switched from a fixed mindset to a growth mindset, and their academic results tend to rise as a result. Joshua Aronson, a frequent collaborator with Claude Steele, and two colleagues conducted a study that compared the effectiveness of a few different mindset-changing interventions on a group of mostly low-income seventh-grade students in Texas. Over the school year, each student in the study worked with a mentor, a college student who met with him or her twice for ninety minutes each time and then communicated with him or her regularly by e-mail. Some students were randomly assigned to hear from their mentors a growth-mindset message such as "Intelligence is not a finite endowment, but rather an expandable capacity that increases with mental work." Students in a control group heard a more standard message about the way that drug use could interfere with academic achievement.

At the end of the year, Aronson and his colleagues compared the two groups' scores on Texas's standardized achievement test, the Texas Assessment of Academic Skills, and the students who had heard a growth-mindset message did significantly better than the students who had heard the anti-drug message. The most impressive effect was seen in the math scores of the female students. The effect of stereotype threat has been well demonstrated in the math scores of girls and women, who seem to be especially anxious in testing situations when they think they might confirm the stereotype that girls are bad in math. In the Texas experiment, girls who received the standard anti-drug message averaged 74 on the test, about eight points below the male students who had heard the same message. The girls who heard a growth-mindset message averaged about 84, closing the gap with the male students completely.

16. Report Cards

Dweck's notion that students do better when they think they can improve their intelligence applies to character as well. At least, that is the idea behind the character report card — that presenting character to students not as a set of fixed traits but as a series of constantly developing attributes will inspire them to improve those traits. I talked about this idea one morning at KIPP Infinity with Mike Witter, a thirty-one-year-old eighth-grade English teacher who seemed hardwired to believe in the growth mindset. "If you're going to be a good teacher, you *have* to believe in malleable intelligence," he told me. "And character is equally malleable. If you teach kids to pay attention to character, then their character will transform."

Perhaps more than any other teacher at the school, Witter had made a concerted effort to get his students to pay attention to character. I visited Witter's class one morning that winter to observe something that David Levin called dual-purpose instruction, teachers deliberately working explicit talk about character strengths into every lesson. Levin wanted math teachers to use the character strengths in word problems; he explained that history teachers could use them in classes about Harriet Tubman and the Underground Railroad. And when I arrived in Witter's class, he was leading a discussion on Chinua Achebe's novel *Things Fall Apart*. Above Witter's head, at the front of the class, the seven character strengths, from optimism to social intelligence, were stenciled in four-inch-high letters, white on blue. He asked his students to rank Okonkwo, the protagonist, on his various character strengths. There was a lot of back-and-forth, but in the end, most students agreed that Okonkwo rated highest on grit and lowest on self-control. Then a student named Yantzee raised his hand. "Can't a trait backfire at you?" he asked.

"Sure, a trait can backfire," Witter said. "Too much grit, like Okonkwo, you start to lose your ability to have empathy for other people. If you're so gritty that you don't understand why everyone's complaining about how hard things are, because nothing's hard for you, because you're Mr. Grit, then you're going to have a hard time being kind. Even love — being too loving might make you the kind of person who can get played." There was a ripple of knowing laughter from the students. "So, yes, character is something you have to be careful about. Character strengths can become character weaknesses."

When I spoke to Witter after the class, he told me that some teachers at KIPP Infinity still weren't convinced of the essential premise behind the report card: that character can change. "That has been part of the process, teachers getting comfortable with this idea. In order to really buy into the character report card, you have to believe in malleable character, and I don't know if every teacher is there yet. I mean, how many times have you heard a grownup say, 'That's just how I am! That's me. Get used to it!'? But if you don't believe that it applies to you, then how can you believe that it applies to children?"

I saw Witter again on report-card night, which at KIPP Infinity middle school fell on a chilly Thursday at the beginning of February. Report-card night is always a big deal at KIPP schools — parents are strongly urged to attend, and at Infinity, almost all of them do — but this particular evening carried an extra level of anxiety for both the administrators and the parents because students would be receiving their very first character report cards, and no one knew quite what to expect.

Logistically, the character report card had been a challenge to pull off for Brunzell and his colleagues. Teachers at three of the four KIPP middle schools in New York City had to grade every one of their students on each of the twenty-four character indicators, and more than a few of them found the process a little daunting. And now that report-card night had arrived, they had an even bigger challenge: explaining to parents just how those precise figures, rounded to the second decimal place, summed up their children's characters. I sat with Witter for a while on a bench down the hall from the band room, listening as he talked through the character report card with Faith Flemister, an African American woman wearing dark red lipstick and a black knit cap, and her son, Juaquin Bennett, a tall, hefty eighth-grader in a gray hooded sweatshirt.

"For the past few years we've been working on a project to create a clearer picture for parents about the character of your child," Witter explained to Flemister. "The categories that we ended up putting together represent qualities that have been studied and determined to be indicators of success. They mean you're more likely to go to college. More likely to find a good job. Even surprising things, like they mean you're more likely to get married, or more likely to have a family. So we think these are really important."

Flemister nodded, and Witter began to work his way down the scores on Juaquin's character report card, starting with the good news: Every teacher had scored him as a perfect 5 on "Is polite to adults and peers," and he did almost as well on "Keeps temper in check." These were both indicators for interpersonal self-control.

"I can tell this is a real strength for you," Witter said, turning to Juaquin. "This kind of self-control is something you've developed incredibly well. So that makes me think we need to start looking at, What's something we can target? And the first thing that jumps out at me is this." Witter pulled out a green felt-tip marker and circled one indicator on Juaquin's report card. "'Pays attention and resists distraction,'" Witter read aloud; this was an indicator for academic self-control. "That's a little lower than some of the other numbers. Why do you think that is?"

"I talk too much in class," Juaquin said a little sheepishly, looking down at his black sneakers. "I sometimes stare off into space and don't pay attention."

The three of them talked over a few strategies to help Juaquin focus more in class, and by the end of the fifteen-minute conversation, Flemister seemed convinced by the new approach. "The strong points are not a surprise," she said to Witter as he got up to talk to another family. "That's just the type of person Juaquin is. But it's good how you pinpoint what he can do to make things easier on himself. Then maybe his grades will pick up."

17. Climbing the Mountain

If each student's first character report card represents the beginning of a conversation he'll have with teachers and administrators at KIPP about his character and how to improve it, then a woman named Jane Martinez Dowling is responsible for the other end of that process. Dowling runs the New York office of KIPP Through College, KIPP's alumni support program, overseeing twenty or so counselors working out of shared office space on the eighth floor of a tall stone building a block from Wall Street. In all, New York KIPP Through College is responsible for about seven hundred KIPP graduates, half still in high school and the other half making their way, with varying degrees of success, through college.

The official KIPP goal for college completion is to have 75 percent of all KIPP middle-school graduates complete a degree from a four-year college within six years of graduating from high school. If you recall that the actual six-year college-graduation rate for Tyrell Vance's class was 21 percent, you get an idea of the challenge Dowling faces. When I visited her office on a cold morning in February of 2011, she handed me a detailed spreadsheet that showed college-attainment data for each KIPP cohort. The numbers were definitely moving in the right direction: the six-year graduation rate had gone up from 21 percent, for the Class of 2003, Tyrell Vance's class, to 46 percent, for the Class of 2005. On the day I visited, Dowling was focused especially on the Class of 2007, which was just about to reach the four-year mark — four years out of high school — the point when the first students could, in theory, be graduating with BAs. Only 26 percent of the students were on track to graduate in four years, according to the spreadsheet, but another 18 percent were still enrolled in college, meaning that they still had the potential to graduate in five or six years.

The Class of 2007, Dowling told me, was academically more talented than the ones that had come before. Many of the students had gone to exclusive boarding schools for high school, and the list of colleges they were attending included Vanderbilt and Columbia. "What we have found is that it's the character piece that has held some of them back," Dowling explained. "There are students who have incredible intellect but don't necessarily channel it in the right direction. There are lots of kids who struggle with procrastination issues, even though they have the ability to get their work done. There are students who are dealing with real social and emotional issues." Seven of the fifty-seven kids in that graduating class, Dowling told me, had experienced serious depression in college. "It's especially pronounced in that class," she said. "They're dealing with family issues, or they have issues just dealing with their peer groups, and that has really held some of them back." Dowling emphasized that most if not all of the kids she was talking about were still on track to graduate. "They're good kids," she said. "But the impact of poverty catches up even with children who are resilient."

She gave me a copy of KIPP's seventy-six-page *College Advisory Playbook,* which the advisers use as they follow their students' progress. It is incredibly detailed, a reflection of KIPP's institutional obsession with data. According to the playbook, each KIPP Through College adviser is supposed to be in touch with each student on his or her roster at least once a month. Every student is given a constantly fluctuating college persistence rating in four categories: academic preparedness, financial stability, socio-emotional wellness, and non-cognitive preparedness, and after each contact with a student, the adviser rates the student as red, green, or yellow in each category. For example, if a student has a job that requires her to work more than twenty hours a week, that's a yellow in academic preparedness. If she has an open case with her college's counseling service, that's a red in socio-emotional wellness. If she "has great difficulty in taking responsibility and completing important tasks," that's a red in noncognitive preparedness. From her desk at any time, Dowling can access a database that displays a glowing red dot for each potential problem area of every student her advisers are working with.

Reading through the playbook on the subway back uptown reminded me how complicated the logistics of success can be. The book is packed with facts and ideas — deadlines for financial-aid forms, notes on picking majors, tips on improving study habits, suggestions for good relations with roommates and professors — information that students who graduate from Riverdale have heard from parents and friends and older siblings for years already, that they've been immersed in, in fact, their whole lives. To KIPP graduates, though, it often feels like a foreign language.

Here's one way of looking at character: It can function as a substitute for the social safety net that students at Riverdale enjoy — the support from their families and schools and culture that protects them from the consequences of occasional detours and mistakes and bad decisions. If you don't have that kind of safety net — and children in low-income families almost by definition do not — you need to compensate in another way. To succeed, you need more grit, more social intelligence, more self-control than wealthier kids. Developing that strength takes a lot of work. But for the KIPP students who do manage to find those skills, who are able to make it through that minefield and graduate from college, it's hard not to think that they will set out into adulthood with some real advantages over their Riverdale counterparts. Not financial advantages, but character advantages. When a KIPP student graduates from college, he will have not only a BA but also something more valuable: the knowledge that he climbed a mountain to get it.

3

HOW TO THINK

_____

1. Sebastian's Blunder

Sebastian Garcia couldn't figure out where he'd gone wrong. One minute he was up by a bishop and a pawn, in good position, feeling strong, looking to start off the 2011 National Junior High Chess Championships with a victory. And the next minute he was in deep trouble, his advantage squandered, his king scurrying across the board like a frightened little mouse, fleeing his opponent's rook. A few moves later, when his defeat was complete, Sebastian limply shook hands with the boy who had beaten him, a sandy-haired kid from a central Ohio suburb, shuffled his way through the cavernous convention-center ballroom where a thousand heads were bowed over chessboards, and slunk back to Union B, the windowless conference room down the hall that was his chess team's temporary home. Sebastian, a short, stocky, quiet Latino with round cheeks and a thick bristle of black hair, was in the sixth grade at Intermediate School 318 in Brooklyn, and two days earlier, along with sixty teammates and a handful of teachers and parents, he had traveled eleven hours in a chartered bus to Columbus, Ohio, for a few days of competitive chess. His weekend was not off to a good start.

The ritual for students on the IS 318 team was that, win or lose, after each game they would come back to the team room for a post-mortem with the school's chess teacher, Elizabeth Spiegel. Sebastian slouched into Union B and approached the small table where Spiegel, tall and slender, sat behind a chessboard.

"I lost," he announced.

"Tell me about your game," Spiegel said. She was in her mid-thirties, dressed all in black, her pale skin made paler by the contrast with her brightly dyed hair, which changed hues somewhat from season to season. For this tournament, she had chosen the deep vermilion of red velvet cake. Sebastian dropped into the chair opposite her and handed her his chess notation book, where he'd scrawled all sixty-five of his moves as well as all of his opponent's.

The other guy was simply better than him, Sebastian explained. "He had good skills," he said, a little plaintively. "Good strategies."

"Well, let's see," said Spiegel, and she took the white pieces and started re-creating the game on the board between them, making each of Sebastian's opponent's moves while Sebastian, as black, re-played his own moves. Sebastian and the Ohio boy had both begun by bringing out a couple of pawns, and white quickly developed his knights, a standard opening called the Caro-Kann, which they'd gone over in chess class back in Brooklyn dozens of times. And then the Ohio boy had pulled one knight back to an unexpected square, so that both of his knights were attacking a single black pawn. Sebastian, nervous, moved another pawn up to defend, but he had stumbled into a trap. His opponent quickly swooped a knight down to capture the defending pawn, and just four moves into the game, Sebastian was down a piece.

Spiegel stared at Sebastian. "How long did you spend on that move?" she asked.

"Two seconds."

Spiegel's face grew cloudy. "We did not bring you here so that you could spend two seconds on a move," she said, a steely edge in her voice. Sebastian looked down. "Sebastian!" He looked up. "This is pathetic. If you continue to play like this, I'm going to withdraw you from the tournament, and you can just sit here with your head down for the rest of the weekend. Two seconds is not slow enough." Her voice softened a little. "Look, if you make a mistake, that's okay. But you do something without even thinking about it? That's not okay. I'm very, very, very upset to be seeing such a careless and thoughtless game."

And then as quickly as the storm had arrived, it passed, and Spiegel was back to moving pieces and examining Sebastian's game. "Nice," she said as he avoided a pawn capture. "Very clever," she said when he took his opponent's knight. They went on like this, move after move, Spiegel praising Sebastian's good ideas, asking him to come up with alternatives to his less-good ones, and again and again reminding him that he had to slow down. "You were playing in some ways an excellent game," she told him, "and then once in a while you moved superfast and you did something really stupid. If you can stop doing that, you're going to do very, very well."

I first met Spiegel in the winter of 2009, after I read an article in the *New York Times* about her team's performance at the National Scholastic K–12 Championship the previous December. The article, by the paper's chess columnist, Dylan McClain, pointed out that IS 318 was in the federal education department's Title I program, meaning that more than 60 percent of the students at the school were from low-income families, and yet at the tournament in question, Spiegel's students had beaten wealthy kids from private schools and magnet schools. I was intrigued, but to be honest, I was also a little skeptical. Hollywood producers and magazine editors love tales of inner-city kids defeating private-school students in chess tournaments, but often, when you look a little more closely at the triumphs, they aren't quite as inspiring as they originally seemed. Sometimes the tournament that the team from the disadvantaged neighborhood won turns out to be a minor one, or the division that the students were competing in was restricted to students below a certain ability rating. Or the low-income kids turn out to be somehow atypical—they go to a selective school with an entrance exam, or they're recent immigrants from Asia or Eastern Europe rather than black or Latino kids from families with long poverty histories. In 2005, to give one example, *New York* magazine ran a long, adulatory profile of the chess team from the Mott Hall School, known as the Dark Knights of Harlem, "a hard-charging bunch of 10-to-12-year-olds from Washington Heights, Inwood, and Harlem" who were competing in a national tournament in Nashville. They did come in second in their division of the sixth-grade tournament, which was a fine achievement — but they were competing in the under-1000 section, meaning they didn't play anybody with a rating over 1000, which is fairly low. And the students had all had to pass an entrance exam to get into Mott Hall, so they were above average to begin with. Plus the team, while technically from Harlem, had only one black player; almost all the others were immigrants born in Kosovo or Poland or Mexico or Ecuador or China.

And so when I showed up at IS 318 on a January morning, I expected to encounter some comparable asterisk. But I couldn't find one. The team is diverse — there are a handful of whites and Asians — but most of the players are black or Hispanic, and the best players are African American. Few students on the team, from what I could tell, faced quite the daunting array of disadvantages and obstacles that the average student at Fenger High School in Roseland did, but with 87 percent of IS 318's students eligible for federal lunch subsidies, the school had come by its Title I designation honestly. IS 318 was in South Williamsburg, near the border of Bedford-Stuyvesant — its most famous graduate was the rapper Jay-Z, who grew up in the nearby Marcy housing project — and the team reflected the student body; the students' families were mostly from the struggling working class, and the majority of their parents were employed but not college educated.

Over the next two years, I returned often to IS 318 — sitting in on classes, accompanying the team to tournaments and chess clubs around New York City, following their progress on Spiegel's blog — and all the while, I was trying to figure out how they did it. The blunt reality is that rich kids win chess tournaments — or, more precisely, rich kids plus the cognitive elite who attend selective schools with competitive entrance exams. Take a look at the team winners, by grade, of the 2010 scholastic tournament in Orlando, held a few months before the Columbus tournament that Sebastian Garcia was playing in:

Kindergarten   Oak Hall School, a private school in
                Gainesville, Florida

First grade   SciCore Academy, a private school in
                New Jersey

Second grade   Dalton School, a private school in New
                York City

Third grade   Hunter College Elementary, an exam
                school in New York City

Fourth grade   Tie between SciCore Academy and
                Stuart Hall School for Boys, a Catholic
                school in New Orleans

Fifth grade   Regnart Elementary, a public school in
                Cupertino, California, home of Apple
                and dozens of software companies

Ninth grade   San Benito Veterans Memorial
                Academy, in southern Texas, a public
                school whose student body is mostly
                Hispanic and low income

Tenth grade   Horace Mann, a private school in New
                York City

Eleventh grade	Solomon Schechter, a private school in a New York City suburb
Twelfth grade	Bronx Science, an exam school in New York City

The winning team in every grade, in other words — with the exception of those outliers from San Benito — came from a private school, an exam school, a parochial school, or a public school populated by the children of Apple engineers.

Except, that is, for the middle-school grades, where the list of winners looked like this:

Sixth grade	IS 318, a low-income public school in Brooklyn
Seventh grade	IS 318, a low-income public school in Brooklyn
Eighth grade	IS 318, a low-income public school in Brooklyn

The students at IS 318 didn't win in just one grade; they won in every grade the school was allowed to enter. The roster of schools they beat reads like a wealthy parent's wish list of the most desirable private schools in the country: Trinity, Collegiate, Spence, Dalton, and Horace Mann in New York City, and exclusive private schools in Boston, Miami, and Greenwich, Connecticut. And the 2010 tournament wasn't a one-time fluke; IS 318 won in all three grades in 2008 as well. (In 2009, they won in the sixth- and seventh-grade divisions but lost the eighth-grade trophy by half a point.)

In the end, it is a simple truth, no caveats or asterisks required: the chess program at Intermediate School 318 is the best middle-school chess program in the United States, bar none. In fact, it is almost certainly the best scholastic chess program in the country at any grade level. The team's reputation has grown in recent years, and they have begun to draw good elementary-school players from around the city, which has added to their advantage. But mostly, they win tournaments because of what Elizabeth Spiegel was sitting in Union B doing that April afternoon: taking eleven-year-old kids, like Sebastian Garcia, who know a little chess but not a lot, and turning them, move by painstaking move, into champions.

By the thirty-fifth move in the game Sebastian was replaying with Spiegel, he had recovered completely from his early errors and taken a clear lead. He pushed his queen deep into enemy territory, putting the white king in check. His opponent drew a pawn up to block the black queen's attack. Sebastian moved his queen two squares ahead: check again. The white king retreated a square, pulling out of the queen's range.

And then, rather than keeping the pressure on the white king, Sebastian went for the easy score: he captured a white pawn with his queen. Once again, he had missed a looming threat: from the other side of the board, his opponent's rook stole Sebastian's bishop, and Sebastian's advantage started to slip away.

"You took the pawn?" Spiegel asked. "Come on. What's a better move?"

Sebastian said nothing.

"What about check?"

Sebastian stared at the board.

"Think about it," Spiegel said. "Remember, when I ask you a question, you don't have to answer right away. But you do have to be right."

Suddenly a bit of a smile crept onto Sebastian's face. "I could win the queen," he said.

"Show me," Spiegel said, and Sebastian made the moves, demonstrating how one more check would have not only saved his bishop but also sent white into a tailspin, forcing the Ohio boy to choose between losing his queen and losing the game.

"This is the thing," Spiegel said evenly, moving the pieces back to where they were when Sebastian had gone for the easy pawn. "Think back on this moment. When you made *this* move" — she captured the white pawn, as Sebastian had done — "you lost the game. If you had made *this* move" — she put the white king in check — "you would have won the game." She leaned back in her chair, her gaze fixed on Sebastian. "It's okay if the loss hurts you a little," she said. "You *should* feel bad. You're a talented player, but you have to slow down and think more. Because now you have" — she checked her watch — "four hours until the next game, which means that you have four hours to think about the fact that you got beat by this kid." She tapped the board. "All because of this one time when you could have slowed down but you didn't."

2. IQ and Chess

On May 11, 1997, at the Equitable Center in midtown Manhattan, Garry Kasparov, who since 1985 had been the world chess champion, resigned after just nineteen moves in the last game of his six-game match against Deep Blue, a chess-playing computer program designed by engineers at IBM. It was Kasparov's second defeat in the match — he had won one game; three others were draws — meaning he had lost the match and, more important, his unofficial title as the "finest chess playing entity on the planet," in the words of the *New York Times* reporter on the scene. There was, in the chess world and beyond it, great consternation over Kasparov's defeat and much anxious discussion about what it meant for the rest of us mortals. (*Newsweek* had run a story about the match a few days earlier; the magazine's cover had proclaimed it "The Brain's Last Stand.") In a mournful postgame news conference, Kasparov said he was ashamed of his loss and mystified by Deep Blue's towering ability. "I'm a human being," he lamented. "When I see something that is well beyond my understanding, I'm afraid."

To many people, Deep Blue's triumph represented not just a challenge to humanity's mastery of chess but an existential threat to our species' unique intelligence; it was as if a school of dolphins had just composed a perfect symphony. Indeed, chess ability has long been considered a simple shorthand for smartness: the more intelligent you are, the better you can play chess, and vice versa. In his 1997 book *Genius in Chess*, the British grand master Jonathan Levitt proposed a precise mathematical relationship between IQ and chess prowess in what he called the Levitt equation:

$$\text{Elo} \sim (10 \times \text{IQ}) + 1000.$$

Elo refers to a player's tournament rating — and in his equation, Levitt explained, he was referring to the highest rating that a player could achieve "after many years of tournament play or study." (That funny squiggle after *Elo* means "is approximately equal to.") So if you had a run-of-the-mill IQ of 100, by Levitt's calculation, the highest rating you could ever hope for was 2000. An IQ of 120 could potentially get you to 2200. And so on. Chess grand masters are usually rated at 2500 or above; according to Levitt's formula, that means they each possess an IQ of at least 150, which is considered genius level.

But not everyone accepts the premise that chess skill is closely and directly related to pure IQ. Jonathan Rowson, a young Scottish grand master who has written a few provocative books about chess, calls the Levitt equation "completely misguided." Rowson has argued that the most important talents in chess are not intellectual at all; they are psychological and emotional. "Most of the major academic studies of chess miss much that is essential to the ways that a chess-player thinks and feels," Rowson wrote in his book *The Seven Deadly Chess Sins*. "They are guilty of thinking of chess as an almost exclusively cognitive pursuit, where moves are chosen and positions understood only on the basis of mental patterns and inferences." In reality, he wrote, if you want to become a great chess player, or even a good one, "your ability to recognize and utilize your emotions is every bit as important as the way you think."

In her chess classes at IS 318 and in her postgame debriefings with students at tournaments like the National Junior High Championships, Spiegel often conveys specific chess knowledge: how to spot the difference between the exchange Slav opening and the semi-Slav; how to weigh the comparative value of your light-square bishop and your dark-square bishop. But most of the time, it struck me whenever I watched her at work, what she was really doing was far simpler, and also far more complicated: she was teaching her students a new way to think. Her methodology was closely related to the metacognitive strategies that Martin Seligman studied and that Angela Duckworth taught. And, to me, anyway, her system seemed inextricably linked to the research neuroscientists have been doing on executive functions — those higher-order mental capacities that some scientists compare to an air traffic control center for the brain.

Two of the most important executive functions are cognitive flexibility and cognitive self-control. Cognitive flexibility is the ability to see alternative solutions to problems, to think outside the box, to negotiate unfamiliar situations. Cognitive self-control is the ability to inhibit an instinctive or habitual response and substitute a more effective, less obvious one. Both skills are central to the training Spiegel gives to her students. To prevail at chess, she says, you need a heightened ability to see new and different ideas: Which especially creative winning move have you overlooked? And which potentially lethal move of your opponent's are you blindly ignoring? She also teaches them to resist the temptation to pursue an immediately attractive move, since that type of move (as Sebastian Garcia found out) often leads to trouble down the road. "Teaching chess is really about teaching the habits that go along with thinking," Spiegel explained to me one morning when I visited her classroom. "Like how to understand your mistakes and how to be more aware of your thought processes."

Before she was a full-time chess teacher at IS 318, Spiegel taught an eighth-grade honors English class at the school, and as an English teacher she was, she says, a bit of a disaster. She taught composition the way she analyzed Sebastian's chess game: When students turned in writing assignments, she went through each assignment sentence by sentence with each student, asking, Well, are you *sure* that's the best way to say what you want to say? "They looked at me like I was insane," she told me. "I would write them these long letters about what they'd written. It would take me the whole evening to do six or seven of them."

Although Spiegel's teaching style might not have been the right fit with an English class, her experience teaching English did help her understand better what she wanted to do in chess class. Rather than follow a set chess curriculum over the course of the year, she decided she would construct her academic calendar as she went, planning lessons based entirely on what her students knew and, more important, on what they didn't know. For instance, she would take her students to a weekend tournament and notice that many of them were hanging pieces, meaning they were leaving pieces undefended, which made them easy targets. The following Monday, she would organize the whole class around how not to hang pieces, reconstructing the students' flawed games on the green felt practice boards hung on hooks at the front of her classroom. Again and again, she would go over her students' games, both individually and as a class, analyzing exactly where a player had gone wrong, what he could have done differently, what might have happened if he had made the better move, and playing out these counterfactual scenarios for several moves before returning to the moment of error.

Sensible though this process might sound, it's actually a pretty unusual way to teach chess, or to learn it. "It's uncomfortable to focus so intensely on what you're bad at," Spiegel told me. "So the way people usually study chess is they read a book about chess, which can be fun and often intellectually amusing, but it doesn't actually translate into skill. If you really want to get better at chess, you have to look at your games and figure out what you're doing wrong."

It's a little like what people ideally get out of psychotherapy, Spiegel says. You go over the mistakes you made — or the mistakes you keep making — and you try to get to the bottom of why you made them. And just like the best therapists, Spiegel tries to lead her students down a narrow and difficult path: to have them take responsibility for their mistakes and learn from them without obsessing over them or beating themselves up for them. "Very rarely do kids have an experience in life of losing when it was entirely in their control," she told me. "But when they lose a chess game, they know that they have no one to blame but themselves. They had everything they needed to win, and they lost. If that happens to you once, you can usually find some excuse, or just never think about it again. When it's part of your life, when it happens to you every single weekend, you have to find a way to separate yourself from your mistakes or your losses. I try to teach my students that losing is something you do, not something you are."

3. Chess Fever

Of course, it's easy to tell kids they should put their losses in perspective and keep their confidence intact despite setbacks. It's harder when you're the person doing the losing. Spiegel plays chess at a very high level herself; although her rating has slipped a bit over the past few years, as she has dedicated more of her time to teaching, she is still one of the top thirty female chess players in the country. But like all great chess players, she loses a lot, and when she does, she often takes to her blog — a popular if offbeat source of news and opinion in the chess world — and castigates herself for everyone to see. "I am such a stupid retarded disgusting mindless child," she wrote in 2007 after losing to a Russian master. "Am I really incapable of calculating simple captures? I officially hate myself."

Spiegel's father taught her the basic chess moves when she was just four years old, but she didn't play chess competitively until she got to sixth grade and signed up for an afterschool chess program at her junior high school in Raleigh, North Carolina. She loved it — not just the chess, which she excelled at, but also the unfamiliar sense of belonging that chess gave her. A socially awkward child before finding chess, she suddenly had a place where she fit in. "I remember feeling so happy and relieved," she told me. "Kids were nice to me because I was good. Adults treated me like I had real opinions. For the first time, I felt like life was getting better." Her chess rating quickly soared

above that of the teacher who ran the chess program, and she realized, to her amazement, that she didn't need his help to continue to
improve; she could just study chess on her own. And if she could
teach herself chess, she figured, she could teach herself math, too,
or anything else. Her ability to master new subjects on her own, a
skill she learned entirely from chess, carried her through her years at
what she describes as "a terrible American high school" and into college, first Duke and then Columbia, where she started off majoring in
math and then after a couple of years switched to English literature.

After graduating, Spiegel stayed in New York and signed up as a
teacher with a nonprofit called Chess-in-the-Schools, an organization that since 1986 has been arranging for chess experts like Spiegel
to spend a few hours a week teaching chess in the city's low-income
public schools. For a few years, Spiegel rotated among a group of four
schools, a day here, a day there, but she liked IS 318 the best, and finally, in 2006, the principal hired her as a full-time chess teacher and
as the coach of the school's traveling chess team.

In the summer of 2005, after several years of playing chess only
halfheartedly, she entered, on a whim, a high-level open tournament
in Phoenix. And to her surprise, she did very well, scoring the highest of any woman at the tournament, which meant that she auto-
matically qualified for the U.S. national championship the following
spring. She was out of her depth, and she knew it; sixty-four men and
women had qualified for the tournament, the finest chess players in
the country, and she was one of the lowest rated. So she poured herself into chess, studying three or more hours a day, five days a week,
staying up all night going over an opening or playing for hours online on the Internet Chess Club website. She improved enough that
she did reasonably well at the tournament—not top ten, but respect-
ably—and afterward, she kept playing with the same fervor. Just as it
had in junior high, chess took over her life. She taught chess all day
and played every night. She lost touch with her friends who didn't
play chess, and other commitments and connections began to slip
away. Playing chess, she wrote on her blog, had become "pretty much

the only time I ever feel anything. The rest of the time, with just a couple exceptions, I am almost completely numb."

Spiegel became more and more cut off from the non-chess world. She has a tendency toward both melancholy and a certain eccentricity, and her increasing social isolation allowed those traits to metastasize. One day, on her blog, she announced bashfully to her readers that she had been on a date the previous Friday. "At some point," she wrote, "he put his arm around me, and I thought, *Wow, I have absolutely no physical contact with human beings anymore.* Ultimately, though, I am proud of myself, because I did not say this to my date, despite the fact that I thought about it for a long time. I realized in time that it is not the sort of thing you say on a date."

Then, over Christmas vacation in 2009, she took an impulsive, romantic trip to the Caribbean with the art teacher from IS 318, a tall, good-looking guy named Jonathan with Mediterranean features and long dark hair, whom she had admired from afar in the teachers' lounge but had considered out of her league. By the time they got back from their week in the Bahamas, they were in love. Four months later, they moved in together, and by the fall of 2010, they were engaged.

Jonathan didn't play chess at all, and as she spent more time with him, Spiegel found her chess fever starting to dissipate. It wasn't that she abandoned chess altogether — she was still teaching it all day at school and coaching her students on Saturdays at scholastic tournaments — but now her free time was spent doing things like riding bikes and eating good food and exploring new neighborhoods and talking about the future, not playing chess online. To me, a non–chess player, this seemed like a positive development. It seemed clear that playing chess all the time didn't make Spiegel very happy, and hanging out with Jonathan did. From her perspective, though, the cost-benefit analysis wasn't so simple. Her official chess rating peaked at 2170, but after Spiegel started dating Jonathan, it slipped down below 2100. She often talked about her desire to get serious about chess again, to play more, to get her rating back up. Rationally, she knew that she was happier than she had been when she was playing chess all the time, but still, she told me, she missed those unhappy, obsessive days all the same.

4. Calibrated Meanness

At the heart of Spiegel's job was a complex balancing act. She wanted to build up her students' confidence, to make them believe in their own ability to overcome stronger rivals and master an impossibly complicated game. But the exigencies of her job — and the particularities of her personality — meant that she spent most of her time telling her students how they were messing up. It's the basic narrative of all postgame chess analysis, in fact: *You thought you had a good idea here, but you were wrong.*

"I struggle with it all the time," she told me one day when I visited her class. "Every day. It's very high on my list of anxieties as a teacher. I feel like I'm very mean to the kids. It kills me sometimes, like I go home and I play through everything I said to every kid and I'm like, 'What am I doing? I'm damaging the children.'"

After the 2010 girls' national tournament (which IS 318 won), Spiegel wrote on her blog:

The first day and a half was pretty bad. I was on a complete rampage, going over every game and being a huge bitch all the time: saying things like "THAT IS COMPLETELY UNACCEPTABLE!!!" to 11-year-olds for hanging pieces or not having a reason for a move. I said some amazing things to kids, including "You can count to two, right? Then you should have seen that!!" and "If you are not going to pay more attention, you should quit chess, because you are wasting everyone's time."

By the end of round three I was starting to feel like an abusive jerk and was about to give up and be fake nice instead. But then in round four everyone took more than an hour and started playing well. And I really believe that's why we seem to win girls' nationals sections pretty easily every year: most people won't tell teenage girls (especially the together, articulate ones) that they are lazy and the quality of their work is unacceptable. And sometimes kids need to hear that, or they have no reason to step up.

Spiegel often defied my stereotype of how a good teacher, especially a good inner-city teacher, should interact with her students. I confess that before meeting her, I had a vision of the ideal inner-city chess teacher that bore a close resemblance to the character played by Ted Danson in *Knights of the South Bronx,* an inspirational 2005 A&E original movie in which Danson leads a ragtag band of kids from the ghetto to victory over a bunch of stuck-up private-school students, handing out hugs and motivational speeches and life lessons along the way. Spiegel is not like this. She does not hug. She clearly is devoted to her students and cares about them deeply, but when a student gets upset after a loss, Spiegel is rarely the one to go over and offer comfort. John Galvin, the vice principal at IS 318, who often came to tournaments as Spiegel's co-coach, was better at that sort of thing, she said; he had more "emotional intelligence."

"I definitely have a warm relationship with a lot of the kids," Spiegel told me at one tournament. "But I think my job as a teacher is to be more like a mirror, to talk about what they did on the chessboard and help them think about it. It's a big thing to offer a kid. They put a lot of work into something, and you really look at it with them on a non-condescending level. That's something that kids don't often get, and in my experience, they really want it. But it's not like I love them and mother them. I'm not that kind of person."

Researchers, including Michael Meaney and Clancy Blair, have demonstrated that for infants to develop qualities like perseverance and focus, they need a high level of warmth and nurturance from their caregivers. What Spiegel's success suggests, though, is that when children reach early adolescence, what motivates them most effectively isn't licking and grooming–style care but a very different kind of attention. Perhaps what pushes middle-school students to concentrate and practice as maniacally as Spiegel's chess players do is the unexpected experience of someone taking them seriously, believing in their abilities, and challenging them to improve themselves.

During the months when I was most actively reporting at IS 318, watching the team prepare for the tournament in Columbus, I was also spending a lot of time at KIPP Infinity, tracking the development of the character report card. And as I shuttled back and forth on the subway between West Harlem and South Williamsburg, I had plenty of time to contemplate the parallels between Spiegel's methods of training her students in chess and the way that teachers and administrators at KIPP talked to their students about day-to-day emotional crises or behavioral lapses. You may recall that KIPP's dean, Tom Brunzell, said he considered his approach to be a kind of cognitive-behavioral therapy. When his students were flailing, lost in moments of stress and emotional turmoil, he would encourage them to do the kind of big-picture thinking — the metacognition, as many psychologists call it — that takes place in the prefrontal cortex: slowing down, examining their impulses, and considering more productive solutions to their problems than, say, yelling at a teacher or shoving another kid on the playground. In her postgame chess analyses, Spiegel had simply developed a more formalized way to do this. Like students at KIPP, IS 318 students were being challenged to look deeply at their own mistakes, examine why they had made them, and think hard about what they might have done differently. And whether you call that approach cognitive therapy or just plain good teaching, it seemed remarkably effective in producing change in middle-school students.

This technique, though, is actually quite rare in contemporary American schools. If you believe that your school's mission or your job as a teacher is simply to convey information, then it probably doesn't seem necessary to subject your students to that kind of rigorous self-analysis. But if you're trying to help them change their character, then conveying information isn't enough. And while Spiegel didn't use the word *character* to describe what she was teaching, there was a remarkable amount of overlap between the strengths David

Levin and Dominic Randolph emphasized and the skills that Spiegel tried to inculcate in her students. Every day, in the classroom and at tournaments, I saw Spiegel trying to teach her students grit, curiosity, self-control, and optimism.

On a couple of occasions, I even saw her use her analytical techniques to teach social intelligence. One day in September, I went with Spiegel and the IS 318 team to a big outdoor chess tournament in Central Park run by Chess-in-the-Schools. It was a hot day, and while I was sitting with Spiegel on the stone steps that led down to Bethesda Fountain, a student came up to us, looking upset, wanting to talk to Spiegel. It was A.J., a student in the seventh grade who had dark skin, short hair, and big, thick Elvis Costello glasses. A.J., I knew, had difficulty in social situations, often losing his way amid the middle-school joking and jockeying, frequently misinterpreting what was going on around him. His story that day came out in a jumble: another IS 318 kid, a recent graduate named Rawn, was threatening to slap A.J., and A.J. wanted Spiegel to do something about it.

"Why does he want to slap you?" Spiegel asked.

A.J. haltingly explained that he had brought his football to the park, and between matches, he and a few of the other boys were tossing it around. A.J. felt hot, and when he went to get a drink, he decided he needed to take his football with him. When he grabbed it and headed off to the drinking fountain, he thought he heard one of the boys call him a bitch. He accused Rawn. Rawn denied it.

"He said, 'Don't you talk to me like that,'" A.J. told Spiegel, sounding aggrieved. "He tells me, 'I will slap you in the mouth.' And I said, 'Why don't you try it?' And then he tried to come over to me and slap my face, but everybody backed him off." It was, in other words, a classic quarrel between boys on the cusp of adolescence: impulsive, awash in hormones, intensely moralistic, somewhat nonsensical.

But rather than take sides or offer some vague bromides about getting along, Spiegel started to break it down like a chess game.

"So, let me see if I understand," Spiegel said, shielding her eyes from the sun and looking up at A.J. "He tried to hit you after you told him to try to hit you?"

"Yeah," A.J. said, a little uncertainly.

"Well, you know, if Rawn didn't say anything to you, and then you were saying stuff back to him? Then he's going to be upset. Does that make sense?"

A.J. stared at her, silent, looking a little like Sebastian Garcia being chastised for losing his bishop.

"My other question would be about the football," Spiegel went on. "You have to understand that people aren't going to like that you're taking your football when they're playing with it. Do you think it would be okay if they used it when you weren't there?"

"No."

"Well, you have to understand, though, that if you're not going to trust them, they're probably not going to be your friends."

A.J. looked frustrated. "Forget it," he said and walked away.

I had actually observed a similar conversation a few months earlier between A.J. and Spiegel. I was sitting in Spiegel's classroom with her, talking chess, and A.J. had come in with a complaint: he'd said something about another kid's mother, and the other kid had called him a name.

At first, I assumed that A.J. was coming to Spiegel for recourse or revenge, so that she would discipline the other student. But after observing the Central Park conversation, it struck me that he was really coming to her for the same reason he came to her for help after a game when he had squandered a lead or hung a queen. He wanted to know how to quit making boneheaded mistakes. He wanted advice on how to get better at what was, to A.J., another incredibly complex game with way too many moving pieces: surviving middle school and getting other kids to like you.

5. Justus and James

When I first saw Spiegel in Columbus, the afternoon before the opening day of the tournament, she looked happy and well rested; she was wearing a crisp white dress shirt and pinstriped tailored pants, eating tangerines and sipping chai tea and going over last-minute chess worksheets with a couple dozen students crammed into her hotel room high above the convention center. Once the competition began, though, her crispness began to fray, and each day her hair grew a little wilder, her eyes a little more glazed. For her, the junior high tournament was the most important competition of the year. "I feel like it's a judgment on my work," she told me that first afternoon. "Everything I do all year comes down to how well we do here." And so she sat in Union B all day, drinking coffee and eating takeout from the food court and worrying.

IS 318 had teams competing in five divisions, and the two that Spiegel took most seriously were K–8 Open and K–9 Open. (*Open* means that there is no upper limit on the ratings of players.) K–9 Open included students up to ninth grade, but it was considered by many coaches to be a less competitive section than K–8 Open (which allowed students only up to eighth grade), since fewer junior high teams competed in K–9. Spiegel thought her team had at least a decent shot at winning both sections, even though no school had ever won K–8 and K–9 in the same year — and even though IS 318 didn't have a ninth grade.

One of the reasons that Spiegel's teams had always done so well in tournaments was that she had what basketball coaches call a deep bench. At most private schools and selective exam schools, you could find a small handful of very good chess players, prodigies from well-off families who had been getting individual coaching since they were quite young. IS 318 didn't attract those privileged kids, but because chess was such an integral part of the school day and the school's culture, Spiegel was instead able to draw dozens of new students each year to chess club, kids who had little or no chess knowledge but who were eager to learn more. She had designed her program to capitalize on that, and after almost a decade at the school, she had built a teaching system that could reliably turn the two dozen or so novices who showed up for chess club in their first week of sixth grade into a collection of 1500s and 1600s, with a few 1800s and 1900s, by the time they finished eighth grade.

Only rarely had an IS 318 student topped 2000, which meant that the school didn't win many individual championships. But Spiegel's approach was the perfect strategy for *team* championships, which were won in each tournament by the school whose top four players together had the most wins. In a team competition, Spiegel knew, it was not the ability of your best player that made the real difference; it was the ability of your fourth-best player. And at IS 318, on any given day, there were ten or more students who could each be the team's fourth-best player.

But in the fall of 2009, Justus Williams arrived at IS 318, and the composition of the team began to change. Justus, who lived in the Bronx, was a cool kid, pensive and rugged, tall and dark-skinned and solidly built. He spoke quietly, and he could be shy around strangers, but he moved with a smooth confidence through the halls of IS 318, one of the few middle schools in the country where being a chess champion earned you respect rather than wedgies. Justus had started playing chess in third grade at PS 70 in the South Bronx, through Chess-in-the-Schools, and his teachers had recognized early on that he was a player of great promise, eager to learn and unusually able to focus and concentrate. Chess-in-the-Schools paid for chess tutors to work with him privately, and his mother, who believed that Justus was destined for greatness, did everything she could to help him improve. By the time Justus started sixth grade at IS 318, his rating was above 2000, hundreds of points higher than any previous incoming student Spiegel had taught and quite close, in fact, to Spiegel's own rating. And while Justus was clearly the best player in sixth grade, there were two other students who arrived with him at IS 318 who also had substantial chess experience: Isaac Barayev, a son of Russian immigrants from Queens who entered sixth grade with a rating of 1500, and James Black Jr., an African American boy from the Brooklyn neighborhood of Bedford-Stuyvesant who had graduated from his local public school with a rating of 1700.

Spiegel had an especially warm relationship with James Black. She had met him when he was still in elementary school, and although his chess ability now rivaled hers, he recognized that she had helped him improve his rating during his time at the school from 1700 to over 2100, a significant leap. James was slight and handsome, with close-shorn hair, a chipped front tooth, and wide, expressive eyes. He was intensely social and loved joking with his classmates. When I visited Spiegel's class, I often found James at the back of the room playing one game and loudly kibitzing the game next to him, telling the other players what moves they should make and occasionally reaching over and making them himself.

Like Justus, James learned how to play chess in third grade when a Chess-in-the-Schools tutor visited his school. At home, he would practice with his father, who had bought James a chess set from Kmart at the first sign of James's interest in the game. James Black Sr. was intensely devoted to his son. He once told me that he had made up his mind, even before James was conceived, that his first child, whether a boy or a girl, would be named James Black Jr.

James Sr. grew up in the Bronx and did well in high school, but he dropped out of college after two years. His dream had always been to join the Marines, but when he left school, he landed a well-paying job behind the deli counter at D'Agostino, the New York City supermarket chain, and he never enlisted. Almost twenty-five years later, Black was still at D'Agostino, still a deli clerk. In his mid-thirties, he'd fallen in love with Tonya Coles, a woman with three children, and together with their baby, James, they formed a blended family. James Sr. told me that he had hoped that his stepchildren would provide good examples for James Jr., but it hadn't worked out that way. One of James's half brothers was convicted of selling drugs when James was a boy and spent almost three years in prison; the other is still in prison for murder, serving twenty years to life. Their problems only increased James Sr.'s focus on his son and his determination that he would succeed. "I tell James, 'I can only say so much to them,'" he told me early in the school year. "'But I can say a lot to you. My job is to guide you to the future.'"

James was an inconsistent student at IS 318. His grades were mostly good, but on the statewide achievement tests in sixth grade, he scored a 2, on a scale of 1 to 4, in both math and reading, which meant he was below grade level and in the lowest third of students in the city as a whole. At school, he had a reputation as a troublemaker, and in sixth grade he was often sent to the principal's office for goofing around in class or saying inappropriate things to his female classmates. Despite his occasional problems in school, though, he was an exceptional student of chess, studying as much as six hours a day, one whole wall of his bedroom filled with thick books of strategy.

6. The Marshall

Six months before the Columbus tournament, I spent a day with James, Spiegel, and half a dozen other IS 318 students at the Marshall Chess Club, which occupies two floors of a beautiful old town house on a tree-lined street in Greenwich Village. The club, considered by many chess players to be the most prestigious in the United States, was founded in 1915 by Frank Marshall, a chess champion of the day, and it has counted some of the best American players among its members. It is an imposing place, especially to young chess aspirants: the ceilings are high, the fireplaces grand, the wood tables polished to a lustrous shine, the walls lined with framed black-and-white photos of legendary players bent over chessboards and sepia-toned group shots of black-tie club dinners from the 1930s.

When Spiegel arrived in New York in her late teens, after transferring from Duke to Columbia, the Marshall was where she hung out, playing in weekend tournaments and soaking up the atmosphere. Now the Marshall offers a few free memberships each year to IS 318, and once a month or so, Spiegel brings a small group of students to play. It is a very different kind of chess experience than what they are used to. Regular scholastic weekend tournaments in New York City are pretty chaotic, hundreds of players and parents stuffed into a public school, moms serving up baked ziti for lunch. Games last only an hour, and IS 318 players usually win or at least do quite well. When students go to the Marshall, though, they generally play in games that last four hours against opponents whose ratings vastly exceeds theirs.

It is an intimidating situation for the students, but Spiegel reminds them that the best way to improve your chess is to play against the best, even if they take you apart.

On the fall day I watched James play at the Marshall, he was paired with Yuri Lapshun, a Ukrainian-born international master who was (and is) one of the thirty or forty best players in the United States. In 2000 and 2001, Lapshun was the Marshall club champion, and on the grand wooden plaque on the wall that lists every club champion since 1917, his name is embossed on two consecutive brass plates. Chess games, especially at the Marshall, often offer odd-looking pairings — the moody Goth teenage girl against the bearded and bespectacled math nerd; the aging tweed-clad Village lunatic against the diminutive young Chinese boy — but Black versus Lapshun was one of the odder ones. Lapshun, in his late thirties, was not only three times James's age but also at least a hundred pounds heavier than him. For most of the four-hour game, Lapshun sat scowling at the board, leaning back in his chair and stroking his thick, retro-Soviet mustache, his big, meaty arms folded over his sizable belly. James sat forward, his chin propped in his hands, threatening to disappear inside his big gray hoodie and oversize jeans, occasionally looking around the room and then back at the board, blinking his long, dark eyelashes. James has a hard time sitting still, and during games he frequently gets up and walks around, checking out other boards, much to the consternation of his teachers and coaches. At one point during his match with Lapshun, James wandered all the way up to the second floor, where Spiegel and I were talking. She yelled at him to get back down to the tournament room and told him that if he didn't stay in his seat for the rest of the game, she'd call his father.

Lapshun was rated 2546 that day, and James was rated 2068. James was, in every way, outmatched — except, somehow, on the board. As early as the sixth move, James surprised Lapshun with some savvy tactics, and by move thirty, it was clear to the various experts and masters observing the game that James was in a dominant position. He had established a suffocating line of defense across the middle of the board, cutting off one move after another for Lapshun, trapping him in an uncomfortable stasis where almost any move he made would lose him a piece or a positional advantage. On the fifty-ninth move, Lapshun resigned.

Afterward, on the upper floor, James went over his game with Spiegel, and Lapshun was gracious enough to analyze the game with them, occasionally adding some dark, fatalistic observations that were made somehow darker by his heavy Eastern-bloc accent: "Eet ees hopeless," he would say, indicating the board. And then, a few moves later, with a mournful shake of his head, "Here I am feen-ished." James demonstrated, move by move, how he had blocked off every chance Lapshun had to escape the paralyzing traps he had set for him, and Spiegel was impressed. He had done more than beat an international master; he had outplayed him from start to finish. It was, she told him, "exceptionally deep chess."

With the victory over Lapshun and some other strong games that fall, James's rating soared past 2150. His short-term goal was to reach 2200, which is a crucial marker for chess players. When you hit 2200, you are certified by the U.S. Chess Federation as a national master. Justus had become a national master in September, a month before James beat Lapshun. In fact, Justus was the youngest African American ever to make master. It looked for a while as though James, who was five months younger than Justus, would beat Justus's youngest-black-master record with ease. But then James's rating seemed to hit a plateau; it actually slipped down to almost 2100 in January, and then it bounced around for a couple of months in the low 2100s. By the time he got on the bus for the trip to the Columbus tournament in April, James had lost his shot at Justus's record, and his rating was stalled at 2156.

7. Mastery

In Columbus, James didn't go over his games with Spiegel; instead, he analyzed them with Matan Prilleltensky, a twenty-three-year-old competitive chess player from Miami who had been working that year as a part-time assistant coach for the IS 318 team while he studied for a master's degree in special education. Prilleltensky's interest in special ed had its roots in his own diagnosis of attention deficit hyperactivity disorder, or ADHD, when he was a child. He had struggled in elementary and middle school, unable to concentrate in class or on his homework for longer than a few minutes. And then he discovered chess. It was, he told me, the first time he had ever felt able to focus on anything. Chess, which requires hours of patient study, seemed an unlikely pursuit for a person with an attention disorder, but Prilleltensky said that the combination was not as odd as it sounded. "A lot of people with attention issues crave intense experiences and serious stimulation," he explained. "They want to be absorbed in some sort of all-encompassing pursuit." For Prilleltensky, chess was in fact the perfect antidote to ADHD; when he sat down at a chessboard, his symptoms all but disappeared.

Prilleltensky became a serious player in high school, reaching a rating of 2000 just after his eighteenth birthday. In college, he continued to play and even won a tournament or two, but he didn't really improve much, and when he graduated, in 2009, his rating was stuck at around 2100. He wanted to get better, but his chess didn't seem to be going anywhere. Then in January of 2010, he played in a tournament in Palatka, Florida; he was on the verge of winning the whole thing when he blew a crucial game. He felt crushed by the defeat, and when he analyzed the game afterward with his opponent, a high-school student, he realized that the other guy hadn't played particularly well — Prilleltensky had beaten himself. It was an awful feeling, he told me later. He was tired of being an unexceptional chess player.

On the way home to Miami, Prilleltensky read a collection of interviews with grand masters that included an e-mail conversation with Jonathan Rowson, the Scottish grand master who had written about the importance of emotion and psychology in chess success. Rowson's comments seemed to speak to Prilleltensky's plight — and they also echoed Angela Duckworth's theory on the crucial difference between motivation and volition. "When it comes to ambition," Rowson wrote, "it is crucial to distinguish between 'wanting' something and 'choosing' it." Decide that you *want* to become world champion,

Rowson explained, and you will inevitably fail to put in the necessary hard work. You will not only not become world champion but also have the unpleasant experience of falling short of a desired goal, with all the attendant disappointment and regret. If, however, you *choose* to become world champion (as Kasparov did at a young age), then you will "reveal your choice through your behavior and your determination. Every action says, 'This is who I am.'"

Inspired by these words, Prilleltensky, in late January of 2010, made a belated New Year's resolution: he would break 2200. He devoted almost a full year to the study of chess, eliminating everything else (except his understanding girlfriend) from his life: no parties, no Facebook, no ESPN, no unnecessary socializing. Just hours and hours of chess. ("This is who I am.") His efforts paid off; on October 10, 2010, his rating hit 2200 for the first time. He was a national master.

I met Prilleltensky soon after he reached his goal, and what surprised me, as I listened to him talk about it, was that he looked back on those monastic months with not just pride in the result but also pleasant memories of the process. What, I asked him, was so fun about a year of complete immersion in chess? "It was mostly the feeling of being intellectually productive," he replied. "So much of the time I feel like I'm not really challenging myself or pushing myself, just kind of wasting my brain. I never feel like that when I'm studying or playing or teaching chess."

I was struck by the word that Prilleltensky used: *productive*. Spiegel chose the same word when she described for me, a little wistfully, what she had lost when she traded all-night online chess obsession for domestic bliss with Jonathan: "I miss how productive I used to be."

This was a puzzle. I could appreciate the appeal of mastering chess, just as I could appreciate the appeal of mastering any other skill I wasn't good at — oil painting, playing jazz trumpet, pole-vaulting — but while I could easily be persuaded that chess was a worthy and challenging intellectual undertaking, *productive* was the last word I would choose to describe it. Chess players, it seemed to me, were quite literally producing nothing. As it happens, this question had come up in the Rowson interview that sparked Prilleltensky's quest for 2200. The interviewer asked Rowson if he was embarrassed to have expended such prodigious mental energy to become a grand master "rather than something worthwhile like a brain surgeon." Rowson acknowledged that "the question of chess being an essentially futile activity has a nagging persistence for me. . . . I occasionally think that the thousands of hours I've spent on chess, however much they have developed me personally, could have been better spent."

But Rowson went on to defend himself and his fellow chess players, and he did so on essentially aesthetic grounds: "Chess is a creative and beautiful pursuit, which allows us to experience a wide range of uniquely human characteristics," he wrote. The game "is a celebration of existential freedom, in the sense that we are blessed with the opportunity to create ourselves through our actions. In choosing to play chess, we are celebrating freedom above utility." In Rowson's eyes, two chess players facing off across a board were making a unique, collaborative work of art, and the better they played, the more beautiful the result.

In his 2008 book *Outliers,* Malcolm Gladwell brought to popular attention Swedish psychologist K. Anders Ericsson's theory that it takes ten thousand hours of deliberate practice to truly master any skill, whether it is playing violin or programming computers. Ericsson based his theory in part on a study of chess mastery. There are no natural-born chess champions, he found; you simply cannot become a grand master without dedicating thousands of hours to play and study. The best chess players started as children, Ericsson discovered; in fact, over the course of chess history, the age at which an aspiring chess champion needed to start playing in order to reach the game's highest levels had steadily fallen. In the nineteenth century, it was possible to start playing chess at seventeen and still become a grand master. Among players born in the twentieth century, though, no one who started playing after the age of fourteen became a grand master.

By the end of the twentieth century, Ericsson found, those who went on to become chess masters had started playing chess at an average age of ten and a half, and the typical grand master had started playing at seven.

The most famous, and notorious, study demonstrating the power of early deliberate practice on success in chess was conducted by Laszlo Polgar, a Hungarian psychologist who, in the 1960s, published a book titled *Bring Up Genius!* The book argued that with enough hard work, parents could turn any child into an intellectual prodigy. When he wrote the book, Polgar was single and childless, and thus in no position to test his theory himself, but he set out to change that, winning the heart of a Hungarian-speaking foreign-language teacher named Klara who was living in Ukraine but was persuaded to move to Budapest by Polgar's letters, which detailed how together they would raise a family of geniuses.

And then, amazingly, they did just that. Laszlo and Klara had three girls, Susan, Sofia, and Judit, and Laszlo homeschooled them all in an academic program that focused almost exclusively on chess (though the girls also learned several foreign languages, including Esperanto). Each girl began studying chess before her fifth birthday, and they were all soon playing eight to ten hours each day. Susan, the oldest, won her first tournament at age four. At fifteen, she became the top-rated female chess player in the world, and in 1991, when she was twenty-one, she became the first female grand master. Her success was an impressive confirmation of her father's contention that geniuses are made, not born — and Susan wasn't even the best chess player in the family. That was Judit, the youngest, who became a grand master at fifteen, breaking Bobby Fischer's record as the youngest person to claim the title. Judit's overall chess ranking peaked in 2005, when she was the eighth-highest-ranked player in the world, with a rating of 2735; she is now universally considered to be the best female chess player ever to walk the planet. (Sofia was pretty good too; her top rating was 2505, at which point she was the sixth-best female player in the world, a stunning accomplishment for anyone but a Polgar.)

If the story of the Polgars is a little spooky, the tale of Gata Kamsky is downright creepy. Kamsky, born in Soviet Russia in 1974, began to study chess at the age of eight under the supervision of his father, a short-tempered former boxer named Rustam. (Gata's mother had left the family when he was a boy.) By twelve, Gata Kamsky was defeating grand masters; in 1989, he and his father defected to the United States, and they were installed in an apartment in Brighton Beach and given a $35,000 annual living allowance by the president of Bear Stearns, who believed that Kamsky was destined to become world champion. At sixteen, Kamsky became a grand master; at seventeen, he won the U.S. chess championship. For all his youthful accomplishments, though, Kamsky got as much if not more recognition for what many considered to be the draconian circumstances of his upbringing. Under his father's tutelage, Kamsky practiced and studied chess fourteen hours a day in the apartment in Brighton Beach; he never attended school, never watched television, played no sports, had no friends. His father became well known in the chess world for his violent temper, frequently screaming at Gata over losses and errors, throwing furniture, and, at one match, allegedly physically threatening his son's opponent.

In 1996, when he was twenty-two, Kamsky quit chess altogether. He married, graduated from Brooklyn College, attended medical school for a year, then got a degree from a Long Island law school but wasn't able to pass the bar exam. His story seemed to be a cautionary tale about how early practice and aggressive parenting can backfire. But then in 2004, Kamsky returned to competitive chess. He started with small tournaments at the Marshall, and within a few years he had surpassed his adolescent achievements, winning the U.S. championship in 2010, nineteen years after he'd first won the title, and then winning it again in 2011. He is now the top-rated chess player in the United States and the tenth best in the world. The effect of those ten thousand hours — although in Kamsky's case, practicing fourteen hours a day throughout his childhood as he did, the true figure might have been twenty-five thousand hours or more — was apparently too powerful to be derailed even by an eight-year hiatus.

8. Flow

When Spiegel and other chess players talk about the childhoods of players like Kamsky and the Polgars, it is often with a mixture of emotions. On the one hand, they acknowledge that a childhood organized obsessively around a single pursuit is unbalanced, if not unhinged. On the other, they can't help but feel a little jealous: *If my father had made me play for ten hours a day, imagine how good I'd be now!* The first time I visited Spiegel's class, she had just returned from a week of helping out at a high-level youth chess camp, five days of analyzing chess problems with the best nine- to fourteen-year-olds in the country. It turned out to be not much fun, she told me. "I felt so stupid," she explained. "It was painful for me to be there because the kids were so much faster than me. I had to ask a nine-year-old to explain a game to me." At one point, she said, she actually slipped away to a bathroom and cried.

While I was writing this chapter, I kept a cheap chess set on the coffee table in my office for reference, and occasionally my son, Ellington, who was two at the time, would wander in and start messing around with the chess set. When he did, I'd take a break. I taught him the names of the various pieces, and he discovered that he liked to knock them all down and then arrange them in attractive patterns on the board. I knew, logically, that Ellington's interest in the chessboard was no more unusual or meaningful than his interest in the paper clips in my desk drawer. But at times, I found myself thinking, *Hmmm, he knows the difference between a rook and a knight, and he's only two. Maybe he's a prodigy! If I teach him now how all the pieces move, and we start playing an hour a day, then by the time he's three . . .*

Tempting though my Polgaresque fantasy was, I resisted. I realized that I didn't actually want Ellington to become a chess prodigy. But when I tried to figure out exactly *why* I felt that way, I found it wasn't easy to explain or to justify. I felt that if Ellington studied chess four hours a day (let alone fourteen), he would be missing out on something. But I wasn't sure if I was right. Was it better to spend your childhood, or your life, a little bit interested in a lot of things (as I tend to be), or a lot interested in one thing? Spiegel and I often debated this question, and I have to admit, she made a convincing case for the benefits of single-minded devotion — a case, in fact, that reminded me very much of Angela Duckworth's definition of grit: self-discipline wedded to a dedicated pursuit of a goal.

"I think it's really liberating for kids to understand what it's like to be passionate about something," Spiegel explained one day at a tournament. "They're having momentous experiences that they'll always remember. I think the worst thing is you look back on your childhood and it's one blur of sitting in class and being bored and coming home and watching TV. At least when the kids on the chess team look back, they'll have the nationals to remember, or one great game they played, or a moment when they were full of adrenaline and trying their hardest."

It may be difficult for an outsider to fully comprehend the allure of chess mastery. When Spiegel was trying to explain it to me, she often referred to the work of Mihaly Csikszentmihalyi, a psychologist who collaborated with Martin Seligman in the early days of positive psychology. Csikszentmihalyi studied what he called optimal experiences, those rare moments in human existence when a person feels free of mundane distractions, in control of his fate, totally engaged by the moment. Csikszentmihalyi came up with a word for this state of intense concentration: *flow*. He wrote that flow moments most often occur "when a person's body or mind is stretched to its limits in a voluntary effort to accomplish something difficult or worthwhile." In his early research, Csikszentmihalyi interviewed chess experts, classically trained dancers, and mountain climbers, and he found that all three groups described flow moments in similar ways, as a feeling of intense well-being and control. During that peak state, one chess player told Csikszentmihalyi, "the concentration is like breathing — you never think of it. The roof could fall in and, if it missed you, you would be unaware of it." (One study found that physiological changes among expert chess players in tournaments mimicked those of athletes in competitions: muscle contractions, increased blood pressure, and breathing rates three times normal.)

You simply don't experience flow if you aren't good at something—I will never feel it at the chessboard. But Justus and James feel it all the time. During one conversation, I asked Spiegel whether she ever felt that her students were sacrificing too much to succeed at chess. She looked at me like I was crazy. "What's missing from that idea is that playing chess is, like, *wonderful*," she said. "There's a joyousness to it. That's when you're happiest or that's when you're most you or that's when you feel your best. It's easy to think of it in terms of the opportunity cost, but I think Justus and James think of it as there's nothing else they'd rather do."

9. Optimism and Pessimism

Psychologists have long suspected that a person needs more than intelligence to achieve chess mastery. But for over a century, researchers have been struggling to figure out just which skills are the important ones. What separates the chess champions from the also-rans if not pure IQ? The first person to study that question seriously was Alfred Binet, a French psychologist who helped create one of the earliest intelligence tests. In the 1890s, people in the chess world and beyond were captivated by the odd phenomenon of blindfold chess, in which masters played chess blindfolded against multiple opponents at once. Binet sought to understand the cognitive ability behind this unusual skill. His hypothesis was that masters of the blindfold game possessed photographic memories. They must have the ability, he thought, to capture a precise visual picture of what was on each board and to hold it in their memories. Binet began interviewing blindfold-chess players, and he quickly discovered that his theory was completely wrong. The players' memories weren't particularly visual at all. Instead, what they remembered were patterns, vectors, even moods—what Binet described as "a stirring world of sensations, images, movements, passions, and an ever changing panorama of states of consciousness."

About fifty years later, in 1946, a Dutch psychologist named Adriaan de Groot picked up on Binet's research and began testing the mental abilities of a collection of chess masters, and his results challenged another long-held belief about chess skill. It had always been assumed that an essential element of chess mastery was rapid calculation; that on each move, the best chess players were able to consider many more possible outcomes than novices were. In fact, de Groot found, a typical chess player with a rating of 2500 considered about the same number of moves as a typical player with a rating of 2000. What gave the higher-ranked players the advantage was that the moves they contemplated somehow turned out to be the right ones. Experience had given them the instincts to know intuitively which potential moves to take seriously; they never even considered the less promising options.

But if the best chess players don't have better visual memories, and they don't analyze potential outcomes more quickly, what *does* set them apart from novices? The answer may have more to do with their ability to perform one particular mental task that relies as much on psychological strengths as on cognitive ability: a task known as falsification.

In the early twentieth century, the Austrian philosopher Sir Karl Popper wrote that the nature of scientific thought was such that one could never truly verify scientific theories; the only way to test the validity of any particular theory was to prove it wrong, a process he labeled falsification. This idea made its way into cognitive science with the observation that most people are actually quite bad at falsification — not just in science but in daily life. When testing a theory, however large or small, an individual doesn't instinctively look for evidence that contradicts it; he looks for data that prove him right, a tendency known as confirmation bias. That tendency and the ability to overcome it turn out to be crucial elements in chess success.

In 1960, an English psychologist (and, as it happens, a chess enthusiast) named Peter Cathcart Wason came up with an ingenious experiment to demonstrate our natural tendency to confirm rather than disprove our own ideas. Subjects were told that they would be

given a series of three numbers that followed a certain rule known
only to the experimenter. Their assignment was to figure out what
the rule was, which they could do by offering the experimenter other
strings of three numbers and asking him whether or not these new
strings met the rule.

The string of numbers the subjects were given was quite simple:

2-4-6.

Try it: What's your first instinct about the rule governing these
numbers? And what's another string you might test with the experimenter in order to find out if your guess is right?

If you're like most people, your first instinct is that the rule is "ascending even numbers" or "numbers increasing by two." And so you
guess something like

8-10-12.

And the experimenter says, "Yes! That string of numbers also
meets the rule." And your confidence rises. To confirm your bril-
liance, you test one more possibility, just as due diligence, something
like:

20-22-24.

"Yes!" says the experimenter. Another surge of dopamine. And
you proudly make your guess: "The rule is: even numbers, ascending
in twos."

"No!" says the experimenter.

It turns out that the rule is "any ascending numbers." So 8-10-12
does fit the rule, it's true, but so does 1-2-3. Or 4-23-512. The only way
to win the game is to guess strings of numbers that would prove your
beloved hypothesis *wrong* — and that is something each of us is con-
stitutionally driven to avoid.

You may tell yourself that you'd never fall for such a trick; you'd be more careful. Perhaps, but if so, you'd be in the minority. In Wason's study, only one in five participants was able to guess the correct rule. And the reason we're all so bad at games like this is the tendency toward confirmation bias: It feels much better to find evidence that confirms what you believe to be true than to find evidence that falsifies what you believe to be true. Why go out in search of disappointment?

It turns out that confirmation bias is a big problem for chess players. Building on Wason's findings, two researchers at the University of Dublin, Michelle Cowley and Ruth Byrne, interviewed two groups of chess players, all members of the Irish Chess Union: one group of experienced novices with ratings around 1500, and one group of experts whose ratings ranged from 2000 to 2500. They presented the players with midgame chess positions and asked them to choose the best next move — and while doing so, to speak into a tape recorder their thought processes: which moves they were considering, what they thought their opponents might do in response to each possible move, how they thought they might respond to each response — exactly the process that every good chess player employs at the board. Cowley and Byrne then used a chess-analysis program called Fritz to see how accurate each player's analysis had been.

Unsurprisingly, the expert players analyzed their positions more accurately than the novices. What was surprising was *how* they were better. In a word, they were more pessimistic. When the novices found a move they liked, they tended to fall prey to confirmation bias, to see only the ways that it could lead to success, ignoring possible pitfalls; the Eeyore-like experts, by contrast, were more likely to see terrible outcomes lurking around every corner. They were able to falsify their hypotheses and thus avoid deadly traps.

When I asked Spiegel about the Dublin study, she said she agreed it was a good idea for a chess player to be a bit pessimistic about the outcome of any particular move. But when it comes to a person's chess ability as a whole, she said, it was better to be *optimistic*. It's like public speaking, she explained: if you're not a bit overconfident when you step up to the microphone, you're in trouble. Chess is inherently painful, she said. "No matter how good you get," she told me, "you never stop making stupid, stupid mistakes that you want to kill yourself for." And so part of getting good at chess is feeling confident that you have within yourself the power to win.

I saw this phenomenon in action on the day that I visited the Marshall Chess Club with Spiegel and her students. In the morning, before Yuri Lapshun lost to James Black, Lapshun played another IS 318 student, Shawn Swindell, a small-framed African American boy in the eighth grade who wore a diamond-stud earring and whose rating at the time was about 1950. When Shawn found out he'd been paired with a player rated more than five hundred points higher than him, he felt doomed. He was assigned the white pieces in the game, which gave him the slight advantage of moving first, and he later told me that his first thought was *What a waste of having white.* James Black, by contrast, entered into his game with Lapshun entirely convinced that he could beat an international master — a belief that might have seemed foolish and brash, but which turned out to be entirely true.

10. Sunday

Each player in Columbus played seven games — two on Friday, three on Saturday, and the final two on Sunday. As of Sunday morning, most of the kids on the IS 318 team hadn't been outside the convention center since the tournament began. They just circled endlessly: the food court, the ballroom where the games were played, their hotel rooms, and the team room in Union B. No one seemed to miss the fresh air. On the scoreboard, IS 318 was comfortably ahead in K–8 and also ahead, though less comfortably, in K–9. James Black had won his first five games and then drew his sixth on Sunday morning. Going into the final round, the K–8 team seemed to be fairly certain to win the team trophy, and James was one of five players tied for first overall. If he won his last game, he could win the individual trophy, something that no player from IS 318 had ever done at junior high nationals.

The K–9 team had a bad Sunday-morning round. Justus lost, somewhat shockingly, and among the other four players with a chance of being one of the top scorers on the team, two lost, one drew, and only one won. They were still in first place going into the final round, but their lead was narrowing. For Spiegel, the situation brought back bad memories of the previous year, when her K–9 team had held a half point lead going into the seventh and final round and then seriously choked: each of the six top players on the team lost his last game, and IS 318 tumbled out of first place to finish in third. ("The scale of the chokage," Spiegel wrote on her blog at the time, was "incredible.")

This year, the final round was scheduled to begin at 2:00 p.m., and at 1:40, James was sitting across a table from Prilleltensky talking strategy. James was playing on board one, meaning that he would be sitting on the risers at the front of the ballroom, separate from and elevated over the other thousand or so other players. He was playing black against Brian Li, an eighth-grade student from a suburb of Washington, D.C., and he had a feeling that Li was going to play the grand prix attack. His conversation with Prilleltensky was technical, most of it well beyond me—Should James play d5 or e5 on his third move? Which piece should attack d6?—but it became clear before long that what James really wanted from Prilleltensky was a confidence boost: some reassurance that James knew the right opening and, even more, that he knew what he was doing in general.

A couple of minutes before two o'clock, the two of them started walking up to the ballroom. James had on a black hoodie and dark jeans, and he looked anxious. They stepped onto the escalator together.

"James, remember: calm, concentrated, confident. Okay?"

James pulled his hood over his head and looked up at the ceiling. "I'm nervous," he said in a quiet voice.

"You're nervous?" said Prilleltensky. He bent down low next to James, a trainer getting his boxer ready for a fight. "You know who's *really* nervous right now, James? Brian Li. You know why? Because Brian Li, probably about twenty minutes ago, went and looked at the pairings, and he found out he was playing *James Black* on board one in the last round. I can tell you right now, James, there is no pairing in the whole tournament, maybe no pairing he's had his entire *life,* that would scare him as much as that one. Right?"

James smiled.

Isaac Barayev, James's teammate, who was a couple of steps ahead of them on the escalator, turned around. "Hey, James," he said. "If you win, I think you got the —"

"Isaac, Isaac, Isaac!" Prilleltensky cut him off. He didn't want James thinking about first-place finishes or trophies or results, just chess. He turned back to James. "Just do your thing, James," he said. "Play slowly, take your time, be confident. You've got this, okay?"

And James did have it, it turned out. He and Brian Li played for three hours and ten minutes. At one point, James thought he was going to have to settle for a draw, but then on the twenty-seventh move, Brian made an unusual exchange, trading his queen for a rook and a bishop, and from that point on, James felt in control. Finally, on the forty-eighth move, his knight captured a critical pawn, and Brian, realizing defeat was inevitable, resigned. James ran back to Union B, where he was enveloped in a flurry of hugs and high-fives. He had won the individual championship, and his victory meant the K–8s had clinched the team championship. (The K–9s hung on to win their division as well.) James pulled out his cell phone to call his father.

Spiegel was thrilled by James's win, but the most emotional moment in the tournament for her came when Danny Feng, a tall, taciturn eighth-grader with long floppy hair, returned to Union B and announced that he had won too, which gave him six victories in the seven-round tournament. It wasn't so much his result that got to her; it was the way he had played. She had been Danny's main chess teacher since the beginning of sixth grade, back when he was a true novice barely aware of how the pieces moved. She had almost literally taught him everything he knew.

Danny set up a board to show his win, and it was a grinding victory — he had made a major error in the opening, losing a pawn right away, a beginner's mistake, but he had slowly fought back until, in the endgame, he had a slight advantage — a rook and a pawn against his

opponent's rook. It was a hard position to win, the kind of endgame
that often concludes in a draw. But Danny had pulled it out, move
by move, slowly edging his pawn forward to the back rank, where it
was promoted to a queen. Usually when Danny analyzed his games
with a teacher or coach, he moved his pieces meekly, but this time he
was slamming them down, like Shawn and James did, clearly proud
of himself. Spiegel couldn't help herself — it was an endgame she had
taught him, and as she watched him execute the last few moves perfectly, she started to cry.

The students watching couldn't quite believe it. Afterward, in the
hotel elevator, Warren Zhang said to Prilleltensky, "Was Ms. Spiegel
really crying over Danny's game?"

"Of course," Prilleltensky replied. "It was a very beautiful game."

11. The Test

The next month, IS 318 almost pulled off an even more remarkable
feat — James, Justus, Isaac, and Danny came within a half point of
winning the high-school nationals, despite the fact that none of them
was in high school. They beat teams from some of the best high
schools in the country — Bronx Science and Stuyvesant in New York,
Whitney Young in Chicago, the Lakeside School (Bill Gates's alma
mater) in Seattle — before losing in the last round to the team from
Hunter College High School.

Despite his resounding victories in Columbus, James Black gained
only eleven rating points in the junior high tournament, moving
from 2149 to 2160 — still forty points to go before making master. The
rest of the spring his rating kept ebbing and flowing, pulling closer
to 2200, then falling back. Finally, on July 17 at the Marshall, James
beat Michael Finneran, an eighteen-year-old from Connecticut, and
his rating hit 2205. He was a national master. At the beginning of
September, James celebrated with a party under some shade trees in
Fulton Park, in the heart of Bedford-Stuyvesant. People sat on folding chairs, and James was presented with a cake topped with an ed-
ible photo image of himself at the chessboard, framed with white

frosting. Maurice Ashley, the first and, so far, only African American grand master, was there, and he inducted James and Justus and Joshua Colas, a twelve-year-old player from White Plains, New York, into a newly founded society called the Young Black Masters Club. Just a year after Justus had become the first African American master under fifteen, there were now three under *thirteen*, a point of pride for not only their families but black chess players and fans across the country.

Spiegel made a speech, and she said that while she was proud of James's accomplishment, she was more proud of the determination he had displayed. She told the story of his past year in chess, how he had often pulled to within a few points of 2200 and then, again and again, slipped back. "Imagine how frustrating that must be," she said to the assembled crowd. "And then add to that frustration the fact that everyone is watching you, asking how you did, expecting you to already be there.

"For more than a year," Spiegel went on, "James studied, solved tactics, played, analyzed his games, confronted his own mistakes and misunderstandings, and he did not give up. In the last year he has played sixty-five tournaments and three hundred and one rated games. He plays in tournaments until eleven o'clock at night, and then gets up early every morning to do thirty minutes of tactics before school. He has worked so hard, so patiently, for so long. That is what I respect the most about James."

In the spring, right after the junior high tournament, Spiegel had given herself a new mission. The following October, thousands of New York City students in the eighth grade would be taking a daunting exam known as the Specialized High School Admissions Test; students who did well would be admitted to one of the city's prestigious selective high schools, including Stuyvesant, Brooklyn Tech, and Bronx Science. She decided that she would volunteer to train James for the test. John Galvin, the vice principal, told her she had given herself an impossible mission, that there was no way a student who consistently scored below average on statewide standardized tests could ace the specialized-school exam. But Spiegel had seen

James absorb chess knowledge astoundingly quickly, and she had faith in her own teaching ability. As she put it to me in an e-mail message in April: "I figure with six months, if he's into it and will do the work, I can teach a smart kid anything, right?"

In the middle of July, though, Spiegel told me she was starting to get discouraged. She was working hard with James on the test, and he was applying himself, even on hot summer days, but she was daunted by how much he did not know. He couldn't locate Africa or Asia on a map. He couldn't name a single European country. When they did reading-comprehension drills, he didn't recognize words like *infant* and *communal* and *beneficial*. By September, they were working together after school and on weekends for hours at a time, and she was starting to despair, trying to keep James's spirits up while her own were sinking. When James would get downhearted and say that he just wasn't any good at analogies or trigonometry, Spiegel would reply cheerfully that it was just like chess: a few years earlier, he had been no good at chess, and then he got specialized training and worked hard and mastered it. "I tell him, 'We're going to give you specialized training in this, too, and then you'll be good at it,'" she said to me. "And then he gets happy, like, 'Okay, no problem.' But I'm not really telling him how hard that is."

James represented, for me (and for Spiegel, I suspect), a challenging puzzle. Here was a young man clearly possessed of a keen intelligence. (Whatever *intelligence* means, you can't beat Ukrainian grand masters without plenty of it.) And he seemed to be a case study in grit: he had a clear goal that he felt passionately about, and he worked hard and tirelessly and effectively toward that goal. (I have never met a twelve-year-old who worked harder at anything.) And yet he was, according to the standard predictors of academic success, below average, destined for a mediocre future at best. When you compare James's prospects to those of Mush or the other young men of Roseland, he seems like an amazing success story. But it's also possible to see in James a less inspiring story, a tale of unfulfilled potential. When Spiegel talked with me that fall about studying for the test with James, she sometimes sounded shocked at how little non-chess information he had been taught thus far in his life. "I feel angry on his behalf," she told me. "He knows basic fractions, but he doesn't know geometry, he doesn't get the idea of writing an equation. He's at the level I would have been at in second or third grade. It feels like he should have learned more."

The specialized-school test is, by design, difficult to cram for. Like the SAT, it reflects the knowledge and skills that a student has accrued over the years, most of which is absorbed invisibly throughout childhood from one's family and one's culture. But what if James had started studying for the specialized-school exam in the third grade instead of the seventh grade? What if he had expended the same energy and received the same help learning math and reading and generalized knowledge as he did with chess? And what if he had worked in every subject with teachers as creative and engaged as Spiegel and Prilleltensky? I have no doubt that he would have conquered the specialized-school exam the same way he conquered the junior high nationals.

Of course, it doesn't make much sense to talk about James in the past tense; he is only twelve, after all. He didn't get into Stuyvesant, in the end, but he still has four years of high school in front of him (four years during which he'll no doubt crush every player on the Stuyvesant chess team). It might not have been possible to turn him into an elite student in six months, as Spiegel had hoped. But how about in four years? For a student with his prodigious gifts, anything seems possible — as long as there's a teacher out there who can make succeeding in school as attractive a prospect as succeeding on the chessboard.

4

HOW TO SUCCEED

---

1. The College Conundrum

For most of the twentieth century, the United States stood alone in
the quality of its higher-education system and the percentage of its
young people who successfully passed through that system. As recently as the mid-1990s, the American college-graduation rate was
the highest in the world, more than twice as high as the average rate
among developed countries. But the global education hierarchy is
now changing rapidly. Many countries, both developed and developing, are in the middle of an unprecedented college-graduation boom,
and just in the past decade or so, the United States has fallen from
first to twelfth in the percentage of its twenty-five- to thirty-four-
year-olds who are graduates of four-year colleges, trailing behind a
diverse list of competitors that includes the United Kingdom, Aus-
tralia, Poland, Norway, and South Korea.

It is not that the overall college-attainment rate in the United States
has gone down — it has just been growing very slowly, while the rates
of other nations have raced ahead. In 1976, 24 percent of Americans
in their late twenties had earned a four-year college degree; thirty
years later, in 2006, the figure had risen to only 28 percent. But that
apparently static number conceals a growing class divide. Between

1990 and 2000, the rate of BA attainment among wealthy students with at least one parent who had graduated from college rose from 61 percent to 68 percent, while, according to one analysis, the rate among the most disadvantaged young Americans—students in the lowest-income quartile whose parents were not college graduates—actually *fell*, from 11.1 percent to 9.5 percent. In this era of rising inequality, that trend might seem unsurprising: just one more indicator of the way the classes are diverging in the United States. But it's worth remembering that for most of the past century, things were very different.

As the Harvard economists Claudia Goldin and Lawrence Katz chronicled in their influential 2008 book *The Race Between Education and Technology*, the story of American higher education in the twentieth century was essentially a story of democratization. Just 5 percent of American males born in 1900 graduated from college, and those 5 percent were the elite in every way: wealthy, white, well connected. But between about 1925 and 1945, the percentage of American men graduating from college doubled, from 5 percent to 10 percent, and then it doubled again between about 1945 and 1965, thanks in no small measure to the GI Bill, which helped put millions of returning American soldiers through college. (For American women, the increase in the college-graduation rate was fairly modest until the early 1960s, but after that, it far outpaced the increase among men.) As a result, American college campuses became less elite and more diverse; the children of factory workers found themselves sitting in lecture halls and science labs next to the children of factory owners. During those years, "upward mobility with regard to education characterized American society," wrote Goldin and Katz. "Each generation of Americans achieved a level of education that greatly exceeded that of the previous one." But now that progress has stopped, or at least stalled, and the nation's higher-education system has ceased to be the instrument of social mobility and growing equality that it was for so much of the twentieth century.

Until recently, education-policy types who concerned themselves with the problems of American higher education were focused mostly on college access — how to increase the number of young people, and especially disadvantaged young people, who graduated from high school and enrolled in college. But over the past few years, it has become clear that the United States does not so much have a problem of limited and unequal college *access;* it has a problem of limited and unequal college *completion.* Among the thirty-four member countries of the Organisation for Economic Co-Operation and Development, or OECD, the United States still ranks a respectable eighth in its college-enrollment rate. But in college completion — the percentage of entering college freshmen who go on to graduate — the United States ranks second to last, ahead of only Italy. Not long ago, the United States led the world in producing college graduates; now it leads the world in producing college dropouts.

What is most puzzling about this phenomenon is that it has taken place at the same time as the value of an American college education has skyrocketed. An American with a BA can now expect to earn 83 percent more than an American with only a high-school diploma. This college-graduate wage premium, as economists call it, is among the highest in the developed world, and it has risen sharply since 1980, when American college graduates earned just 40 percent more than high-school graduates. As Goldin and Katz put it, a young American today who is able to complete college but does not do so "is leaving large amounts of money lying on the street."

So we are left with a conundrum: Why are so many American students dropping out of college just as a college degree has become so valuable and just as young people in the rest of the world have begun to graduate in such remarkable numbers?

2. The Finish Line

The best answer to this question so far came in a 2009 book titled *Crossing the Finish Line: Completing College at America's Public Universities,* a collaboration between two former college presidents, both economists — William G. Bowen, the president of Princeton University from 1972 to 1988, and Michael S. McPherson, who served for almost a decade as the president of Macalester College in Minnesota. Because of their standing in the education establishment, Bowen and McPherson — along with a third coauthor, a researcher named Matthew Chingos — were able to persuade sixty-eight public colleges, as well as the College Board and ACT, to give them access to detailed academic data covering about two hundred thousand students. They found in the data some surprising facts about which students successfully complete college, which ones drop out, and why.

In certain quarters, the college-dropout phenomenon has been explained as a problem of excessive and unrealistic ambition on the part of many students, especially low-income students. The conservative author Charles Murray argued in his 2008 book *Real Education* that the true crisis in American higher education is not that too *few* young Americans are getting a college education; it is that too *many* are. Because of Americans' natural tendency toward "educational romanticism," Murray wrote, we push students to go to college who are simply not smart enough to be there. High-school guidance counselors and college-admissions officers, lost in "a fog of wishful thinking, euphemisms, and well-intentioned egalitarianism," encourage low-IQ, low-income students to attend colleges that are too intellectually demanding; when those students discover that they don't possess the intelligence necessary to do the work, they drop out. Murray, the coauthor of *The Bell Curve,* is perhaps the country's best-known cognitive determinist, and his thesis in *Real Education* is a pure expression of the cognitive hypothesis: what matters in success is IQ, which is fixed quite early in life; education is not so much about providing skills as it is about sorting people and giving those with the highest IQs the opportunity to reach their full potential.

But when Bowen, McPherson, and Chingos took a close look at their data, they found that low-income students generally weren't overreaching their abilities when they chose their colleges; many of them, in fact, were attending schools well *below* what their GPAs and standardized-test scores qualified them for. This phenomenon, which the authors labeled undermatching, didn't happen much with well-off students; it was a problem that almost exclusively affected disadvantaged teenagers. In North Carolina, the state for which the researchers were able to gather the most complete data, three out of four high-income students with the GPAs and test scores needed to gain admission to one of the state's highly selective public colleges went on to attend a highly selective school. For them, the system worked. But among students who had those same lofty academic credentials but didn't have parents who had attended college themselves, only a third chose to go to a highly selective school. And choosing a less challenging college didn't make it more likely that those highly qualified students would graduate — it had the opposite effect. Undermatching, the authors found, was almost always a big mistake.

But the information on undermatching, important though it was, was not the most surprising or significant finding in *Crossing the Finish Line*. The authors also discovered that the most accurate predictor of whether a student would successfully complete college was not his or her score on the SAT or the ACT, the two standardized college-admissions tests. In fact, it turned out that, except at the most highly selective public universities, ACT scores revealed very little about whether or not a student would graduate from college. The far better predictor of college completion was a student's high-school GPA.

To people involved in the college-admissions process, this finding came as something of a shock; it was essentially a repudiation of one of the founding tenets of the late-twentieth-century American meritocracy. In *The Big Test*, Nicholas Lemann's history of standardized college-admissions testing, he explains that the SAT was invented, in the years after World War II, because of growing skepticism about the predictive power of high-school grades. How were college-admissions officials supposed to compare a 3.5 student at a suburban high school in California with a 3.5 student at a rural high school in the Pennsylvania countryside or at an urban school in the South Bronx? The SAT was designed to correct that problem, to provide an objective tool that would distill a student's ability to thrive in college down to a single, indisputable number. But at the colleges that Bowen and Chingos and McPherson examined, high-school grades turned out to be excellent predictors of college graduation — no matter where the student attended high school. It was true that a student with a 3.5 GPA from a high-quality high school was somewhat more likely to graduate from college than a student with a 3.5 GPA from a low-quality high school, but the difference was surprisingly modest. As the authors put it, "Students with very good high school grades who attended not-very-strong high schools nonetheless graduated in large numbers from whatever university they attended."

And when Angela Duckworth, the guru of self-control and grit at the University of Pennsylvania, analyzed GPA and standardized-test scores among middle-school and high-school students, she found that standardized-test scores were predicted by scores on pure IQ tests and that GPA was predicted by scores on tests of self-control. Put Duckworth's findings together with the discoveries in *Crossing the Finish Line*, and you reach a rather remarkable conclusion: whether or not a student is able to graduate from a decent American college doesn't necessarily have all that much to do with how smart he or she is. It has to do, instead, with that same list of character strengths that produce high GPAs in middle school and high school. "In our view," Bowen, Chingos, and McPherson wrote, "high school grades reveal much more than mastery of content. They reveal qualities of motivation and perseverance — as well as the presence of good study habits and time management skills — that tell us a great deal about the chances that a student will complete a college program."

It's possible, of course, that once a student reaches adolescence, those skills and habits are no longer teachable. It may be that at that point, either you have them or you don't, and if you have them, you're likely to graduate from college, and if you don't, you're not. But consider Elizabeth Spiegel's ability to reconstruct the thinking skills of her middle-school chess players. Think of the way Lanita Reed helped Keitha Jones change her whole outlook on life — essentially helping her rewire her personality — at the advanced age of seventeen. In each case, a teacher or mentor found a way to help a student achieve a rapid and unexpected transformation by using what James Heckman would call noncognitive skills and David Levin would call character strengths. What if we could do that for large numbers of teenagers — not to help them attain chess mastery or persuade them to quit fighting in school but to help them develop precisely those mental skills and character strengths they would need to graduate from college?

3. One in Thirty

Jeff Nelson, the CEO of OneGoal, doesn't seem like a revolutionary when you first meet him. He's fresh-faced and clean-cut and midwesternly polite, with a tuft of blond hair sticking up over his forehead that makes him look a little like the comic-book character Tintin. He wears button-down shirts and keeps to a button-down schedule; once, when I made arrangements to talk to him on the phone, he e-mailed me in advance with a point-by-point agenda for our call that included three "objectives" and allocated ten minutes for "wrap up." He seems most at home when surrounded by the typical tools of the modern education reformer — PowerPoint presentations, management consultants, strategic plans, venti lattes — and yet his vision of education reform is a profoundly unorthodox one, a thorough challenge to the cognitive hypothesis.

Nelson grew up in Wilmette, an affluent bedroom community that is part of the comfortable, Caucasian suburban enclave north of Chicago where John Hughes set *Home Alone* and *The Breakfast Club.* It is a mostly Democratic town, a reliable haven for progressive causes and notions of social justice, though those notions are often expressed in an abstract, distant way, through donations to Amnesty International or Habitat for Humanity or petitions supporting the refugees of Darfur. From an early age, though, Nelson was drawn to an issue closer to home: the challenges faced by children growing up in the metropolis fifteen miles to his south. In eighth grade, Nelson read Alex Kotlowitz's book *There Are No Children Here,* the harrowing story of two African American boys living in the Henry Horner Homes, a dismal and dangerous high-rise housing project on Chicago's West Side. The book, Nelson told me, "crushed my view of the world a little bit. It sparked something in me."

Nelson went on to attend New Trier Township High School, which is legendary in the Chicago area for its lush campus and lavish facilities, all underwritten by the property taxes assessed on the luxurious homes of Wilmette and the surrounding towns. The crusading journalist Jonathan Kozol, in his 1991 book *Savage Inequalities,* chose New Trier as his archetypal suburban high school of privilege, cataloging its dance studios and fencing rooms and Latin classes and contrasting the "superfluity of opportunity" its students enjoyed to the "denial of opportunity" experienced by students at Du Sable High, a South Side school that, Kozol wrote, would be "shunned — or, probably, shut down — if it were serving a white middle-class community." Nelson read Kozol's book in his freshman sociology class at the University of Michigan, and it only increased the sense of urgency he felt, his growing determination to find a way to reverse the patterns that Kozol described; to bring at least a small measure of the opportunity enjoyed by students at New Trier to students at schools like Du Sable.

After graduating, Nelson joined Teach for America and taught sixth grade at a struggling, high-poverty South Side public school called O'Keeffe Elementary, a mile or so from Du Sable. He was a gifted classroom instructor, raising his students' reading and math ability by an average of two years' worth of progress for each year he taught them and, in his second year, winning recognition as the best Teach for America teacher in the Chicago region. He was a coach of the school's football team and helped start a student council, and he became close with many of his students, visiting them at home and getting to know their parents.

From his first day at O'Keeffe, Nelson talked to his students incessantly about college. All of them were African Americans from low-income families, and few of them had parents who were college graduates — but that didn't matter, Nelson promised them; if they worked hard, they could and would go to college and graduate. Then one morning in April of 2006, Nelson picked up the *Chicago Tribune* and read a front-page story, based on a report by the Consortium on Chicago Schools Research, that challenged that promise. According to the consortium, just eight of every one hundred students who started high school in the Chicago public schools would go on to earn four-year-college degrees. For African American boys, the odds were even worse: fewer than one in thirty black male high-school freshmen in the city would graduate from a four-year college by the time they were twenty-five. For Nelson, the numbers were profoundly unsettling: even if he was able to create the most effective sixth-grade classroom in the city, could that possibly be enough to help his students overcome those terrible odds?

Nelson's experience at O'Keeffe Elementary convinced him of two things: first, that he would spend the rest of his life working in the field of education reform. And second, that despite his success in the classroom, he wasn't meant to be a teacher. As he was preparing to leave O'Keeffe, Teach for America's national office offered him a job as the organization's executive director for Chicago, a big responsibility for a twenty-four-year-old. It seemed like his dream job, but at the last minute, for reasons he couldn't quite understand let alone put into words, he turned it down. It was an agonizing decision. Saying no to Teach for America "frustrated me beyond belief," he told me. "I was so close to having found the right way to make a big impact, but for some reason it didn't feel like the right role."

The *Tribune* story had helped convince him that there was a missing piece in the education-reform landscape, a program or a system or a tool that could help kids like the ones he taught at O'Keeffe not only make it to college but also graduate. "I desperately wanted to find an organization, or start one, that closed the gap between high school and college," he told me. "Every one of us in Teach for America was working so hard and creating results in our classrooms, but if our kids didn't go on to graduate from college, who the hell cared?"

Turning down the Teach for America job sent Nelson into a crisis of the spirit, a period of deep inner turmoil that lasted almost six months. He had always been a hyper-busy person, a workaholic even in high school, and suddenly he had no official responsibilities, noth-

ing to do but think about his life and where it was going and what it
meant. Occasionally that fall, he got calls from some of the parents
of the students he had taught the year before at O'Keeffe. The kids
were in seventh grade now, and the gains they had made the previous year were slipping away, the parents said. Distraught, they asked
Nelson what they could do to get their kids back on track. One even
broke down in tears on the phone. Nelson didn't know what to say.
He didn't know how to help.

Nelson started praying regularly, looking for answers, for some re-
lief from his growing depression. He began to make a ritual of visiting
a different place of worship every day — one day going to a Catholic
Mass, the next a Baha'i temple. He went into therapy. He wrote pages
and pages of poetry. It was a strange and intense period for Nelson,
and when he talks about it now, he sounds like he still isn't quite sure
what to make of it. But what he thinks he was looking for, he says, was
vocation. He was trying to find his mission.

4. The Call

In January of 2007, Nelson got a call from Eddie Lou, a young Chicago venture capitalist who a few years earlier had set up a small nonprofit with two friends, one of whom, Matt King, was a teacher at the
Dunbar vocational high school, on the South Side. Their fledgling
organization, which they'd named the Urban Students Empowered
Foundation, managed and supported an afterschool program that
King ran for a handful of juniors and seniors at Dunbar. It was a kind
of college-prep boot camp: King tutored the students so they could
increase their GPAs and improve their ACT scores, helped them figure out which colleges they should apply to, walked them through
the financial-aid process, talked to them about how to survive at college. Though the program was small — King's first class of seven students had graduated and were freshmen in college, and there was a
second class of seven who were seniors at Dunbar — it was producing
some impressive results. The students had raised their ACT scores,
on average, from about 15 to around 18 over the course of their junior

year, moving them from about the fifteenth percentile nationally to about the thirty-fifth percentile. Their GPAs improved as well, and all of the students who entered the program made it to college.

Lou, a serial entrepreneur who had been involved in several tech start-ups, wanted to expand the program beyond a single afterschool class — but then King landed a job as a vice principal at a local charter school and decided he couldn't keep running the program. So Lou and King and their third partner, a doctoral student at Northwestern named Dawn Pankonien, went looking for a new executive director, someone who could not only revive King's program but also turn it into something more ambitious. They interviewed more than twenty candidates, but none of them seemed like the right fit. They were on the verge of shutting down the organization altogether when, through a mutual acquaintance at Teach for America, they found Jeff Nelson.

That winter, Nelson was finally beginning to feel like he was emerging from his long season in the wilderness, and when Lou called, it seemed like perfect timing. The board of directors — the three founders, plus a couple of finance guys — offered him the job of executive director, and he quickly accepted, he told me, "without doing a lot of due diligence." If he had, he might have learned before his first day on the job that the organization had no employees, no office space, no business plan, and just six thousand dollars in the bank, enough to cover operating expenses for ten days. At the end of that first day, it dawned on Nelson that he had somehow managed to turn down a job with the biggest and most established education-reform organization in the country in order to take a position with one of the smallest and least established. Oddly, it felt like the right move.

Nelson told the board he needed six weeks to come up with a plan for the future of the organization. He recruited two Teach for America teachers to work for him as unpaid interns during their summer vacation. Pankonien offered to work without pay for a few months as well. She was renting a room from a guy she knew who was a trader at the Mercantile Exchange, and the guy said they could use his apartment during the day when he was on the trading floor. And so that

became the unofficial headquarters for the organization that summer — the four of them sitting on couches in a commodity trader's
living room, using their own cell phones and laptops. The one as-
set the organization owned was a printer. Five years later, Urban
Students Empowered has a new name — OneGoal — an administra-
tive staff of fifteen, an annual budget of $1.7 million, and more than
twelve hundred students at twenty Chicago high schools enrolled in
a three-year course modeled on King's program but much bigger and
more intensive.

Nelson's belief is that underperforming high-school students can
relatively quickly transform themselves into highly successful college
students — but that it is almost impossible for them to make that transition without the help of a highly effective teacher. So Nelson and his
team scour the city looking for and signing up motivated, ambitious
high-school teachers, sometimes at charter schools, but more often
at traditional Chicago high schools in low-income neighborhoods.
(Fenger is one of those schools.) OneGoal has signed a unique partnership deal with the Chicago public schools that lets the organization work directly with individual teachers to help them run the
OneGoal programs. The teachers remain regular full-time employees of the public-school system, though they get stipends on top of
their salaries for the extra work they do. Once a teacher is signed up
with OneGoal, he or she will recruit and select a class of twenty-five
students in their sophomore year — not the highest-scoring kids, not
the ones who can already see the path to college, but underperforming students who show at least some spark of ambition. (The average
GPA of incoming students is 2.8.) And then the teacher sticks with
that same class of students for three years. In junior and senior year,
OneGoal is a full-time academic course, with a curriculum designed
by Nelson and his team. The class usually meets once a day through
the end of senior year. And when the students are freshmen in college, the teacher keeps in close touch with them, by phone and e-mail
and Facebook, answering questions, holding regular online conferences, providing support and advice.

There are three main elements to the OneGoal curriculum. The first and most straightforward is an intensive unit of ACT prep in junior year, designed to give students the essential content knowledge and test-taking strategies to raise their scores from terrible to not bad. These days, OneGoal teachers are regularly able to match Matt King's accomplishment, helping their students improve by about three points on the ACT over the course of their junior year, moving them from about the fifteenth percentile to the thirty-fifth percentile.

The second element is what Jeff Nelson calls a "road map to college." When Nelson was planning the curriculum that first summer, he often found himself thinking of the process at New Trier: the school's college-counseling office employs eight full-time counselors, who begin working on college planning with students and their parents early in the sophomore year. "It's a machine," Nelson told me with a laugh. "They give you an incredibly clear and structured path from the middle of high school through the day you step onto a college campus." He recognized that he couldn't afford to transplant New Trier's entire college-prep machine to the South Side. "But there were pieces of what was happening at New Trier," he said, "that I thought could be translated to low-income schools and could make a massive difference." So OneGoal students get help not just with applications but also with their entire college-admission strategy: choosing match schools rather than undermatch schools; deciding whether to apply to schools close to home or far away; writing appealing application essays; finding scholarships. (One morning in a OneGoal class at a Chicago high school I watched as the school's college counselor ran through a list of increasingly obscure scholarships. "Is anyone here Greek?" she asked. Twenty-five black and Latino faces looked back at her skeptically. "Do we have any multiracial students?" she asked hopefully. "Yeah," replied one impeccably dressed African American boy, deadpan. "South Side black and West Side black.")

But still, Nelson said, "it was obvious to us that the road map was not going to be enough. We could give our students a very clear idea of how to get to college, but we also needed to train them to succeed once they got there. We needed to teach students to be highly effective people."

For this third part of the equation, Nelson was influenced by the high-school research done by the Consortium on Chicago Schools Research, and particularly the work of an analyst there named Melissa Roderick. In a 2006 paper, Roderick identified as a critical component of college success "noncognitive academic skills," including "study skills, work habits, time management, help-seeking behavior, and social/academic problem-solving skills." Roderick, who borrowed the term *noncognitive* from James Heckman's work, wrote that these skills were at the center of an increasingly dire mismatch between American high schools and American colleges and universities. When the current high-school system was developed, she wrote, the primary goal was to train students not for college but for the workplace, where at the time "critical thinking and problem-solving abilities were not highly valued." (This was the era that Bowles and Gintis, the anti-conscientiousness Marxist economists, were writing about.) And so the traditional American high school was never intended to be a place where students would learn how to think deeply or develop internal motivation or persevere when faced with difficulty—all the skills needed to persist in college. Instead, it was a place where, for the most part, students were rewarded for just showing up and staying awake.

For a while, Roderick wrote, this formula worked well. "High school teachers could have very high workloads and manage them effectively because they expected most of their students to do little work," she recounted. "Most students could get what they and their parents wanted, the high school credential, with little effort." There was, she wrote, "an unwritten contract between students and teachers that said, 'Put up with high school, do your seat time, and behave properly, and you will be rewarded.'"

But then the world changed, and the American high school didn't. As the wage premium paid to college graduates increased, high-school students voiced an increasing desire to graduate from college — between 1980 and 2002, the percentage of American tenth-graders who said they wanted to obtain at least a BA doubled, from 40 percent to 80 percent. But most of those students didn't have the nonacademic skills — the character strengths, as Martin Seligman would put it — they needed to survive in college, and the traditional American high school didn't have a mechanism to help them acquire those skills. This is what Nelson is trying to change, and he believes this third element of the OneGoal strategy is at the heart of the program's nascent success.

Nelson knew when he started that he couldn't remake the entire high-school experience for his students. But he thought that perhaps he didn't need to. By helping students develop the specific nonacademic skills that would lead most directly to college success, he believed he could compensate, relatively quickly, for the serious gap in academic ability that separated the average senior at a Chicago public high school from the average American college freshman. Nelson, using instinct more than research, identified five skills, which he called leadership principles, that he wanted OneGoal teachers to emphasize: resourcefulness, resilience, ambition, professionalism, and integrity. Those words now permeate the program — they're even more ubiquitous than Seligman and Peterson's seven character strengths are at KIPP Infinity.

"We know that most of our kids are going to arrive in college academically behind their peers," Nelson explained to me one morning. "We can help them improve their ACT scores significantly, but it is unlikely that we'll be able to close the gap on those tests entirely, simply because of the K-through-twelve system that our students grew up in. But what we also know, and what we tell our students, is that there is a way for them to offset that disparity. And the key is those five leadership abilities."

5. ACE Tech

For four decades, the Robert Taylor Homes loomed over the South Side, the largest of Chicago's postwar housing projects: twenty-eight

high-rise concrete monoliths extending for almost two miles down a
narrow strip of land between State Street and the Dan Ryan Expressway. Almost as soon as construction on the projects was completed,
in the early 1960s, the buildings began to descend into disrepair,
violence, and chaos, and in the 1970s and 1980s, the Robert Taylor
Homes were considered, according to the Chicago Housing Authority, "the worst slum area in the United States"; in 1980, one in nine
murders in Chicago took place in those ninety-two acres. At the projects' high point, which is to say their low point, more than twenty-
five thousand people lived in the Robert Taylor Homes, at least two-
thirds of them children, the large majority of whom were living with
single mothers on welfare. The projects are gone now, torn down in
Chicago's latest attempt at urban renewal, but nothing has been built
in their place. And when you drive down State Street today, there is
just an eerie emptiness where the towers once stood, a weird inner-
city pastoral of grass, weeds, and concrete punctuated by a few old,
lonely churches that managed to escape the wrecking ball.

At the south end of that long stretch of nothingness, down by Fifty-
Fourth Street, there is a small outcropping of intact structures — a few
houses, mostly boarded up; a liquor store; a pizza place; a pawnshop;
and a storefront Baptist church, now closed. And then, in a two-story
blue-brick building just north of the old church, there is, of all things,
a school: ACE Tech Charter High School. Given the pervasive bleak-
ness of the surroundings, it is hard to imagine anything very positive
coming out of that building, and in fact, ACE Tech is not at all a
high-achieving school: in 2009, just 12 percent of the school's juniors
met or exceeded the standards on the statewide achievement test,
and since its founding in 2004, the school has never made "adequate
yearly progress," the benchmark set by the federal No Child Left Behind law. But it was at ACE Tech, soon after Jeff Nelson took over in
2007, that OneGoal introduced its new methods. First, there was an
afterschool program much like Matt King's, held two hours a week
for a class of juniors and seniors; then, in 2009, Nelson brought in the
full-time, in-class, three-year, teacher-led model that is now the One-
Goal standard. (It is a coincidence, but perhaps an apt one, that ACE

Tech is only a few blocks away from Du Sable High, the school that Jonathan Kozol presented in *Savage Inequalities* as the tragic counterpoint to Nelson's alma mater of New Trier.)

The person who pioneered both iterations of the OneGoal program at ACE Tech was Michele Stefl, an English teacher now in her early thirties who grew up in Chicago's southwestern suburbs and started teaching at ACE Tech in 2005. Nelson hired her as one of OneGoal's first contract teachers soon after he took the position as executive director. I followed a class of Stefl's OneGoal students throughout their senior year, observing as she guided them through the college-admissions process. There were, inevitably, plenty of low moments for her students — suspensions, unplanned pregnancies, college rejections — but in the Sahara of failure that surrounded ACE Tech, Stefl's classroom felt, on most days, like an oasis of hope and possibility.

Stefl was not an educational romantic; she was plainspoken and pragmatic, blunt about the school's inadequacies and the reality of how far behind her students were. One morning toward the end of her students' junior year, she talked to them about their personal essays, which, she said, were going to be essential parts of successful college applications. "Remember who you are competing against," she said. "You are competing against people who have ACT scores of thirty-plus. You are competing with kids who, in all honesty, have received a better education than many of you. We're trying to make up for that now, but the level still isn't where it should be. And that's unfair, unfortunately, okay?" She held up a sample essay. "So this is where it has to come from. What life experiences have you had to get where you are today?"

When selecting this class of students for the OneGoal program, back in the spring of 2009, when they were sophomores, Stefl had taken pains not to pick the highest-scoring students or the ones from the most competent families; in fact, she did the opposite of creaming: during the process, if a student revealed that there was a college graduate anywhere in her immediate family, Stefl would gently tell the student that the program was meant not for her but for her peers with fewer resources and greater need. As a result, one of Stefl's biggest challenges was simply to convince her OneGoal students that they each had the potential for a successful life, despite all the evidence to the contrary they saw in their neighborhood and, often, in their families.

When I sat in Stefl's class, I frequently found myself thinking about the research that the Stanford psychologist Carol Dweck had done on the growth mindset. To recap briefly: Dweck found that students who believed intelligence was malleable did much better than students who believed intelligence was fixed. David Levin's project at KIPP in New York City essentially expanded Dweck's mindset idea into the message that character is malleable too. It seemed that what Stefl was attempting to do was convince her students that not just their intelligence and their character but their very *destinies* were malleable; that their past performance was not an indication of their future results. She was not preaching a gospel of empty self-esteem or wishful thinking. Her message to her students was that they could grow and improve and achieve at a much higher level than they had before but that it would take a lot of hard work, a lot of perseverance, and a lot of character — or, as they put it in class, leadership skills.

When I spoke with Angela Duckworth about the OneGoal program, she pointed out something I hadn't thought of: that the ACT-prep component of the OneGoal curriculum might actually be serving two purposes. First, on a practical level, improving their scores by a few points would give students access to more and higher-quality colleges. But second, and perhaps more important, the experience of improving one's outcome on a test that ostensibly measures intelligence serves as an unforgettable reinforcement of the growth-mindset message: *You can get smarter. You can do better.*

Some of Stefl's students took this message to heart more than others did. Even in their senior year, many still didn't quite seem to believe that they belonged in college, and their families were not always helpful in underscoring Stefl's message. One boy who got into Purdue University was convinced by his mother to attend the two-year community college down the street instead so that he wouldn't be so far from home. At the opposite end of the spectrum — the confident, optimistic end — was Kewauna Lerma.

6. Test Scores

As I described in the introduction to this book, when I met Kewauna halfway through her junior year, I was struck by the remarkable turn-around she had made in her life: from a troubled childhood marred by multiple risk factors and plenty of adverse experiences, through a difficult and delinquent period in middle school, to a successful high-school career and an intense determination to succeed at college and beyond. During the two years that she and I kept in touch, her home life was never easy, and her family's finances were always perilous — her mother received about five hundred dollars a month in disability benefits, and that, plus food stamps, was the family's only income. But somehow Kewauna seemed able to ignore the day-to-day indignities of life in poverty on the South Side and instead stay focused on her vision of a more successful future. "Nobody wants a dumb girl," she told me in one of our first conversations. "Nobody wants a failure. I always wanted to be one of those business ladies walking downtown with my briefcase, everybody saying, 'Hi, Miss Lerma!'" To get her hands on that briefcase, Kewauna knew, she needed at least a bachelor's degree, and despite the fact that no one in her family had ever been to college, she was certain that she could and would obtain one.

By the fall of her senior year, Kewauna was consumed with the process of applying to college. But she was starting from scratch in learning about the system — Was there really both a DePaul University and a DePauw University? — and at the beginning of the year, she had a tendency to go a little overboard. In September, she told me she was planning to apply to twenty-three colleges, including some highly competitive ones like Duke and the University of Chicago. By some measures, Duke was not an entirely unreasonable goal for Kewauna. She had finished her junior year as an almost-straight-A student — there were a few A minuses on her final transcript, but not a single B—despite a demanding course load that included honors algebra II, honors American literature, sociology, and biology. But there was a problem: she had not done at all well on the ACT.

On the first practice ACT test, at the beginning of her junior year, Kewauna got an 11, which is a very low score: it placed her at the first percentile nationally, behind 99 percent of all American high-school juniors. She worked hard on ACT training throughout her junior year, studying many hours each week with an online service called PrepMe that OneGoal had contracted with, and walking into the official ACT test in April, she felt much better prepared than she'd felt for her practice test. But it turned out to be a frustrating day for her nonetheless. There was still so much on the test that she didn't know, and even in sections where she was familiar with the material, she wasn't able to get through the questions as quickly as she wanted. "When I got out of the test, I was crying," she told me. "I told Miss Stefl I thought I wasn't going to get into college at all. I was really mad at myself." When she got her results back a month or so later, she had scored a 15. That meant she had improved by an impressive four points since her diagnostic test, but it also meant she was only at the fifteenth percentile nationally. The Chicago public schools' average is 17. ACT's official standard for college-readiness is 20. Incoming students at Duke usually score above 30. (The maximum possible score is 36.)

Charles Murray would almost certainly have found Kewauna's college ambitions distressing. In *Real Education,* he argued that only students who score in the top 20 percent of the population on tests of cognitive ability should attend college; in his ideal world, only the top 10 percent would go. The idea that someone who scored in the bottom half of a standardized achievement test's distribution, let alone in the bottom fifth, like Kewauna did, might seriously aspire to college would strike him, one imagines, as pure lunacy. "As long as it remains taboo to acknowledge that college is intellectually too demanding for most young people, we will continue to create crazily unrealistic expectations among the next generation," Murray wrote. Students who score in the bottom third on cognitive tests like the

ACT are unsuited for college, he wrote; they are also "just not smart enough to become literate or numerate in more than a rudimentary sense."

Jeff Nelson looks at the ACT quite differently than Charles Murray does. "I think the ACT is a very good measure of how effective your education has been," he told me. "But I don't think it's a good measure of intelligence. The average incoming score of our students is hovering around a fourteen, or the tenth percentile. And I adamantly do not believe that ninety percent of students at that age are actually more intelligent than the students we're working with. What I *do* believe is that ninety percent of the population is receiving a better education than our students have received."

For Nelson, the distinction is in some ways a semantic one. You can call the quality that the ACT measures intelligence if you want, but regardless of what you call it, he believes, the ability to get a high score on the test is not essential to college success and college persistence. Nelson bases that belief on his reading of Melissa Roderick's work and on the book *Crossing the Finish Line* but also on the real-life experiences of OneGoal's alumni, who consistently attend schools that their ACT scores say should be out of their league and then regularly succeed at levels that their ACT scores suggest should be impossible. "Noncognitive skills like resilience and resourcefulness and grit are highly predictive of success in college," Nelson told me. "And they can help our students compensate for some of the inequality they have faced in the education system." A student like Kewauna, Nelson said, "will show up on campus with many important tools for success that other students do not have. And those skills are going to be more useful in getting her to graduation day than a good score on the ACT."

7. Kewauna's Ambitions

When Kewauna's mother, Marla McConico, was a junior in high school, back in the late 1980s, she took the ACT with the rest of her class. She doesn't remember her exact score, but it wasn't very good.

"After I got those scores back, I felt so like a failure," she told me when I visited with her and Kewauna one fall day. "I thought, 'I can't get into college with these scores.' So I just didn't bother with it."

Kewauna's relationship with her mother was close but often fraught, and her strategy in life sometimes seemed to be to do the exact opposite of whatever her mother had done when she was Kewauna's age. Her mother fell in love with Kewauna's father as a teenager and made a series of shortsighted decisions as a result; Kewauna kept her boyfriend at a distance, determined not to make her college decisions based on his plans. Her mother took her eyes off her academic goals; Kewauna's remained fixed on hers. Her mother was derailed by a bad ACT score; Kewauna was determined to overcome her own bad ACT score.

But as Kewauna proceeded through the fall of her senior year, her mood grew heavier, and when I spoke with her one afternoon in the middle of October, she sounded uncharacteristically pessimistic about her future. She had started to hear back about some of the scholarships that she had applied for, and she was getting turned down for each one, she presumed because of her ACT score. "I'm getting kind of depressed about the whole situation," she told me. "I worked so hard on all those applications, and I really do need that money for college."

We talked a lot that day about her years at Plymouth Middle School, which she attended back when she lived in Minnesota. Kewauna traced a lot of her current academic difficulties to sixth grade, when, because of her poor grades and bad behavior, she was placed in a remedial class called WINGS. Officially, WINGS stood for Working Innovatively Now for Graduation Success, but Kewauna told me that at Plymouth, the joke was that it was called WINGS because the kids used to sit in class all day just eating chicken wings. That was an exaggeration, she said—but not much of one. "We never did *anything* in that class," she said. "It was for kids who needed help, but they didn't give us any help. We didn't read. We didn't study. We just played video games and watched movies and ate popcorn. It was fun, but that's why I'm struggling with the ACT now. That's why I'm getting denied from scholarships. Those two years were when we were supposed to be learning punctuation, commas, metaphors, all that stuff. When they bring it up today, they say, 'Remember when we learned this?' And I'm like, 'No, I don't! I never learned any of that.'"

Kewauna's other lingering regret was that during her freshman year of high school at ACE Tech, when she had had a chance to start over, she had squandered it, skipping class, goofing around, hanging out with her friends instead of studying. She got mostly Cs and Ds that year. She even failed phys ed. "I wasn't thinking about the future," she told me. "At that point, I just wanted to have fun." She was only fourteen, and she didn't think anything mattered; it wasn't until she was a sophomore and started applying herself a little more that she learned that her GPA was cumulative all through high school, which meant that her freshman grades would directly affect her college prospects. That was why, in her junior and senior years, she became so preoccupied with keeping a near-perfect GPA — doing extra-credit work, staying after school to get help from her teachers. Still, she sometimes talked about her past like it was a stain on her record that she would never be able to erase.

The college Kewauna had set her sights on most intently was the University of Illinois at Urbana-Champaign, the flagship college of the state's university system, rated by *U.S. News & World Report* as the thirteenth-best public university in the country. Urbana is about two and a half hours south of Chicago, which felt like the right distance to Kewauna — not so far that she'd get homesick, but still far enough for her to feel independent. She had visited the campus on a OneGoal field trip in her junior year, and she loved it: the quad, the student center, the lecture halls, the Applebee's. "That's my dream, number-one, please-let-me-get-in school," she told me. "If I don't get in, I'm going to cry for like six days."

But by the beginning of February, Kewauna had scaled back her college ambitions a bit. She had applied to the University of Chicago, the most prestigious college in the state, but she told me she no longer wanted to go there even if she did get in. She had been admitted to a couple of her safety schools, including the University of Illinois in

Chicago, but she was hoping for something better. She hadn't given up on Urbana — that was still her first choice — but she now had a clear second choice as well: Western Illinois University, in Macomb, which was somewhat less competitive than Urbana but still had an average incoming ACT score of 21, well above Kewauna's score. She had visited Western the previous year, and she had warm memories: "I fell in love with that school," she told me. "I felt really comfortable there. The people were friendly. The dorm rooms — everything was perfect."

That winter, she developed what seemed to me a more stoic, far-sighted view of her college future than she had had when I met her. "If I don't get into one of my top schools, maybe I wasn't meant to go there," she told me. "I would be disappointed, but I would work hard wherever I got in, and then maybe after a year or two I could transfer to one of my number-one schools." She had decided to quit beating herself up about the mistakes she made in her freshman year too. "I can't keep saying, 'Oh my goodness! I messed up my freshman year,'" she told me. "It's already done. I did what I did. It's a lesson for me. And when I go to college, I'll make sure that this time I don't make the same mistakes in freshman year. I'm going to be on task. Plan things out. Have a schedule, be really organized, be focused, meet the right people."

February was an anxious month; Kewauna kept checking the mail, calling admissions offices just to make sure they had everything they needed from her. Finally, at the end of the month, she got good news: she had been accepted to Western Illinois. Because of her low ACT score, she was enrolled in a special freshman-support program that would provide her with extra tutoring and counseling in her first year. Three of Kewauna's close friends from ACE Tech got into Western as well, and together they made plans to head to Macomb.

8. Closing the Gap

Recently, two labor economists at the University of California, Philip Babcock and Mindy Marks, analyzed surveys of time use by college students from the 1920s through the present. They found that in 1961, the average full-time college student spent twenty-four hours a week studying outside of the classroom. By 1981, that had fallen to twenty hours a week, and in 2003, it was down to fourteen hours a week, not much more than half of what it had been forty years earlier. This phenomenon transcended boundaries: "Study time fell for students from all demographic subgroups," Babcock and Marks wrote, "for students who worked and those who did not, within every major, and at four-year colleges of every type, degree structure, and level of selectivity." And where did all those extra hours go? To socializing and recreation, mostly. A separate study of 6,300 undergraduates at the University of California found that students today spend fewer than thirteen hours a week studying, while they spend twelve hours hanging out with friends, fourteen hours consuming entertainment and pursuing various hobbies, eleven hours using "computers for fun," and six hours exercising.

To many observers, these statistics are cause for alarm. But Jeff Nelson sees this situation as an opportunity for his students. He recalled for me his own freshman year at the University of Michigan, when he did what a lot of other upper-middle-class kids do at the beginning of their college careers: he didn't work very hard. For some affluent students, freshman year is about drinking heavily; for others, it's about pledging a fraternity or trying to write for the student newspaper. That time is certainly not always wasted, but it generally doesn't contribute much to a student's academic outcomes. And so Nelson sees freshman year as a "magical timeframe" for OneGoal students "where they can radically close the achievement gap." As Nelson explained his theory in one of our early conversations, "Freshman year is this unique moment in time. Kids who have not had to persevere as much walk into college and they coast, for the most part. Or they're partying too hard. And in that moment, if our kids are working diligently and building relationships with professors and studying and using all of the skills that we've trained them to use, they can close the gap. We've seen it time and time again, that all of a sudden a kid who might have been three or four grade levels behind in high school has caught up in a really significant way to his peers by the beginning of sophomore year."

Her first fall at Western Illinois, Kewauna took introductory courses — English 100, Math 100, Sociology 100. None of them was easy for her, but the course she found most challenging was Biology 170, Introduction to Health Careers. The professor was a popular lecturer, so the class was pretty full, and most of the students were upperclassmen. On the first day of class, Kewauna did what Michele Stefl had recommended: she politely introduced herself to the professor before class, and then she sat in the front row, which until Kewauna sat down was occupied entirely by white girls. The other African American students all tended to sit at the back, which disappointed Kewauna. ("That's what they *expect* you to do," she said when we talked by phone that fall. "Back in the civil rights movement, if they told you you had to sit in the back, you wouldn't do it.")

Her biology professor used a lot of scientific terms in his lectures that Kewauna wasn't familiar with. So she came up with a strategy: every time he used a word she didn't understand, she wrote it down and put a red star next to it. At the end of the class, she waited until all the other students who wanted to talk to the professor had taken their turns, and then she went through each red-starred word with him, one by one, asking him to explain them.

Kewauna spent a lot of time interacting with all her professors, in fact. She was a regular at office hours, and she e-mailed them whenever she wasn't clear on assignments. She also tried to make one or two acquaintances among the students in each of her classes, so that if she needed help with homework and couldn't reach the professor, she'd have someone to ask. Through her freshman-support program, she found a writing tutor — she had always had "grammar issues," she told me, as well as trouble with spelling and punctuation — and she made a practice of going over with her tutor every paper she wrote before handing it in. Finally, in December, she felt she had internalized enough about comma splices and dependent clauses, and she handed in her final English paper without going over it with the writing tutor. She got an A.

Still, it was a difficult semester for Kewauna. She was always short
of money and had to economize everywhere she could. At one point,
she ran out of money on her meal card and just didn't eat for two
days. She was studying all the time, it felt like. Every paper was a
challenge, and at the end of the semester, she stayed up practically
all night, three nights in a row, studying for finals. But her hard work
was reflected in her final grades that semester: two B pluses, one A,
and, in biology, an A plus. When I spoke to her a few days before
Christmas, she sounded a bit depleted, but proud too. "No matter
how overwhelming it is, no matter how exhausting it is, I'm not going to give up," she said. "I'm never the type to give up. Even when
I played hide-and-go-seek when I was little, I would be outside till
eight o'clock, until I found everyone. I don't give up on nothing, no
matter how hard."

Kewauna's grades actually improved in her second semester, and at
the end of her freshman year, her cumulative GPA stood at 3.8. There
were still three years to go, lots of time for things to go wrong, for setbacks and mistakes and crises. But Kewauna seemed certain of where
she was heading and why — almost unnervingly so. What was most
remarkable to me about Kewauna was that she was able to marshal
her prodigious noncognitive capacity — call it grit, conscientiousness,
resilience, or the ability to delay gratification — all for a distant prize
that was, for her, almost entirely theoretical. She didn't actually *know*
any business ladies with briefcases downtown; she didn't even know
any college graduates except her teachers. It was as if Kewauna were
taking part in an extended, high-stakes version of Walter Mischel's
marshmallow experiment, except in this case, the choice on offer was
that she could have one marshmallow now or she could work really
hard for four years, constantly scrimping and saving, staying up all
night, struggling, sacrificing — and then get, not two marshmallows,
but some kind of elegant French pastry she'd only vaguely heard of,
like a Napoleon. And Kewauna, miraculously, opted for the Napoleon, even though she'd never tasted one before and didn't know anyone who had. She just had faith that it was going to be delicious.

Not all of Kewauna's fellow OneGoal students are going to take to the deal with the same conviction. And it won't be clear for another couple of years whether the leadership skills Kewauna and her classmates were taught are powerful enough to get them through four years of college. But so far, OneGoal's overall persistence numbers are quite good. Of the 129 students, including Kewauna, who started OneGoal as juniors at ten Chicago high schools in the fall of 2009, ninety-four were enrolled in four-year colleges as of May 2012. Another fourteen were enrolled in two-year colleges, for an overall college-persistence total of 84 percent. Which left only twenty-one students who had veered off the track to a college degree: twelve who left OneGoal before the end of high school, two who joined the military after high school, two who graduated from high school but didn't enroll in college, and five who enrolled in college but dropped out in their freshman year. The numbers are less stellar but still impressive for the pilot-program cohort, students for whom OneGoal was a weekly afterschool class. Three years out of high school, 66 percent of the students who enrolled in the program as high-school juniors are still enrolled in college. Those numbers grow more significant when you recall that OneGoal teachers are deliberately selecting struggling students who seem especially unlikely to go to college.

Jeff Nelson would be the first to admit that what he has created is far from a perfect solution for the widespread dysfunction of the country's human-capital pipeline. Ideally, we should have in place an education and social-support system that produces teenagers from the South Side who *aren't* regularly two or three or four years behind grade level. For now, though, OneGoal and the theories that underlie it seem like a most valuable intervention, a program that, for about fourteen hundred dollars a year per student, regularly turns underperforming, undermotivated, low-income teenagers into successful college students.

5

A BETTER PATH

1. Dropping Out

In the fall of 1985, when I was a freshman at Columbia University, at the same precarious stage of life as Kewauna Lerma in the fall of 2011, I did something Kewauna is determined never to do: I dropped out of college. It felt at the time like a weighty and fateful choice, and it still does. It is a decision, in fact, that I have revisited many times over the last twenty-five years, often with regret. I certainly thought about it a lot while reporting this book. When I was sitting in room 104 of ACE Tech Charter High School with Kewauna and the rest of Michele Stefl's OneGoal class, I would sometimes feel a little ashamed, to be honest: graduating from college was such a consuming goal for those students, and I often wished that when I was their age, I had thought as hard and as responsibly as they were doing about what I wanted from my college experience.

It hasn't escaped my attention that many of the researchers I've written about in this book — everyone from James Heckman to Angela Duckworth to Melissa Roderick to the authors of *Crossing the Finish Line* — have identified dropping out of high school or college as a symptom of substandard noncognitive ability: low grit, low perseverance, bad planning skills. And I think it's true that I was lacking in some of those important skills when I made my decision to leave. But my reporting for this book has also provided me with a more generous way to interpret my choice. It came in my conversations with Dominic Randolph, the head of the Riverdale Country School, who made a persuasive case that failure — or at least the real risk of failure — could often be a crucial step on the road to success. Randolph was worried, you'll recall, that his mostly affluent students, caught up in the modern American meritocratic machine of private schools, private tutors, Ivy League colleges, and safe careers, were being short-changed by their families and their school and even their culture by not being given enough genuine opportunities to overcome adversity and thus develop their character. "The idea of building grit and building self-control is that you get that through failure," Randolph told me. "And in most highly academic environments in the United States, no one fails anything."

I wrote an article about KIPP and Riverdale and character, drawn from the reporting I did for this book, that was published in the *New York Times Magazine* in September of 2011. The article produced an unexpected flood of responses from readers, many of whom said they related to Randolph's ideas about failure and success. Some of them contributed comments on the *Times*'s website about their own experiences, like "Dave," who wrote that he had been one of the kids Randolph was talking about, the ones who got high test scores and lots of praise but never developed the grit that came from confronting real challenges. "I'm left now, in my thirties," Dave wrote, "often wondering how much more I could have accomplished if I wasn't terrified of failure, and prone to shying away from ventures where my success wasn't guaranteed."

Not long after the article was published, and while I was immersed in the research on college persistence, I found myself wondering anew about my decision to drop out. Why had I done it? I dug through a box of old papers from that era, looking for clues, and I discovered a letter that I'd almost forgotten, a long exegesis of my decision to quit that I wrote in my Columbia dorm room over Thanksgiving weekend that freshman fall. It was eight pages long, single spaced — and, to give you an idea of the technological age we're talking about, it was written not only in longhand but in cursive. I pulled out the letter — it had a couple of coffee stains, but it was still legible — sat down in my office, took a deep breath, and reread it. It was, as you can imagine, pretty embarrassing. There is no soul more overwrought than that of an eighteen-year-old trying to make a life-changing decision. But I was glad I had found the letter, and despite its moments of adolescent insufferability, I felt a good deal of compassion for my conflicted younger self.

I had been a high-achieving student in high school, with good grades and good standardized-test scores. I arrived at college excited but confused, lost on a campus and in a city where I didn't know a soul. I was glad to be in New York but less glad to be sitting in lecture halls. Even in high school, while I was being such a responsible student, I had felt grave doubts about my relationship with formal education. I had a rebellious streak — I was a teenage Kerouac reader — and like millions of high-school rebels before me, I was convinced that what I was learning in the classroom didn't really matter, man. And on that November day at Columbia, I decided I had finally had enough. "I have been being educated for fifteen years and three months, which is 84 percent of my life," I wrote, with characteristic precision (for the record, I was counting from the first day of nursery school). "Going to school is all I know. Education is a game, and let's face it: I'm good at it. I know the rules; I know how to perform all the required tasks. I even know how to win. But I'm sick of the game. I want to cash in my chips."

It is always hard, the eighteen-year-old me wrote, to quit doing something that everyone tells you you're good at in order to do something you've never tried before. But that was precisely what I felt I needed: to do something uncertain, unsafe; something I didn't know if I could succeed at. The specific trial I fixed upon for myself was a long journey, an odyssey of sorts: I would take some of the money I was about to spend on my next semester's tuition, buy a touring bicycle and a tent, and pedal my way, alone, from Atlanta to Halifax, sleeping in state parks and the backyards of strangers. It was an odd idea. I'd never been on a long bicycle trip before, and I'd never been on even a short one by myself. I'd never been to the American South. I wasn't particularly good at talking to strangers. But I somehow felt compelled to subject myself to this mission. I had a notion that I might learn more along the road than I would on campus. "This may be a total failure, a flop, a disaster of gargantuan proportions," I wrote. "It may be the most irresponsible thing I'll ever do. But it may be the most responsible."

A couple of days after the *New York Times Magazine* story on KIPP and Riverdale came out, a reader sent me an e-mail message saying he thought I should watch the commencement address that Steve Jobs gave at Stanford University in 2005. There were a lot of parallels, he wrote, between Jobs's thoughts on failure and character and the debates that I'd tried to capture in the article. After Jobs's untimely death, the Stanford speech got a lot of attention, but as it happened, this was a few weeks before he died, and I'd never seen or read it. I clicked the YouTube link the reader had sent and watched Jobs speak, and I soon realized I didn't know much about his life story. Watching that speech, I learned that in his freshman year, Jobs had dropped out of college — Reed College, in Oregon. And believe me, if decades after you drop out of college, you're still trying to justify your decision, there's nothing more reassuring than finding out that one of the most successful and creative businessmen of modern times did the same thing. And what's more, that he had no regrets. In his speech, Jobs explained that dropping out had "been one of the best decisions I ever made." It even paid off for him, and for Apple, in one very specific way: Freed from course requirements, Jobs sat in on courses that interested him more than his assigned classes had, including one on calligraphy and typography. "I learned about serif and sans serif typefaces, about varying the amount of space between different letter combinations, about what makes great typography great," Jobs said. "None of this had even a hope of any practical application in my life" — until, of course, a decade later, when he and Steve Wozniak were designing the Macintosh and decided to include, for the first time, creative typography in a personal computer. That flourish helped distinguish the Mac from everything that had come before.

What struck me most about Jobs's speech, though, was the story he told about his greatest failure: being fired from Apple, the company he created, just after his thirtieth birthday. "What had been the focus of my entire adult life was gone, and it was devastating," he said. "I was a very public failure." What he wasn't able to see at the time, Jobs said, but that became clear later was that the experience of such a dramatic failure allowed him to reorient himself and his work in a way that led to his greatest successes: buying and transforming Pixar, getting married, returning to Apple rejuvenated. As Jobs put it in his speech: "The heaviness of being successful was replaced by the lightness of being a beginner again, less sure about everything." That was, I think, exactly what I was looking for in that Columbia dorm room: the lightness of being a beginner.

A month or so after writing my dropout letter, I did, indeed, drop out. I bought a bike and a tent and a Coleman stove and a one-way plane ticket to Atlanta, and from there I bicycled to Halifax, through many rainstorms, flat tires, and strange encounters. It took me two months, and at the end of the journey, I felt it was the best thing I'd ever done. I gave college another try a few months later, back in my native Canada — McGill University, in fact, where a decade or so later Michael Meaney would begin to discover such amazing things about rat mothers and their licking habits. And then three semesters after that, I dropped out again to take an internship at *Harper's Magazine*. This time, the dropping-out stuck. I never went back to college, never got a BA, and, haltingly, I began a career as a magazine editor and a journalist. I didn't go on to found Apple, or even NeXT (Jobs's failed computer company), and in fact I continued for the next two decades to struggle with some of the same questions I had been wrestling with in that dorm room — *Should I do something I'm good at or something I love? Take a chance or play it safe?* — until on another fall morning, twenty-four years after dropping out of Columbia, I found myself dropping out of another esteemed New York City institution, the *New York Times,* again without much of a safety net. This time, the strange adventure I set out on was not to pedal a bicycle halfway across the country; it was to write a book. This one.

2. High-LG Parenting

These days, when I contemplate success and failure, I think less frequently about my own prospects and more often about those of my son, Ellington. I figure I've already turned out more or less the way I'm going to turn out. But Ellington? Anything could happen. I started reporting this book right around the time he was born, and it will be published just after his third birthday, so the years I spent working on it coincided almost exactly with the period in his life that neuroscientists tell us is the most critical in a child's development. The experience of writing the book—and especially encountering the brain research that I wrote about in chapter 1—has profoundly affected the way I think about what it means to be a parent.

When Ellington was born, I was like most anxious parents under the influence of the cognitive hypothesis, worried that he wasn't going to succeed in life unless I broke out the brain-building flashcards and the Mozart CDs in the maternity ward and then kept bombarding him with them until he got a perfect score on his preschool-admission test. But the brain researchers whose work I had begun to read pointed me in a different direction. Yes, they said, those first few years are critically important in the development of a child's brain. But the most significant skills he is acquiring during those years aren't ones that can be taught with flashcards.

It is not as if I suddenly stopped caring about Ellington's being able to read and write and add and subtract. But I became convinced that those particular skills would come to him sooner or later no matter what I did, simply because he was growing up surrounded by books and had two parents who liked to read and were comfortable with numbers. What I felt less confident about were his character skills.

Yes, it feels a little ridiculous to use the word *character* when you're talking about a toddler. And yes, the development of an individual's character depends on all sorts of mysterious interactions among culture and family and genes and free will and fate. But to me, the most profound discovery this new generation of neuroscientists has made is the powerful connection between infant brain chemistry and adult psychology. Lying deep beneath those noble, complex human qualities we call character, these scientists have found, is the mundane, mechanical interaction of specific chemicals in the brains and bodies of developing infants. Chemistry is not destiny, certainly. But these scientists have demonstrated that the most reliable way to produce an adult who is brave and curious and kind and prudent is to ensure that when he is an infant, his hypothalamic-pituitary-adrenal axis functions well. And how do you do that? It is not magic. First, as much as possible, you protect him from serious trauma and chronic stress; then, even more important, you provide him with a secure, nurturing relationship with at least one parent and ideally two. That's not the whole secret of success, but it is a big, big part of it.

When Ellington was an infant, the research that influenced me most was Michael Meaney's. It's a little embarrassing to admit, but while I was playing with baby Ellington, I was often thinking about baby rats. I spent a lot of time, in fact, mulling over exactly what it might mean to be a high-licking-and-grooming human parent. Those high-LG dams, I realized, were not helicopter parents. They didn't hover anxiously. They weren't constantly licking and grooming their pups. They did their LG-ing mostly in one very specific situation: when their pups were stressed out. It was almost as if the dams were trying to teach their pups, through repetition, a valuable skill: how to manage their inflamed stress systems and restore them to a resting state. The equivalent skill for human infants, I think, is being able to calm down after a tantrum or a bad scare, and that's what I concentrated on trying to help Ellington learn how to do. To be clear: I didn't lick my son. I didn't even really groom him much, to be honest. But if there is a human equivalent to high-LG parenting, it involves a lot of comforting and hugging and talking and reassuring. And my wife, Paula, and I both did a lot of that when Ellington was little. My guess is that doing those things with Ellington in his infancy will turn out to have made a bigger difference in his character, and in his ultimate happiness and success, than anything else we do.

As Ellington grew older, though, I found, as countless parents had found before me, that he needed something more than love and hugs. He also needed discipline, rules, limits; someone to say no. And what he needed more than anything was some child-size adversity, a chance to fall down and get back up on his own, without help. This was harder for Paula and me — it came less naturally to us than the hugging and comforting — and I know that it is just the beginning of the long struggle we will face, as all parents do, between our urge to provide everything for our child, to protect him from all harm, and our knowledge that if we really want him to succeed, we need to first let him fail. Or more precisely, we need to help him learn to *manage* failure. This idea — the importance of learning how to deal with and learn from your own failures — is a common thread in many of the chapters in this book. It's what Elizabeth Spiegel, the chess coach, was such an expert at. She took it for granted that her students were going to fail a lot. Every chess player does. As she saw it, her job was not to prevent them from failing; it was to teach them how to learn from each failure, how to stare at their failures with unblinking honesty, how to confront exactly why they had messed up. If they could do that, she believed, they would do better next time. Just like Steve Jobs at Apple the second time around.

When I spoke to teachers and administrators at Riverdale Country School and, later on, to the many private-school parents and teachers and alumni who had read the *Times Magazine* article on character and wanted to talk about it, this was exactly what they were most worried about — that their children were so overly protected from adversity that they weren't developing the ability to overcome failure and learn from it. Reporting at Riverdale, I often felt that I had stumbled upon a pervasive, if still somewhat inchoate, anxiety within the contemporary culture of affluence, a feeling that something had gone wrong within the traditional channels of American meritocratic pursuit, that young people were graduating from our finest institutions of higher learning with excellent credentials and well-honed test-taking skills and not much else that would allow them to make their own way in the world. There are fewer entrepreneurs graduating from our best colleges these days; fewer iconoclasts; fewer artists; fewer everything, in fact, except investment bankers and management consultants. Recently, the *New York Times* reported that 36 percent of new Princeton graduates in 2010 took jobs in the finance industry, and another 26 percent took jobs in a category that Princeton labels services, which features, prominently, management consulting. More than half of the class, in other words, was going into investment banking or consulting—and this after the near-collapse of the finance industry in 2008. (Before the economic crisis, about three-quarters of Princeton graduates went into one of those two careers.)

To some analysts, the fact that we are sending so many of our best and brightest young people into professions that are, let's say, not known for their high level of personal fulfillment or deep social value is simply the continuation of the phenomenon that so many Riverdale teachers spoke to me about: kids who worked very hard but never had to make a difficult decision or confront a real challenge and so entered the adult world competent but lost. In 2010, an economics blogger and law professor named James Kwak wrote an insightful blog post addressing this issue, "Why Do Harvard Kids Head to Wall Street?" After Kwak graduated from Harvard, he, like so many of his classmates, went to work as a management consultant. And he explained that the reason that path is so well trod is not the money, though that doesn't hurt. It's that the firms make the path and the decision so easy to take and so hard to resist.

The typical contemporary Harvard undergraduate, Kwak wrote, "is driven more by fear of not being a success than by a concrete desire to do anything in particular." The postcollege choices of Ivy League students, he explained, "are motivated by two main decision rules: (1) close down as few options as possible; and (2) only do things that increase the possibility of future overachievement." Recruiters for investment banks and consulting firms understand this psychology, and they exploit it perfectly: the jobs are competitive and high status, but the process of applying and being accepted is regimented and predictable. The recruiters also make the argument to college seniors that if they join Goldman Sachs or McKinsey and Company or any similar firm, they're not really *choosing* anything — they're just going to spend a couple of years making money and, perhaps, recruiters suggest, doing some good in the world, and then at some point in the future they'll make the *real* decision about what they want to do and who they want to be. "For people who don't know how to get a job in the open economy," Kwak wrote, "and who have ended each phase of their lives by taking the test to do the most prestigious thing possible in the next phase, all of this comes naturally."

3. A Different Challenge

If you're an undergraduate at Harvard, your struggles with the challenges of character might land you in a less-than-inspiring investment-banking job. If you're a teenager growing up on the South Side of Chicago, though, they might land you in jail, or at least at the Vivian E. Summers Alternative High School. And while it is hard to argue that the general public has a responsibility to help Ivy League grads reach their full potential, it is easier to make the case that society has an important role to play in the successful development of children growing up in poverty and adversity. Liberals and conservatives differ sharply on what the government should do to aid families in poverty, but just about everyone agrees that it should do *something*. Helping to alleviate the impact of poverty and providing young people with opportunities to escape it: that has historically been one of the essential functions of any national government, right up there with building bridges and defending borders. Poll numbers from an ongoing survey of attitudes by the Pew Research Center show that most Americans concur. Although public support for aid to the poor has weakened somewhat since 2008, as it often does during economic hard times, a clear majority of Americans still agree with the statements "The government should guarantee every citizen enough to eat and a place to sleep" and "It is the responsibility of the government to take care of people who can't take care of themselves." And when the issue is framed in terms of *opportunity*, the public consensus is much more clear and unwavering: since 1987, when Pew started asking these questions, between 87 percent and 94 percent of respondents in every poll have agreed with the statement "Our society should do what is necessary to make sure that everyone has an equal opportunity to succeed."

But while Americans remain as committed as ever to helping their less fortunate neighbors succeed, something important *has* changed in the past few decades: what was once a noisy and impassioned national conversation about how best to combat poverty has faded almost to silence. Back in the 1960s, poverty was a major focus of public debate. You couldn't be a serious policy intellectual without weighing in on the issue. During the Johnson administration, the place to be for smart, ambitious young people in Washington was the Office of Economic Opportunity, the command center for the War on Poverty. In the 1990s, there was once more a robust public discussion of poverty, much of it centered on the issue of welfare reform. But now those debates have all but disappeared. We have a Democratic president who spent the early part of his career personally fighting poverty, working in the same neighborhoods that YAP's advocates are working in today — doing a pretty similar job, in fact. But as president, he has spent less time talking publicly about poverty than any of his recent Democratic predecessors.

It is not that poverty itself has disappeared. Far from it. In 1966, at the height of the War on Poverty, the poverty rate was just under 15 percent; in 2010, it was 15.1 percent. And the child poverty rate is substantially *higher* now. In 1966, the rate stood at a little more than 17 percent. Now the figure is 22 percent, meaning that between a fifth and a quarter of American children are growing up in poverty.

So if poverty is at least as big an issue today as it was in the 1960s, why have we mostly stopped talking about it — in public, at least? I think the answer has partly to do with the psychology of public intellectuals. The War on Poverty left some very deep scars on the well-educated idealists who waged it, creating a kind of posttraumatic stress disorder for policy wonks. Remember, President Kennedy first talked about putting an end to poverty at about the same time he promised to put a man on the moon. The early 1960s was an era of great optimism and hope in Washington, and the Apollo missions fulfilled that hope. They were a huge national triumph, and their message was that if we as a nation set our minds to a problem, we could solve it.

Except we didn't solve poverty. Some of the interventions that made up the War on Poverty were effective — but plenty of them weren't. And plenty more seemed to do more harm than good. And if you're someone who believes that smart people working through government can solve big problems, that is a harsh truth to acknowledge. It is painful to admit that making a significant dent in poverty has turned out to be a lot harder than we thought — and even more painful to admit that forty-five years later, we still don't know quite what to do.

Something else has happened in the past decade or so that also helps explain why the poverty debate disappeared: it merged with the education debate. Education and poverty used to be two very separate topics in public policy. There was one conversation about the New Math and Why Johnny Can't Read. And then there was another conversation about slums and hunger and welfare and urban renewal. But increasingly, there's just one conversation, and it's about the achievement gap between rich and poor — the very real fact that overall, children who grow up in poor families in the United States are doing very badly in school.

There are several reasons behind this merger. The first goes back to *The Bell Curve,* the controversial 1994 book about IQ by Charles Murray and Richard Herrnstein. Despite what I and many others believe to be its flawed conclusion — that racial differences on achievement tests are most likely the result of genetic differences between the races — *The Bell Curve* carried within it a very important new observation, which was that academic grades and achievement-test results are very good predictors of all kinds of outcomes in life: not just how far you'll go in school and how much you'll earn when you get out, but also whether you'll commit crimes, whether you'll take drugs, whether you'll get married, and whether you'll get divorced. What *The Bell Curve* showed was that kids who do well in school tend to do well in life, whether or not they come from poverty. Which led to an intriguing idea, one that appealed to social reformers all along the political spectrum: if we can help poor children improve their academic skills and academic outcomes, they can escape the cycle of poverty by virtue of their own abilities and without additional handouts or set-asides.

In the late 1990s and early 2000s, this idea gained momentum because of two important phenomena. One was the passage of the No Child Left Behind law, in 2001. For the first time, the law forced states and cities and individual schools to compile detailed information on how their students were performing — and not just the student population as a whole but individual subgroups as well: minority students, low-income students, English-language learners. Once those numbers started coming in, the achievement gaps they reflected became impossible to avoid or deny. In every state, in every city, at every grade level, in almost every school, students from low-income homes were doing much worse than students from middle-class homes — they were two or three grade levels behind, on average, by the time they left middle school. And the achievement gap between rich and poor was getting worse every year.

The other phenomenon was the emergence of a group of schools that seemed to defy the achievement gap: the KIPP schools and others in the same mold, like Amistad Academy in New Haven, Roxbury Prep in Boston, and North Star Academy in Newark. The initial wave of astounding test scores that David Levin and Michael Feinberg and other educators were able to help their students produce captured the public's imagination. It seemed these teachers had come up with a reliable, replicable model for inner-city-school success.

And so these three facts came together to form a powerful syllogism for people who cared about poverty: First, scores on achievement tests in school correlate strongly with life outcomes, no matter what a student's background. Second, children in low-income homes did much worse on achievement tests than children in middle-income and high-income homes. And third, certain schools, using a very different model than traditional public schools, were able to substantially raise the achievement-test scores of low-income children. The conclusion: if we could replicate on a big, national scale the accomplishments of those schools, we could make a huge dent in poverty's impact on children's success.

This was a very different way of looking at poverty than what had come before. It was exciting to many people, myself included, primarily because so much else *hadn't* worked. We'd tried welfare payments to poor mothers, we'd tried housing subsidies, we'd tried Head Start, we'd tried community policing. And for the most part, poor children weren't doing any better. But now it seemed that if we could make public schools more effective — much more effective — the schools could become a more powerful antipoverty tool than anything we had previously tried. It was a transformative idea. And it sparked a movement: the education-reform movement.

4. A Different Kind of Reform

In the movement's earliest days, its proponents hadn't quite decided what they were moving toward. They shared a vision — a national landscape of schools that performed as well for low-income children as KIPP schools did — but they disagreed on which policy mechanisms might best help to realize that vision. Was it vouchers? A national curriculum? More charter schools? Smaller class size? Now, a decade later, education reformers have mostly united around one specific issue: teacher quality. The consensus of most reform advocates is that there are far too many underperforming teachers, especially in high-poverty schools, and the only way to improve outcomes for students in these schools is to change the way teachers are hired, trained, compensated, and fired.

This argument has its intellectual roots in a handful of research papers published in the late 1990s and early 2000s by economists and statisticians, including Eric Hanushek, Thomas Kane, and William Sanders, that claimed it was possible to identify, through a statistical method known as value-added, two distinct groups of teachers: those who could regularly raise the achievement level of their students and those whose students consistently fell behind. This idea led to a theory of change: if an underperforming low-income student was assigned for multiple years in a row to a high-quality teacher, his test scores should continually and cumulatively improve, and after three or four or five years, he would close the achievement gap with his better-off peers. And to take the idea one step further: if school systems and teacher contracts could somehow be overhauled so that *every* low-income student had a high-performance teacher, the achievement gap could be eliminated altogether.

In the past few years, this theory has been embraced at the highest levels of government. The main education initiative of the Obama administration, in fact, has been to offer states competitive incentives to rewrite or amend their laws governing the teaching profession. Many states have taken the federal government up on the offer, with the result that various experimental notions on teacher compensation, evaluation, and tenure are now being tested, in a variety of forms, in school systems across the country. At the same time, the Gates Foundation, which spends more money on education than any other philanthropy, has embarked on a three-hundred-million-dollar research project called Measures of Effective Teaching to try to answer definitively the questions of what good teaching is and how to create a better national teaching force.

Despite this consensus among reformers, the national push on teacher quality has been quite controversial. Teacher unions, especially, fear that it is a not-so-subtle attempt to undermine many of the professional protections that they have fought for over the past several decades. And whatever your opinion on unions, the fact is that the research on teachers remains inconclusive in some important ways. First, we don't yet know how to reliably predict who will be a top-tier teacher in any given year. Sometimes teachers who seem to be failures suddenly make great strides with their students. Sometimes brilliant teachers suddenly go downhill. And we still don't know if it's true that a string of excellent teachers will produce a cumulative positive effect on the performance of low-income students. It *seems* to make sense that having a top-tier teacher three years in a row would raise a student's achievement three times as much as his having a top-tier teacher for a single year — but it might not. Maybe the effect fades out after a single year. So far, there's just no solid evidence one way or the other.

It's true that the current system has tended for many years to assign the least capable teachers to the students who are most in need of excellent teaching. That's a serious problem. But somehow we've allowed reform of teacher tenure to become the central policy tool in our national effort to improve the lives of poor children. And even those original papers, the ones by Hanushek and others that are now cited by reform advocates, concluded that variations in teacher quality probably accounted for less than 10 percent of the gap between high- and low-performing students.

This is the downside to conflating the education debate with the poverty debate — you can get distracted from the real issue. You start thinking that the only important question is, How do we improve teacher quality?, when really that is just a small part of a much broader and more profound question: What can we as a country do to significantly improve the life chances of millions of poor children?

And as the poverty debate has disappeared inside the education-reform debate, we've also lost track of another important fact: many of the most popular school reforms, including those high-performing charter schools, seem to work best with the most able low-income children, and they often don't work very well with the least able. The problem is that the broad-brush way that the federal education department defines financial need tends to disguise this fact. The only official indicator of the economic status of an American public-school student today is his or her eligibility for a school-lunch subsidy, a government benefit that is offered to any family whose annual income falls below 185 percent of the poverty line, which in 2012 meant $41,348 for a family of four. So when a particular reform or school is touted as improving outcomes for low-income students, we need to remember that the education department's low-income designation covers about 40 percent of American children, including some who are growing up in families that most of us would define as working class or even middle class. (In the Chicago public schools, just one student in eight *doesn't* qualify for a lunch subsidy.) Within the education department's cohort of low-income students, about half are genuinely poor, meaning living below the poverty line. And then half of *those* students, about 10 percent of all American children, are growing up in families that earn less than half of the poverty line. For a family of four, that means an income of less than about $11,000 a year.

And if you're one of the more than seven million American children growing up in a family earning less than $11,000 a year, you are confronted with countless obstacles to school success that children in families earning $41,000 a year likely are not. There are the straightforward financial considerations — your family probably can't afford adequate shelter or nutritious food, let alone new clothes or books or educational toys. But the most serious obstacles to learning that you face most likely transcend what your family can or cannot buy. If your family makes that little money, there is almost certainly no adult in your home who is employed full-time. That may simply be because jobs are scarce, but it also may be because your parent or parents have other obstacles to employment, such as disability, depression, or substance abuse. Statistically, you are likely being raised by a poorly educated, never-married single mother. There's also a good chance statistically that your caregiver has been reported to a child-welfare agency because of a suspicion of abuse or neglect.

We know from the neuroscientists and the psychologists that students growing up in these homes are more likely to have high ACE scores and less likely to have the kinds of secure attachment relationships with caregivers that buffer the effects of stress and trauma; this in turn means they likely have below-average executive-function skills and difficulty handling stressful situations. In the classroom, they are hampered by poor concentration, impaired social skills, an inability to sit still and follow directions, and what teachers perceive as misbehavior.

Despite these children's intense needs, school reformers have not been very successful at creating interventions that work for them; they have done much better at creating interventions that work for children from better-off low-income families, those making $41,000 a year. *No one* has found a reliable way to help deeply disadvantaged children, in fact. Instead, what we have created is a disjointed, ad hoc system of government agencies and programs that follow them haphazardly through their childhood and adolescence.

This dysfunctional pipeline starts in overcrowded Medicaid clinics and continues through social-service and child-welfare offices and hospital emergency rooms. Once students get to school, the system steers them into special education, remedial classes, and alternative schools, and then, for teenagers, there are GED programs and computer-assisted credit-recovery courses that too often allow them to graduate from high school without decent skills. Outside of school, the system includes foster homes, juvenile detention centers, and probation officers.

Few of the agencies in this system are particularly well run or well staffed (there is no Teach for America equivalent sending in waves of eager and idealistic young college graduates to work in them), and their efforts are rarely well coordinated. For the children and families involved, dealing with these agencies tends to be frustrating and alienating and often humiliating. The system as a whole is extremely expensive and wildly inefficient, and it has a very low rate of success; almost no one who passes through it as a child graduates from college or achieves any of the other markers of a happy and successful life: a good career, an intact family, a stable home.

But we could design an entirely different system for children who are dealing with deep and pervasive adversity at home. It might start at a comprehensive pediatric wellness center, like the one that Nadine Burke Harris is now working to construct in Bayview–Hunters Point, with trauma-focused care and social-service support woven into every medical visit. It might continue with parenting interventions that increase the chance of secure attachment, like Attachment and Biobehavioral Catch-up, or ABC, the program developed at the

University of Delaware. In prekindergarten, it might involve a program like Tools of the Mind that promotes executive-function skills and self-regulation in young children. We'd want to make sure these students were in good schools, of course, not ones that track them into remedial classes but ones that challenge them to do high-level work. And whatever academic help they were getting in the classroom would need to be supplemented by social and psychological and character-building interventions outside the classroom, like the ones Elizabeth Dozier has brought to Fenger or the ones that a group called Turnaround for Children provides in several low-income schools in New York City and Washington, D.C. In high school, these students would benefit from some combination of what both One-Goal and KIPP Through College provide — a program that directs them toward higher education and tries to prepare them for college not only academically but also emotionally and psychologically.

A coordinated system like that, targeted at the 10 to 15 percent of students at the highest risk of failure, would be expensive, there's no doubt. But it would almost certainly be cheaper than the ad hoc system we have in place now. It would save not only lives but money, and not just in the long run, but right away.

5. The Politics of Disadvantage

Talking about the influence of family on the success and failure of poor children can be an uncomfortable proposition. Education reformers prefer to locate the main obstacles to success within the school system, and they take it as an article of faith that the solutions to those obstacles can be found in the classroom as well. Reform skeptics, by contrast, often blame out-of-school factors for the underperformance of low-income children, but when they list those factors — and I've read a lot of these lists — they tend to choose ones that don't have much to do with family functioning. Instead, they identify largely impersonal influences like toxins in the environment, food insecurity, inadequate health care and housing, and racial discrimination. All of those problems are genuine and important. But they don't accurately represent the biggest obstacles to academic success that poor children, especially very poor children, often face: a home and a community that create high levels of stress, and the absence of a secure relationship with a caregiver that would allow a child to manage that stress.

So when we're looking for root causes of poverty-related under-achievement, why do we tend to focus on the wrong culprits and ignore the ones that science tells us do the most damage? I think there are three reasons. The first is that the science itself is not well known or well understood, and part of why it's not well understood is that it is dense and hard to penetrate. Any time you need to use the term *hypothalamic-pituitary-adrenal* in order to make your point, you've got trouble.

Second, those of us who don't live in low-income homes are understandably uneasy talking about family dysfunction in those homes. It's rude to discuss other people's parenting practices in a critical way in public. It's especially rude when you're talking about parents who don't have the material advantages that you do. And when the person making the comments is white and the parents in question are black, everyone's anxiety level increases. This is a conversation that inevitably unearths painful issues in American politics and the American psyche.

Finally, there is the fact that the new science of adversity, in all its complexity, presents a real challenge to some deeply held political beliefs on both the left and the right. To liberals, the science is saying that conservatives are correct on one very important point: *character matters*. There is no antipoverty tool we can provide for disadvantaged young people that will be more valuable than the character strengths that Keitha Jones and Kewauna Lerma and James Black possess in such impressive quantities: conscientiousness, grit, resilience, perseverance, and optimism.

Where the typical conservative argument on poverty falls short is that it often stops right there: Character matters . . . and that's it. There's not much society can do until poor people shape up and somehow develop better character. In the meantime, the rest of us are off the hook. We can lecture poor people, and we can punish them if they don't behave the way we tell them to, but that's where our responsibility ends.

But in fact, this science suggests a very different reality. It says that the character strengths that matter so much to young people's success are not innate; they don't appear in us magically, as a result of good luck or good genes. And they are not simply a choice. They are rooted in brain chemistry, and they are molded, in measurable and predictable ways, by the environment in which children grow up. That means the rest of us — society as a whole — can do an enormous amount to influence their development in children. We now know a great deal about what kind of interventions will help children develop those strengths and skills, starting at birth and going all the way through college. Parents are an excellent vehicle for those interventions, but they are not the only vehicle. Transformative help also comes regularly from social workers, teachers, clergy members, pediatricians, and neighbors. We can argue about whether those interventions should be provided by the government or nonprofit organizations or religious institutions or a combination of the three. But what we can't argue anymore is that there's nothing we can do.

When advocates for a new way of thinking about children and disadvantage make their case, they often base it in economics: as a nation, we should change our approach to child development because it will save us money and improve the economy. Jack Shonkoff, the director of the Center on the Developing Child at Harvard, has argued persuasively that an effective program of support for parents of low-income children while their kids are young would be much less expensive and more effective than our current approach of paying later on for remedial education and job training. James Heckman has taken the math a step further, calculating that the Perry Preschool produced between seven and twelve dollars of tangible benefit to the American economy for every dollar that was invested in it.

But powerful though this economic case can be, the argument that resonates more with me is a purely personal one. When I spend time with young people growing up in adversity, I can't help but feel two things. First, a sense of anger for what they've already missed. When Kewauna talks about the feeling of being warehoused in the WINGS classroom in her Minnesota middle school, watching movies and eating popcorn while the other kids learned math and metaphors, I feel the way Elizabeth Spiegel felt when she realized how little James Black had been taught about the world beyond the chessboard: I get mad on Kewauna's behalf. She has to work twice as hard now as a result.

And to her credit, she *is* working twice as hard. Which leads to my second reaction: a feeling of admiration and hope when I watch young people making the difficult and often painful choice to follow a better path, to turn away from what might have seemed like their inevitable destiny. James and Keitha and Kewauna are all working far harder than I ever did as a teenager to remake themselves and improve their lives. And every day they pull themselves up one more rung on the ladder to a more successful future. But for the rest of us, it's not enough to just applaud their efforts and hope that someday, more young people follow their lead. They did not get onto that ladder alone. They are there only because someone helped them take the first step.

Acknowledgments

Gratitude is one of the seven character strengths that the teachers at KIPP and Riverdale are trying to nurture in their students, and I'm glad to have a chance to exercise it here for a few paragraphs: not enough space to thank all the people who helped me with this book, but enough to mention at least a few.

My reporting benefited from the generosity and wisdom of many scholars and researchers, but I am especially grateful to James Heckman, Clancy Blair, Nadine Burke Harris, and Angela Duckworth, who not only shared with me their deep knowledge of their own fields but also helped me see connections that transcended traditional academic and scientific boundaries: the links between developmental psychology and labor economics; between criminology and pediatric medicine; between stress hormones and school reform.

My thanks go as well to the educators who let me watch them work and took such great care in explaining why they did what they did, especially Elizabeth Spiegel, Jeff Nelson, David Levin, Elizabeth Dozier, Dominic Randolph, Tom Brunzell, K. C. Cohen, Michele Stefl, and Lanita Reed. Steve Gates might not describe himself as an educator, but I include him in this category as well; he certainly educated me, and his guidance and generosity enriched the time I spent in Roseland.

I'm very grateful to the dozens of young people in Chicago and New York and San Francisco who told me their stories and answered my questions about their lives with honesty, insight, and grace, especially Keitha Jones, Monisha Sullivan, Thomas Gaston, James Black, and Kewauna Lerma.

My thanks to everyone at Houghton Mifflin Harcourt who made this book a reality, especially my editor, Deanne Urmy, whose contributions are apparent on every page. I'm grateful to my agent, David McCormick, for his unwavering faith in this project, and to my speaking agent, Alia Hanna Habib, for all her support, encouragement, and advice. Thanks to Emmy Liss, who provided me with research assistance; she expanded my understanding of what it means for a child to grow up in deep disadvantage. Thanks to Charles William Wilson, who was intrepid and painstaking as he fact-checked much of the manuscript. I'm grateful as well to Katherine Bradley and her colleagues at the CityBridge Foundation for their help and support in the early stages of my reporting.

I'm indebted to the friends and colleagues who read drafts and sections of this work and offered me advice, including Matt Bai and James Forman Jr., as well as two outstanding magazine editors, Vera Titunik and Daniel Zalewski, who helped turn some of my reporting for this book into articles for the *New York Times Magazine* and *The New Yorker,* respectively. Two more editors, both indispensable: When I could not find my way into or out of a chapter, my first call was invariably to Joel Lovell, who always had a solution. And after I finished a first draft of the book, Ira Glass guided me through some critical revisions, reading and offering advice on multiple drafts; I felt lucky to have the benefit of his keen eyes and ears.

I send heartfelt thanks to the family and friends who offered support and counsel and welcome distraction along the way, including Susan Tough, Anne Tough, Allen Tough, Jack Hitt, Michael Pollan, Ethan Watters, Ann Clarke, Matt Klam, Kira Pollack, James Ryerson, Elana James, and Ilena Silverman.

Above all, my thanks go to Paula, Ellington, and Georgie, for their help, their support, and their love. In the acknowledgments of my last book, I promised Paula that this one would be easier, and it wasn't. But she persevered anyway, with patience and good humor and large helpings of grit. The research papers I immersed myself in while writing this book taught me a great deal about the transformative power of a family's love — but that knowledge is nothing compared to what I learn from her each day.

Notes on Sources

Introduction

xii *a program called Tools of the Mind:* For more on Tools of the Mind,
    see Paul Tough, "Can the Right Kinds of Play Teach Self-Control?,"
    New York Times Magazine, September 25, 2009.

xiii *the Rug Rat Race:* Garey Ramey and Valerie A. Ramey, *The Rug Rat
    Race* (Cambridge, MA: National Bureau of Economics Research,
    January 2010).

    "Age 3 is the sweet spot": Kate Zernike, "Fast-Tracking to Kindergar-
    ten?," *New York Times,* May 13, 2011.

    You can trace its contemporary rise: Carnegie Task Force on Meeting
    the Needs of Young Children, *Starting Points: Meeting the Needs of
    Our Youngest Children* (New York: Carnegie Corporation of New
    York, 1994).

xiv *One of the most famous of these studies:* Betty Hart and Todd R.
    Risley, *Meaningful Differences in the Everyday Experience of Young
    American Children* (Baltimore: Paul H. Brookes, 1995).

xviii *At age twenty-two, Heckman found:* James J. Heckman, John Eric
    Humphries, and Nicholas S. Mader, "The GED," in *Handbook of the
    Economics of Education,* vol. 3, eds. Eric A. Hanushek et al. (Ox-
    ford: Elsevier, 2011), 455, figure 9.16. For more on Heckman's GED
    research, see James J. Heckman, Jingjing Hsse, and Yona Rubinstein,

"The GED Is a 'Mixed Signal': The Effect of Cognitive and Non-Cognitive Skills on Human Capital and Labor Market Outcomes," unpublished paper, revised March 2002; and James J. Heckman and Yona Rubinstein, "The Importance of Noncognitive Skills: Lessons from the GED Testing Program," *American Economic Review* 91, no. 2 (May 2001).

xix *"Inadvertently, the GED has become a test"*: Pedro Carneiro and James J. Heckman, "Human Capital Policy," in *Inequality in America: What Role for Human Capital Policies?*, eds. James J. Heckman and Alan B. Krueger (Cambridge, MA: MIT Press, 2003), 141.

xx *the Perry students were more likely to graduate*: James J. Heckman, Seong Hyeok Moon, Rodrigo Pinto, Peter A. Savelyev, and Adam Yavitz, "The Rate of Return to the High/Scope Perry Preschool Program," *Journal of Public Economics* 94, nos. 1 and 2 (February 2010). For more on Perry, see James Heckman, Lena Malofeeva, Rodrigo Pinto, and Peter Savelyev, "Understanding the Mechanisms Through Which an Influential Early Childhood Program Boosted Adult Outcomes," unpublished paper, November 23, 2011.

xx *"personal behavior" and "social development"*: James Heckman, Lena Malofeeva, Rodrigo Pinto, and Peter Savelyev, "Enhancements in Noncognitive Capacities Explain Most of the Effects of the Perry Preschool Program," unpublished paper, January 13, 2010.

1. How to Fail (and How Not To)

3 *he placed Fenger in the most dire category*: Michael Martinez, "City's Schools Now Thinking Small," *Chicago Tribune*, September 20, 1996.
hiring an outside contractor: Lynn Schnaiberg, "Scores Up But Schools No Better," *Catalyst Chicago*, March 2001.
He created a freshman academy: Martinez, "City's Schools."
a math-and-science academy: Jody Temkin, "Last-Minute Decisions Keep Fenger on Its Toes," *Catalyst Chicago*, October 1999.
he made Fenger a magnet school: Michael Martinez, "Magnet Programs to Expand in City Schools," *Chicago Tribune*, March 16, 2001.
Duncan chose Fenger as one of the pilot schools: David Mendell, "City Dropouts Target of Grant," *Chicago Tribune*, April 18, 2006.
the total bill for the citywide project: Sarah Karp, "If at First You Don't Succeed . . . Turnaround and Go Big," *Catalyst Chicago*, January 16, 2009.

3 *"a truly historic day"*: Mendell, "City Dropouts."

4 *Fenger was switched over*: Karp, "If at First"; Sarah Karp, "Putting the

Brakes on High School Transformation," *Catalyst Chicago,* April 28, 2009.

5 *eighty-three school-age teenagers were murdered:* Sarah Karp, "Youth Murders Up, Money for School Violence Prevention in Doubt," *Catalyst Chicago,* January 28, 2011.

9 *"Turning Gold into Lead":* English translation of Vincent Felitti, "Belastungen in der Kindheit und Gesundheit im Erwachsenenalter: die Verwandlung von Gold in Blei," *Zeitschrift für Psychosomatische Medizin und Psychotherapie* 48 (2002).

10 *Over the course of a few years:* Shanta R. Dube, et al., "Childhood Abuse, Household Dysfunction, and the Risk of Attempted Suicide Throughout the Life Span," *Journal of the American Medical Association* 286, no. 24 (December 26, 2001).

two-thirds of the patients had experienced: Ibid.

they "stunned us": Robert Anda, "The Health and Social Impact of Growing Up with Adverse Childhood Experiences," unpublished paper, www.acestudy.org.

Compared to people with no history of ACEs: Robert Anda, Vincent Felitti, et al., "The Enduring Effects of Abuse and Related Adverse Experiences in Childhood: A Convergence of Evidence from Neurobiology and Epidemiology," *European Archives of Psychiatry and Clinical Neurosciences* 56 (2006). For more on the ACE data, see Vincent J. Felitti and Robert F. Anda, "The Relationship of Adverse Childhood Experiences to Adult Medical Disease, Psychiatric Disorders, and Sexual Behavior: Implications for Healthcare," in *The Hidden Epidemic: The Impact of Early Life Trauma on Health and Disease,* eds. Ruth A. Lanius, Eric Vermetten, and Clare Pain (Cambridge: Cambridge University Press, 2010); Valerie J. Edwards et al., "The Wide-Ranging Health Outcomes of Adverse Childhood Experiences," in *Child Victimization,* eds. K. A. Kendall-Tackett and S. M. Giaromoni (Kingston, NJ: Civic Research Institute, 2005); and Vincent J. Felitti, Paul Jay Fink, Ralph E. Fishkin, and Robert F. Anda, "An Epidemiologic Validation of Psychoanalytic Concepts: Evidence from the Adverse Childhood Experiences (ACE) Study of Childhood Trauma and Violence," in *Trauma und Gewalt* 1 (2006).

twice as likely to smoke: Anda, Felitti, et al., "Enduring Effects."

11 *twice as likely to have heart disease:* Edwards et al., "Wide-Ranging Health Outcomes."

twice as likely to have liver disease: Maxia Dong et al., "Adverse Childhood Experiences and Self-Reported Liver Disease," *Archives of Internal Medicine* 163 (September 8, 2003).

thirty times more likely to have attempted suicide: Dube et al., "Childhood Abuse."

forty-six times more likely to have injected drugs: Felitti and Anda, "Relationship of Adverse Childhood Experiences."

their risk of ischemic heart disease: Felitti et al., "Epidemiologic Validation."

12 *When a potential danger appears:* For this description of stress function, I'm relying on Robert M. Sapolsky, *Why Zebras Don't Get Ulcers* (New York: St. Martin's Press, 1994); Seymour Levine, "Stress: An Historical Perspective," in *Handbook of Stress and the Brain, Part 1: The Neurobiology of Stress,* eds. T. Steckler, N. H. Kalin, and J.M.H.M. Reul (Amsterdam: Elsevier, 2005); and Center on the Developing Child at Harvard University, *The Foundations of Lifelong Health Are Built in Early Childhood* (Cambridge, MA: Center on the Developing Child, 2010).

13 *Bruce McEwen, a neuroendocrinologist:* My knowledge of Bruce McEwen's work comes from conversations with him as well as from Bruce S. McEwen, "Protection and Damage from Acute and Chronic Stress," *Annals of the New York Academy of Sciences* 1032 (2004); Sapolsky, *Zebras Don't Get Ulcers;* and Teresa Seeman et al., "Modeling Multisystem Biological Risk in Young Adults: The Coronary Artery Risk Development in Young Adults Study," *American Journal of Human Biology* 22 (2010).

16 *researchers, led by Teresa Seeman:* Seeman et al., "Modeling Multisystem Biological Risk"; and Teresa Seeman et al., "Socio-Economic Differentials in Peripheral Biology: Cumulative Allostatic Load," *Annals of the New York Academy of Sciences* 1186 (2010).

17 *Among her patients with an ACE score of 0:* Nadine J. Burke, Julia L. Hellman, Brandon G. Scott, Carl F. Weems, and Victor G. Carrion, "The Impact of Adverse Childhood Experiences on an Urban Pediatric Population," *Child Abuse and Neglect* 35, no. 6 (June 2011).

46 percent of kindergarten teachers: Sara E. Rimm-Kaufman, Robert C. Pianta, and Martha J. Cox, "Teachers' Judgments of Problems in the Transition to Kindergarten," *Early Childhood Research Quarterly* 15, no. 2 (2000).

Head Start teachers reported: Janis B. Kupersmidt, Donna Bryant, and Michael T. Willoughby, "Prevalence of Aggressive Behaviors Among Preschoolers in Head Start and Community Child Care Programs," *Behavioral Disorders* 26, no. 1 (November 2000).

18 *compared them to a team of air traffic controllers:* Center on the Developing Child at Harvard University, "Building the Brain's 'Air Traffic Control' System: How Early Experiences Shape the Development

of Executive Function," working paper 11 (Cambridge, MA: Center on the Developing Child, February 2011).

19 *two researchers at Cornell University:* Gary W. Evans and Michelle A. Schamberg, "Childhood Poverty, Chronic Stress, and Adult Working Memory," *Proceedings of the National Academy of Sciences* 106, no. 16 (2009).

21 *something uniquely out of balance about the adolescent brain:* Laurence Steinberg, "A Behavioral Scientist Looks at the Science of Adolescent Brain Development," *Brain and Cognition* 72 (2010).

two separate neurological systems: Laurence Steinberg, "A Social Neuroscience Perspective on Adolescent Risk-Taking," *Developmental Review* 28, no. 1 (March 2008); Laurence Steinberg, "A Dual Systems Model of Adolescent Risk-Taking," *Developmental Psychobiology* 52, no. 3 (April 2010).

26 *Researchers from Northwestern University:* Karen M. Abram et al., "Posttraumatic Stress Disorder and Trauma in Youth in Juvenile Detention," *Archives of General Psychiatry* 61 (April 2004).

Academically, they were severely behind the curve: Roseanna Ander, Philip J. Cook, Jens Ludwig, and Harold Pollack, *Gun Violence Among School-Age Youth in Chicago* (Chicago: University of Chicago Crime Lab, 2009).

28 *researchers in Meaney's lab noticed a curious thing:* Dong Liu et al., "Maternal Care, Hippocampal Glucocorticoid Receptors, and Hypothalamic-Pituitary-Adrenal Responses to Stress," *Science* 277, no. 5332 (September 12, 1997).

29 *Researchers counted every instance of maternal licking and grooming:* Christian Caldji et al., "Maternal Care During Infancy Regulates the Development of Neural Systems Mediating the Expression of Fearfulness in the Rat," *Proceedings of the National Academy of Sciences* 95, no. 9 (April 28, 1998).

30 *a number of cross-fostering experiments:* Christian Caldji, Josie Diorio, and Michael J. Meaney, "Variations in Maternal Care in Infancy Regulate the Development of Stress Reactivity," *Biological Psychiatry* 48, no. 12 (December 15, 2000).

31 *It goes much deeper than that:* Ian C. G. Weaver et al., "Epigenetic Programming by Maternal Behavior," *Nature Neuroscience* 7, no. 8 (August 2004); Robert M. Sapolsky, "Mothering Style and Methylation," *Nature Neuroscience* 7, no. 8 (August 2004).

using the brain tissue of human suicides: Patrick O. McGowan et al., "Epigenetic Regulation of the Glucocorticoid Receptor in Human Brain Associates with Child Abuse," *Nature Neuroscience* 12, no. 3 (March 2009); Steven E. Hyman, "How Adversity Gets Under the

Skin," *Nature Neuroscience* 12, no. 3 (March 2009); Hanna Hoag, "The Painted Brain: How Our Lives Colour Our Minds," *Montreal Gazette*, January 18, 2011.

32 *Clancy Blair, a researcher in psychology at NYU:* Clancy Blair et al., "Salivary Cortisol Mediates Effects of Poverty and Parenting on Executive Functions in Early Childhood," *Child Development* 82, no. 6 (November/December 2011).

When mothers scored high on measures of responsiveness: Clancy Blair et al., "Maternal and Child Contributions to Cortisol Response to Emotional Arousal in Young Children from Low-Income, Rural Communities," *Developmental Psychology* 44, no. 4 (2008). See also Clancy Blair, "Stress and the Development of Self-Regulation in Context," *Child Development Perspectives* 4, no. 3 (December 2010).

Gary Evans, the Cornell scientist: Gary W. Evans et al., "Cumulative Risk, Maternal Responsiveness, and Allostatic Load Among Young Adolescents," *Developmental Psychology* 43, no. 2 (2007).

33 *Attachment theory was developed in the 1950s and 1960s:* Robert Karen, *Becoming Attached: First Relationships and How They Shape Our Capacity to Love* (New York: Oxford University Press, 1998).

35 *Egeland and Sroufe began tracking this group:* My knowledge of the Minnesota study comes mostly from conversations with Byron Egeland, Alan Sroufe, Andrew Collins, and other researchers; from L. Alan Sroufe, Byron Egeland, Elizabeth A. Carlson, and W. Andrew Collins, *The Development of the Person: The Minnesota Study of Risk and Adaptation from Birth to Adulthood* (New York: Guilford Press, 2005); from Alan Sroufe and Daniel Siegel, "The Verdict Is In: The Case for Attachment Theory," *Psychotherapy Networker* (March/April 2011); and from Karen, *Becoming Attached*.

two-thirds of children in the Minnesota study: Sroufe et al., *Development of the Person*, 132.

36 *When teachers ranked students on indicators of dependency:* Ibid., 133.

When teachers and other children were surveyed: Ibid., 139–41.

more self-confident, more curious: L. Alan Sroufe, "Attachment and Development: A Prospective, Longitudinal Study from Birth to Adulthood," *Attachment and Human Development* 7, no. 4 (December 2005): 357.

early parental care predicted which students would graduate: Sroufe et al., *Development of the Person*, 211, 228; Shane Jimerson, Byron Egeland, L. Alan Sroufe, and Betty Carlson, "A Prospective Longitudinal Study of High School Dropouts Examining Multiple Predictors Across Development," *Journal of School Psychology* 38, no. 6 (2000).

could have predicted with 77 percent accuracy: Sroufe et al., *Development of the Person,* 210; Jimerson et al., "A Prospective Longitudinal Study."

39 *In one study, Dante Cicchetti:* Dante Cicchetti, Fred A. Rogosch, and Sheree L. Toth, "Fostering Secure Attachment in Infants in Maltreating Families Through Preventive Interventions," *Development and Psychopathology* 18, no. 3 (2006).

An intervention called Multidimensional: Megan R. Gunnar, Philip A. Fisher, and the Early Experience, Stress, and Prevention Network, "Bringing Basic Research on Early Experience and Stress Neurobiology to Bear on Preventive Interventions for Neglected and Maltreated Children," *Development and Psychopathology* 18, no. 3 (2006).

Attachment and Biobehavioral Catch-up: Mary Dozier et al., "Developing Evidence-Based Interventions for Foster Children: An Example of a Randomized Clinical Trial with Infants and Toddlers," *Journal of Social Issues* 62, no. 4 (2006).

40 *After just ten home visits:* Kristin Bernard et al., "Enhancing Attachment Organization Among Maltreated Children: Results of a Randomized Clinical Trial," *Child Development* 83, no. 2 (March 2012).

42 *Heather Mac Donald, an Olin fellow:* Heather Mac Donald, "Chicago's Real Crime Story," *City Journal,* Winter 2010.

2. How to Build Character

49 *who won them (and their parents) over:* Jay Mathews, *Work Hard. Be Nice.: How Two Inspired Teachers Created the Most Promising Schools in America* (Chapel Hill, NC: Algonquin Books of Chapel Hill, 2009), 160.

the highest scores of any school in the Bronx: Abby Goodnough, "Structure and Basics Bring South Bronx School Acclaim," *New York Times,* October 20, 1999.

50 *a front-page story on KIPP in the* New York Times: Jodi Wilgoren, "Seeking to Clone Schools of Success for the Poor," *New York Times,* August 16, 2000.

completed a four-year college degree: KIPP pays particular attention to the six-year graduation figure because it is the generally accepted benchmark for college-graduation statistics. As of the spring of 2012, nine years after the students in KIPP Academy's Class of 2003 were scheduled to graduate from high school, two members of the cohort are still enrolled in a BA program and on track to graduate this year, which will put the class's total graduation rate at 26 percent.

Three other students have earned two-year degrees. The remaining twenty-five students have no postsecondary degree.

53 Learned Optimism, *a book by Martin Seligman:* Martin E. P. Seligman, *Learned Optimism: How to Change Your Mind and Your Life* (New York: A. A. Knopf, 1991).

a "severe low mood": Ibid., 13.

54 *permanent, personal, and pervasive:* Ibid., 44.

58 *a "manual of the sanities":* Christopher Peterson and Martin E. P. Seligman, *Character Strengths and Virtues: A Handbook and Classification* (Oxford: Oxford University Press, 2004), 4.

a "science of good character": Ibid., 9.

works from Aristotle to Confucius: Ibid., 15.

59 *"Virtues," they wrote, "are much more interesting":* Ibid., 10.

"the good life": Ibid., 4.

a big national push for character education: See, e.g., Roger Rosenblatt, "Teaching Johnny to Be Good," *New York Times Magazine,* April 30, 1995; and Charles Helwig, Elliot Turiel, and Larry Nucci, "Character Education After the Bandwagon Has Gone," paper presented in L. Nucci (chair), "Developmental Perspectives and Approaches to Character Education," symposium conducted at the meeting of the American Educational Research Association, Chicago, March 1997.

60 *A national evaluation of character-education programs:* Social and Character Development Research Consortium, *Efficacy of Schoolwide Programs to Promote Social and Character Development and Reduce Problem Behavior in Elementary School Children* (Washington, DC: National Center for Education Research, Institute of Education Sciences, U.S. Department of Education, 2010); Sarah D. Spark, "Character Education Found to Fall Short in Federal Study," *Education Week,* October 21, 2010.

In his 2008 book: David Whitman, *Sweating the Small Stuff: Inner-City Schools and the New Paternalism* (Washington, DC: Thomas B. Fordham Institute, 2008).

"not just how to think but how to act": Ibid., 3.

61 *"The problem, I think, is not only the schools":* Martin E. P. Seligman, *Flourish: A Visionary New Understanding of Happiness and Well-Being* (New York: Free Press, 2011), 103.

For her first-year thesis: Angela Lee Duckworth and Martin E. P. Seligman, "Self-Discipline Outdoes IQ in Predicting Academic Performance of Adolescents," *Psychological Science* 16, no. 12 (2005).

62 *an ingenious experiment to test the willpower:* Walter Mischel, "From Good Intentions to Willpower," in *The Psychology of Action: Link-*

ing Cognition and Motivation to Behavior, eds. Peter M. Gollwitzer and John A. Burgh (New York: Guilford Press, 1996); Jonah Lehrer, "Don't!," *New Yorker*, May 18, 2009.

Children who had been able to wait for fifteen minutes: Lehrer, "Don't!"

63 *think of the marshmallow as a puffy round cloud:* Walter Mischel, Yuichi Shoda, and Monica L. Rodriguez, "Delay of Gratification in Children," *Science* 244, no. 4907 (May 26, 1989).

64 *a researcher named Calvin Edlund:* Calvin V. Edlund, "The Effect on the Behavior of Children, as Reflected in the IQ Scores, When Reinforced After Each Correct Response," *Journal of Applied Behavior Analysis* 5, no. 3 (Fall 1972).

65 *two researchers from the University of South Florida:* Joy Clingman and Robert L. Fowler, "The Effects of Primary Reward on the I.Q. Performance of Grade-School Children as a Function of Initial I.Q. Level," *Journal of Applied Behavior Analysis* 9, no. 1 (Spring 1976).

66 *giving blood donors a small financial stipend:* Steven D. Levitt and Stephen J. Dubner, *Freakonomics: A Rogue Economist Explores the Hidden Side of Everything* (New York: HarperCollins, 2005).

He tested several different incentive programs: Roland G. Fryer Jr., "Financial Incentives and Student Achievement: Evidence from Randomized Trials," *Quarterly Journal of Economics* 126 (2011); Roland G. Fryer, "Teacher Incentives and Student Achievement: Evidence from New York City Public Schools," NBER Working Paper 16850 (Cambridge, MA: National Bureau of Economic Research, March 2011); Roland G. Fryer Jr., "Aligning Student, Parent, and Teacher Incentives: Evidence from Houston Public Schools," NBER Working Paper 17752 (Cambridge, MA: National Bureau of Economic Research, January 2012); Amanda Ripley, "Should Kids Be Bribed to Do Well in School?," *Time* (April 8, 2010); Elizabeth Green, "Study: $75M Teacher Pay Initiative Did Not Improve Achievement," *Gotham Schools* (March 7, 2011).

67 *Segal wanted to test how personality:* Carmit Segal, "Working When No One Is Watching: Motivation, Test Scores, and Economic Success," *Management Science* (in press).

71 *Big Five conscientiousness was embraced:* See, e.g., "Introduction: Personality and Industrial and Organizational Psychology," in *Personality Psychology in the Workplace*, eds. Brent W. Roberts and Robert Hogan (Washington, DC: American Psychological Association, 2001); and Robert Hogan, *Personality and the Fate of Organizations* (Mahwah, NJ: Lawrence Erlbaum Associates, 2007).

it predicts so many outcomes: Brent W. Roberts et al., "The Power of Personality: The Comparative Validity of Personality Traits, So-cioeconomic Status, and Cognitive Ability for Predicting Impor-tant Life Outcomes," *Perspectives on Psychological Science* 2 (2007); Angela Lee Duckworth and Kelly M. Allred, "Temperament in the Classroom," in *Handbook of Temperament*, eds. R. L. Shiner and M. Zentner (New York: Guilford Press, in press).

In their 1976 book: Samuel Bowles and Herbert Gintis, *Schooling in Capitalist America: Educational Reform and the Contradictions of Economic Life* (New York: Basic Books, 1976).

72 *"to be properly subordinate":* Ibid., 130.

"conscientious, responsible, insistently orderly": Ibid., 135.

They gave low ratings to employees: Ibid., 137–38.

73 *"there is no true disadvantage":* Peterson and Seligman, *Character Strengths and Virtues,* 515.

Overcontrolled people are "excessively constrained": Tera D. Letzring, Jack Block, and David C. Funder, "Ego-Control and Ego-Resiliency: Generalization of Self-Report Scales Based on Personality Descrip-tions from Acquaintances, Clinicians, and the Self," *Journal of Re-search in Personality* 39, no. 4 (August 2005).

In 2011, that pool of evidence grew further: Terrie E. Moffitt et al., "A Gradient of Childhood Self-Control Predicts Health, Wealth, and Public Safety," *Proceedings of the National Academy of Science* 108, no. 7 (February 2011). See also Paul Solman, "Self-Controlled Kids Prosper as Adults: 'Fatalistically Depressing'?," *PBS NewsHour,* June 13, 2011.

74 *Duckworth developed a test to measure grit:* Angela Lee Duckworth and Patrick D. Quinn, "Development and Validation of the Short Grit Scale (Grit-S)," *Journal of Personality Assessment* 91, no. 2 (2009); and Angela L. Duckworth, Christopher Peterson, Michael D. Matthews, and Dennis R. Kelly, "Grit: Perseverance and Passion for Long-Term Goals," *Journal of Personality and Social Psychology* 92, no. 6 (2007).

78 *a national organization called the Character Education Partner-ship:* Character Education Partnership, *Performance Values: Why They Matter and What Schools Can Do to Foster Their Development* (Washington, DC: Character Education Partnership, April 2008).

82 *"unexpectedly high rates of emotional problems":* Madeline Levine, *The Price of Privilege: How Parental Pressure and Material Advantage Are Creating a Generation of Disconnected and Unhappy Kids* (New York: HarperCollins, 2006), 21.

"intense feelings of shame and hopelessness": Ibid., 30.

83 *To Luthar's surprise, she found the affluent teenagers:* Suniya S. Luthar and Chris C. Sexton, "The High Price of Affluence," in *Advances in Child Development,* vol. 32, ed. R. V. Kail (San Diego: Academic Press, 2004), 143; Suniya S. Luthar and Karen D'Avanzo, "Contextual Factors in Substance Use: A Study of Suburban and Inner-City Adolescents," *Development and Psychopathology* 11, no. 4 (1999).

in an even more affluent town: Luthar and Sexton, "High Price of Affluence," 134.

multiple persistent problems: Suniya S. Luthar and Shawn J. Latendresse, "Children of the Affluent: Challenges to Well-Being," *Current Directions in Psychological Science* 14, no. 1 (February 2005): 51.

"excessive achievement pressures and isolation from parents": Luthar and Sexton, "High Price of Affluence," 135.

Kindlon discovered disproportionately high levels of anxiety: Dan Kindlon, *Too Much of a Good Thing: Raising Children of Character in an Indulgent Age* (New York: Hyperion, 2001), 10.

84 *parents making more than one million dollars a year:* Ibid., 18, 246.

87 *"tell students exactly how they are expected to behave":* Whitman, *Sweating the Small Stuff,* 3.

some of Levin's harsher moments of discipline: Mathews, *Work Hard,* 214.

88 *"models an atmosphere of punitive dependence":* Tom Brunzell, "Kaboom! Confronting Student Resistance at the Moment of Impact: A Case Study of KIPP Infinity Charter School," unpublished thesis (December 2006), 1.

Only 24 percent of the incoming students: Ibid., 20.

91 *"before puberty, but late enough in childhood":* Seligman, *Learned Optimism* (second edition), ix.

93 *"creates a strong association between future and reality":* Angela Lee Duckworth, Teri Kirby, Gabriele Oettingen, and Anton Gollwitzer, "Mental Contrasting with Implementation Intentions Improves Academic Performance among Economically Disadvantaged Children," *Journal of Applied Developmental Psychology* (in press).

Oettingen has demonstrated the effectiveness: Ibid., 7.

94 *"provide structure, preparing us for encounters":* David A. Kessler, *The End of Overeating: Taking Control of the Insatiable American Appetite* (New York: Rodale, 2009), 190.

96 *before trying a ten-hole mini golf course:* Jeff Stone, Christian I. Lynch, Mike Sjomeling, and John M. Darley, "Stereotype Threat Effects on Black and White Athletic Performance," *Journal of Personality and Social Psychology* 77, no. 6 (December 1999).

When people in their sixties: Claude Steele, *Whistling Vivaldi: And Other Clues to How Stereotypes Affect Us* (New York: W. W. Norton, 2010), 99.

97 *the malleability of intelligence:* See, e.g., Joshua Aronson, Carrie B. Fried, and Catherine Good, "Reducing the Effects of Stereotype Threat on African American College Students by Shaping Theories of Intelligence," *Journal of Experimental Social Psychology* 38, no. 2 (March 2002).

Dweck divides people into two types: Carol S. Dweck, *Mindset: The New Psychology of Success* (New York: Ballantine Books, 2008).

students' mindsets predict their academic trajectories: Lisa S. Blackwell, Kali H. Trzesniewski, and Carol S. Dweck, "Implicit Theories of Intelligence Predict Achievement across an Adolescent Transition: A Longitudinal Study and an Intervention," *Child Development* 78, no. 1 (January/February 2007): 251.

a growth-mindset message: Catherine Good, Joshua Aronson, and Michael Inzlicht, "Improving Adolescents' Standardized Test Performance: An Intervention to Reduce the Effects of Stereotype Threat," *Applied Developmental Psychology* 24, no. 6 (December 2003).

3. How to Think

107 *after I read an article in the* New York Times: Dylan Loeb McClain, "For School, National Chess Champions in 3 Grades," *New York Times,* December 20, 2008.

108 *"a hard-charging bunch of 10-to-12-year-olds":* Mark Jacobson, "Mr. Times and His Knights of the Square Table," *New York,* May 21, 2005.

Take a look at the team winners: 2010 National K–12 Championships, United States Chess Federation website; see http://www.uschess.org/tournaments/2010/k12/?page=RESULTS.

112 *"finest chess playing entity on the planet":* Bruce Weber, "Swift and Slashing, Computer Topples Kasparov," *New York Times,* May 12, 1997.

Newsweek *had run a story:* Steven Levy, "Man vs. Machine," *Newsweek,* May 5, 1997.

"I'm a human being": Weber, "Swift and Slashing."

113 *what he called the Levitt equation:* Jonathan Levitt, *Genius in Chess: Discover and Develop Your Chess Talent* (Seattle: International Chess Enterprises, 1997), 40.

"completely misguided": Jonathan Rowson, "Beyond the Illusion of 'Talent,'" *New in Chess,* June 2009.

"*Most of the major academic studies of chess*": Jonathan Rowson, *The Seven Deadly Chess Sins* (London: Gambit Publications, 2000), 16.

"*your ability to recognize and utilize your emotions*": Ibid., 17.

116 "*I am such a stupid retarded disgusting mindless child*": Elizabeth Vicary, "North American Open Round Two: Why Am I Such a Huge Baby?," Elizabeth Vicary's Blog, December 31, 2007, http://lizzyknowsall.blogspot.com/2007/12/north-american-open-round-two-why-am-i.html. (Elizabeth Spiegel's maiden name was Vicary. She was married in 2011.)

118 "*I am almost completely numb*": Elizabeth Vicary, "I Hate Myself," Elizabeth Vicary's Blog, July 13, 2008, http://lizzyknowsall.blogspot.com/2008/07/i-hate-myself.html.

"*he put his arm around me*": Elizabeth Vicary, "My Weekend: A Date, a Saturday Tournament, the Bus to Saratoga Springs," Elizabeth Vicary's Blog, March 2, 2009, http://lizzyknowsall.blogspot.com/2009/03/my-weekend-date-saturday-tournament-bus.html.

119 "*The first day and a half was pretty bad*": Elizabeth Vicary, "Thoughts on Girls, High School Nationals," Elizabeth Vicary's Blog, April 20, 2010, http://lizzyknowsall.blogspot.com/2010/04/thoughts-on-girls-high-school-nationals.html.

126 *One of James's half brothers was convicted*: Dylan Loeb McClain, "One Move Ahead of Opponents, and Two Ahead of Trouble," *New York Times* City Room Blog, June 28, 2011.

130 "*When it comes to ambition*": Aaron and Claire Summerscale, *Interview with a Grandmaster* (London: Everyman Chess, 2001), 126.

131 *Inspired by these words:* Matan Prilleltensky, "Choosing to Break 2200," *Chess Life Online,* January 15, 2011.

132 "*Chess is a creative and beautiful pursuit*": Aaron and Claire Summerscale, *Interview,* 128.

Malcolm Gladwell brought to popular attention: Malcolm Gladwell, *Outliers: The Story of Success* (Boston: Little, Brown and Company, 2008).

133 *the typical grand master had started playing at seven:* K. Anders Ericsson, Ralf Th. Krampe, and Clemens Tesch-Romer, "The Role of Deliberate Practice in the Acquisition of Expert Performance," *Psychological Review* 100, no. 3 (1993).

Polgar was single and childless: Carlin Flora, "The Grandmaster Experiment," *Psychology Today,* July 1, 2005.

Each girl began studying chess: David Shenk, *The Immortal Game: A History of Chess* (New York: Anchor Books, 2007), 132.

134 *they were installed in an apartment in Brighton Beach*: Fred Waitz-kin, "A Father's Pawn," *New York Times Magazine,* May 13, 1990.

    got a degree from a Long Island law school: Dylan Loeb McClain, "A Chess Master Returns Older, and Maybe Wiser," *New York Times,* January 27, 2008.

136 *Csikszentmihalyi studied what he called optimal experiences:* Mihaly Csikszentmihalyi, *Flow: The Psychology of Optimal Experience* (New York: Harper and Row, 1990), 3.

    "when a person's body or mind is stretched to its limits": Ibid.

    "the concentration is like breathing": Ibid., 53–54.

    physiological changes among expert chess players: Robert M. Sapol-sky, *Why Zebras Don't Get Ulcers* (New York: St. Martin's Press, 1994), 419–20.

137 *what they remembered were patterns, vectors, even moods:* My knowledge of Binet's chess research comes from Shenk, *Immortal Game;* Philip E. Ross, "The Expert Mind," *Scientific American,* August 2006; and Adriaan D. de Groot, *Thought and Choice in Chess* (Amsterdam: Amsterdam Academic Archive, 2008).

    "a stirring world of sensations": Shenk, *Immortal Game,* 127.

138 *In fact, de Groot found:* Ross, "The Expert Mind."

140 *In Wason's study, only one in five participants:* Michelle Cowley and Ruth M. J. Byrne, "When Falsification Is the Only Path to Truth," unpublished paper, 2004.

    Cowley and Byrne then used a chess-analysis program: Michelle Cowley and Ruth M. J. Byrne, "Chess Masters' Hypothesis Testing," unpublished paper, 2004.

    they tended to fall prey to confirmation bias: Ibid.; Mark Peplow, "Science Secret of Grand Masters Revealed," *Nature,* August 6, 2004; Jonathan Rowson, *Chess for Zebras: Thinking Differently about Black and White* (London: Gambit Publications, 2005), 35–36.

144 *"It was a very beautiful game"*: Elizabeth Vicary, "A Game That Made Me Cry," Elizabeth Vicary's Blog, May 3, 2011, http://lizzyknowsall. blogspot.com/2011/05/game-that-made-me-cry.html.

145 *"Imagine how frustrating that must be"*: Elizabeth Vicary, "James Black's Master Celebration Party," Elizabeth Vicary's Blog, September 5, 2011, http://lizzyknowsall.blogspot.com/2011/09/james-blacks-master-celebration-party.html.

4. How to Succeed

148 *As recently as the mid-1990s:* Organisation for Economic Co-Operation and Development, *Education at a Glance: OECD Indicators*

(Paris: OECD Centre for Educational Research and Innovation, 1995), 20.

the United States has fallen from first: Organisation for Economic Co-Operation and Development, *Education at a Glance 2011: OECD Indicators* (Paris: OECD Publishing, 2011), 40, table A1.3a, tertiary-type-A results. (These figures are for 2009, the most recent available. The United States was tied for twelfth in this category with Japan.)

it has just been growing very slowly: Ibid., 69, table A3.2.

In 1976, 24 percent of Americans: "Percent of People 25 Years and Over Who Have Completed High School or College, by Race, Hispanic Origin and Sex: Selected Years 1940 to 2010," U.S. Census Bureau, Current Population Survey, Educational Attainment, table A-2, http://www.census.gov/hhes/socdemo/education/data/cps/historical/index.html.

149 *the rate among the most disadvantaged young Americans:* William G. Bowen, Matthew M. Chingos, and Michael S. McPherson, *Crossing the Finish Line: Completing College at America's Public Universities* (Princeton, NJ: Princeton University Press, 2009), 27. Other scholars believe that college-completion rates have been rising for disadvantaged students, though more slowly than they have been rising for wealthy students. See, e.g., Martha J. Bailey and Susan M. Dynarski, "Gains and Gaps: Changing Inequality in U.S. College Entry and Completion," NBER Working Paper 17633 (Cambridge, MA: National Bureau of Economic Research, December 2011).

But between about 1925 and 1945: Claudia Goldin and Lawrence Katz, *The Race Between Education and Technology* (Cambridge, MA: Harvard University Press, 2008), 248.

"upward mobility with regard to education": Ibid., 290.

"Each generation of Americans": Ibid., 289.

education-policy types who concerned themselves: David Leonhardt, "The College Dropout Boom," *New York Times,* May 24, 2005; Sarah Turner, "Going to College and Finishing College: Explaining Different Educational Outcomes," in *College Choices: The Economics of Where to Go, When to Go, and How to Pay for It,* ed. Caroline M. Hoxby (Chicago: University of Chicago Press, 2004), 14; and Tamar Lewin, "Once a Leader, U.S. Lags in College Degrees," *New York Times,* July 23, 2010.

150 *the United States still ranks a respectable eighth:* OECD, *Education at a Glance 2011,* 316, table C2.1.

But in college completion: Organisation for Economic Co-Operation and Development, *Education at a Glance 2008: OECD Indicators* (Paris: OECD Publishing, 2008), 96, chart A4.2; 92, chart A4.1.

can now expect to earn 83 percent more: David Leonhardt, "Even for Cashiers, College Pays Off," *New York Times,* June 25, 2011.

among the highest in the developed world: OECD, *Education at a Glance 2011,* 150, table A8.2a.

it has risen sharply: Goldin and Katz, *The Race,* 290, figure 8.1.

American college graduates earned just 40 percent more: Leonhardt, "Even for Cashiers."

"is leaving large amounts of money": Goldin and Katz, *The Race,* 325.

151 *data covering about two hundred thousand students:* David Leonhardt, "Colleges Are Failing in Graduation Rates," *New York Times,* September 9, 2009.

Americans' natural tendency toward "educational romanticism": Charles Murray, *Real Education: Four Simple Truths for Bringing America's Schools Back to Reality* (New York: Crown Forum, 2008), 11.

"a fog of wishful thinking": Ibid., 12.

152 *students who had those same lofty academic credentials:* Bowen, Chingos, and McPherson, *Finish Line,* 104, 110.

the most accurate predictor of whether a student: Ibid., 113.

he explains that the SAT was invented: Nicholas Lemann, *The Big Test: The Secret History of the American Meritocracy* (New York: Farrar, Straus and Giroux, 2000).

high-school grades turned out to be excellent predictors: Bowen, Chingos, and McPherson, *Finish Line,* 122.

153 *"Students with very good high school grades":* Ibid.

And when Angela Duckworth: Angela Duckworth, Patrick Quinn, and Eli Tsukayama, "What No Child Left Behind Leaves Behind: The Roles of IQ and Self-Control in Predicting Standardized Achievement Test Scores and Report Card Grades," *Journal of Educational Psychology,* in press, 2011.

"high school grades reveal much more": Bowen, Chingos, and McPherson, *Finish Line,* 123.

154 *Alex Kotlowitz's book:* Alex Kotlowitz, *There Are No Children Here: The Story of Two Boys Growing Up in the Other America* (New York: Anchor Books, 1991).

155 *contrasting the "superfluity of opportunity":* Jonathan Kozol, *Savage Inequalities: Children in America's Schools* (New York: Crown Publishers, 1991), 67.

"shunned—or, probably, shut down": Ibid., 68.

156 *read a front-page story:* Jodi S. Cohen and Darnell Little, "Of 100 Chicago Public School Freshmen, Six Will Get a College Degree," *Chicago Tribune,* April 21, 2006. After the *Tribune* article came out, the consortium report was updated and corrected to show that eight of every one hundred Chicago high-school freshmen would earn a college degree, not six of every one hundred.

just eight of every one hundred students: Melissa Roderick, Jenny Nagaoka, and Elaine M. Allensworth, *From High School to the Future* (Chicago: Consortium on Chicago Schools Research, 2006).

fewer than one in thirty black male: Cohen and Little, "Of 100 Chicago Public School Freshmen, Six Will Get a College Degree"; Roderick, Nagaoka, and Allensworth, *From High School to the Future*; e-mail communication with Emily Krone of the Consortium on Chicago Schools Research. The *Tribune* story showed that the odds were one in forty; that figure changed when the report was updated.

161 *"study skills, work habits, time management":* Melissa Roderick, *Closing the Aspirations-Attainment Gap: Implications for High School Reform* (New York: MDRC, April 2006), 25.

"critical thinking and problem-solving abilities": Ibid., 26.

"High school teachers could have very high workloads": Ibid., 22–23.

162 *the percentage of American tenth-graders:* Ibid., 3.

163 *"the worst slum area in the United States":* Pam Belluck, "Razing the Slums to Rescue the Residents," *New York Times,* September 6, 1998.

one in nine murders in Chicago: William Julius Wilson, *The Truly Disadvantaged* (Chicago: University of Chicago Press, 1987), 25.

single mothers on welfare: Ibid.

167 *The Chicago public schools' average is 17:* Rosalind Rossi, "CPS High School ACT Scores Go Down — and They Go Up," *Chicago Tribune,* November 3, 2011.

only students who score in the top 20 percent: Murray, *Real Education,* 67, 75.

"As long as it remains taboo": Ibid., 104.

168 *"just not smart enough":* Ibid., 44.

171 *Recently, two labor economists:* Philip Babcock and Mindy Marks, "Leisure College, USA: The Decline in Student Study Time," *AEI Education Outlook* (Washington, DC: American Enterprise Institute for Public Policy Research, August 2010); Philip Babcock and Mindy Marks, "The Falling Time Cost of College: Evidence from Half a Century of Time Use Data," unpublished paper (March 24, 2010).

172 *A separate study of 6,300 undergraduates:* Steven Brint and Allison

M. Cantwell, *Undergraduate Time Use and Academic Outcomes: Results from UCUES 2006* (Berkeley, CA: Research and Occasional Paper Series, Center for Students in Higher Education, University of California, Berkeley, October 2008).

5. A Better Path

177 *I wrote an article about KIPP and Riverdale:* Paul Tough, "What If the Secret to Success Is Failure?," *New York Times Magazine*, September 18, 2011.

"*I'm left now, in my thirties*": See http://community.nytimes.com/comments/www.nytimes.com/2011/09/18/magazine/what-if-the-secret-to-success-is-failure.html?permid=141#comment141.

179 "*one of the best decisions I ever made*": "'You've Got to Find What You Love,' Jobs Says," *Stanford Report,* June 14, 2005.

184 *There are fewer entrepreneurs:* Paul Kedrosky and Dane Stangler, *Financialization and Its Entrepreneurial Consequences* (Kansas City, MO: Kauffman Foundation Research Series, March 2011).

36 percent of new Princeton graduates: Catherine Rampell, "Out of Harvard, and Into Finance," *New York Times* Economix blog, December 21, 2011.

an insightful blog post addressing this issue: James Kwak, "Why Do Harvard Kids Head to Wall Street?," Baseline Scenario blog, May 4, 2010, http://baselinescenario.com/2010/05/04/why-do-harvard-kids-head-to-wall-street/.

185 *The recruiters also make the argument:* Marina Keegan, "Another View: The Science and Strategy of College Recruiting," *New York Times* DealBook blog, November 9, 2011.

an ongoing survey of attitudes by the Pew Research Center: "September 22–25, 2011, Omnibus," Pew Research Center.

186 *In 1966, at the height of the War on Poverty:* Carmen DeNavas-Walt, Bernadette D. Proctor, and Jessica C. Smith, U.S. Census Bureau, Current Population Reports, *Income, Poverty, and Health Insurance Coverage in the United States: 2010* (Washington, DC: U.S. Government Printing Office, 2011), 14, figure 4.

And the child poverty rate: "Poverty Among Children," Congressional Budget Office, December 3, 1984; DeNavas-Walt, Proctor, and Smith, *Income, Poverty,* 17, figure 4.

187 *The first goes back to* The Bell Curve: Richard J. Herrnstein and Charles Murray, *The Bell Curve: Intelligence and Class Structure in American Life* (New York: Free Press, 1994). See also James J. Heck-

man, "Lessons from the Bell Curve," *Journal of Political Economy* 103, no. 5 (1995).

188 *gap between rich and poor was getting worse:* Sean F. Reardon, "The Widening Achievement Gap Between the Rich and the Poor," in *Whither Opportunity?*, eds. Greg Duncan and Richard Murnane (New York: Russell Sage, 2011). See also Sabrina Tavernise, "Education Gap Grows Between Rich and Poor, Studies Say," *New York Times,* February 9, 2012.

189 *The consensus of most reform advocates:* Steven Brill chronicles the way that the broad education-reform movement became a narrowly focused teacher-quality movement in Steven Brill, *Class Warfare: Inside the Fight to Fix America's Schools* (New York: Simon and Schuster, 2011).

This argument has its intellectual roots: William L. Sanders and June C. Rivers, *Cumulative and Residual Effects of Teachers on Future Student Academic Achievement* (Knoxville: University of Tennessee Value-Added Research and Assessment Center, November 1996); William L. Sanders and Sandra P. Horn, "Research Findings from the Tennessee Value-Added Assessment System (TVAAS) Database: Implications for Educational Evaluation and Research," *Journal of Personnel Evaluation in Education* 12, no. 3 (1998); Heather R. Jordan, Robert L. Mendro, and Dash Weerasinghe, *Teacher Effects on Longitudinal Student Achievement: A Report on Research in Progress* (Dallas: Dallas Public Schools, July 1997); Kati Haycock, "Good Teaching Matters . . . a Lot," *Thinking K–16* 3, no. 2 (Summer 1998); Eric A. Hanushek, John F. Kain, and Steven G. Rivkin, "Teachers, Schools, and Academic Achievement," NBER Working Paper 6691 (Cambridge, MA: National Bureau of Economic Research, August 1998); Eric A. Hanushek, "Efficiency and Equity in Education," *NBER Reporter* (Spring 2001); Robert Gordon, Thomas J. Kane, and Douglas O. Staiger, *Identifying Effective Teachers Using Performance on the Job,* Hamilton Project White Paper 2006-01 (Washington, DC: Brookings, 2006).

190 *brilliant teachers suddenly go downhill:* See, e.g., Michael Marder, "Visualizing Educational Data," unpublished paper, Department of Physics, University of Texas at Austin, February 9, 2011; and Michael Marder, "Failure of U.S. Public Secondary Schools in Mathematics: Poverty Is a More Important Cause than Teacher Quality," unpublished paper, 2011.

191 *teacher quality probably accounted for less than 10 percent:* Hanushek, Kain, and Rivkin, "Teachers, Schools"; Eric Eide, Dan Goldhaber,

and Dominic Brewer, "The Teacher Labour Market and Teacher Quality," *Oxford Review of Economic Policy* 20, no. 2 (Summer 2004): 232.

$41,348 for a family of four: United States Department of Agriculture Food and Nutrition Service, *National School Lunch Program Fact Sheet* (Washington, DC: United States Department of Agriculture Food and Nutrition Service, October 2011).

192 *covers about 40 percent of American children:* U.S. Census Bureau, Current Population Survey, *2011 Annual Social and Economic Supplement,* http://www.census.gov/hhes/www/cpstables/032011/pov/new01_185_01.htm.

just one student in eight doesn't qualify: As of the spring of 2012, 87 percent of Chicago public school students are low-income by federal education standards. "Stats and facts" page, Chicago Public Schools website, http://www.cps.edu/about_cps/at-a-glance/pages/stats_and_facts.aspx.

about 10 percent of all American children: DeNavas-Walt, Proctor, and Smith, *Income, Poverty,* 19, table 6.

an income of less than about $11,000 a year: Ibid., 61. See also Hope Yen and Laura Wides-Munoz, "Poorest Poor in US Hits New Record: 1 in 15 People," Associated Press, November 3, 2011.

more than seven million American children: DeNavas-Walt, Proctor, and Smith, *Income, Poverty,* 19, table 6.

196 *an effective program of support for parents:* See, for instance, Jack Shonkoff, speech at the NBC News Education Nation Summit, September 26, 2011, http://developingchild.harvard.edu/index.php/resources/multimedia/lectures_and_presentations/education_nation/.

between seven and twelve dollars of tangible benefit: James J. Heckman, Seong Hyeok Moon, Rodrigo Pinto, Peter A. Savelyev, and Adam Yavitz, "The Rate of Return to the High/Scope Perry Preschool Program," *Journal of Public Economics* 94, nos. 1 and 2 (February 2010).

Index